Damnatio Memoriae

THE SHALL NOT BE FORGOTTEN

A study of the Francoist genocide
of Cordoba 1936-1949

VOLUME III
DESCENT INTO THE BLUE HELL

Annotated English Translation of
La Victoria Sangrienta by
FRANCISCO MORENO GÓMEZ

by

MAGDALENA GORRELL JAÉN

Towards the retrieval of the Historic Memory of Spain

Damnatio Memoriae Vol. 3 by Magdalena Gorrell Jaén

ISBN 978-1-970072-41-9 (Paperback)
ISBN 978-1-970072-42-6 (Hardback)

This book is written to provide information and motivation to readers. Its purpose is not to render any type of psychological, legal, or professional advice of any kind. The content is the sole opinion and expression of the author, and not necessarily that of the publisher.

Printed in the United States of America.

New Leaf Media, LLC
175 S. 3rd Street, Suite 200
Columbus, OH 43215
www.thenewleafmedia.com

VOLUME III
Descent into the Blue Hell

CONTENTS

TABLES

APPENDIXES

One of things that I truly desire, which is why I have agreed to speak
of everything that we have endured, is because above all, I want this to
serve as an example to others, that they might know just what a Fascist
regime and dictatorship such as have suffered is like. As I bear witness,
I describe and explain all that we suffered and how we lived during the
eleven years that I was held in jail, every day under the threat of death
and what this did to the children and what it meant for my family.
I am willing to make all of this known as a living witness to all.

Antonia Garcia, one of the 11,000 women imprisoned in
Ventas Prison, Madrid

INTRODUCTION

Mass imprisonment or the severe deprivation of physical liberty, is considered a crime against humanity under International Law, especially in the Rome Statute that postulates the jurisdiction of the International Criminal Court, under Article 7 (e) as 'imprisonment or other severe deprivation of physical liberty in violation of fundamental rules of international law'.

The phenomenon of mass imprisonments under Franco was not a logistic aberration, nor an unwanted excess of zeal, nor a simple question of public order. First of all, the phenomenon of widespread imprisonments was an expression of the State's intemperate violence.[i] Secondly, it was a criminal project for secluding its opponents and for providing a means of repressing, punishing, eliminating and re-educating the disaffected and for exploiting them in the form of slave labour. Thirdly, this project had much in common with the III Reich's criminal dogma[ii], that is, with the European Totalitarian and Fascist project. Beginning in 1933, the mass Nazi imprisonments had the same goals as Francoism: to exclude, select, punish and terrorize political

---

[i]   Michael Ricards. *Un tiempo de silencio. La guerra civil y la cultura de la represión en la España de Franco, 19361945.* Critica, Barcelona, 1999, p. 30.

[ii] Renzo Stroscio, "Hacia una tipologia de los campos de concentración y exterminio nacionalsocialistas", *Congreso. Los campos de concentración y el mundo penitenciario en España durante la guerra civil y el franquismo.* Critica, Barcelona, 2000, pp. 77 et al.

opponents. The Nazi and Francoist penal complexes (concentration camps and prisons) are symbols of the darkest and most shameful period in Humanity. This continues to be a serious concern, especially in Spain where there is such a tendency to sugar-coat, trivialize, ridicule and deny, these events.

There still has been no serious investigation into what occurred in the Francoist jails in 1941. That year, as in Mauthausen, those who were deprived their liberty under Franco fell by the thousands, like flies. No one has yet offered a detailed explanation for why and how this period became known as the Francoist Auschwitz of 1941. As we shall see in Cordoba, most individuals died in prison than were executed by firing squads during the post-war period. A huge mortality rate in all Francoist prisons that dropped like a stone in 1942, as it did in Mauthausen, when Spain's 'brother regimes' exchanged their policy of exterminating their opponents for a slave labour strategy.

The massive overcrowding in the prisons was, in itself, an exterminating factor. The official number of imprisoned at the end of 1939 was given as 270,719 in a December 1945 report entitled Brief Summary of the Work of the Ministry of Justice for the Spiritual Pacification of Spain. The validity of this report which has been and continues to be frequently quoted, is extremely dubious. First, because the report was published soon after the end of WW II when Franco was not interested in having scandalous data regarding the number of political prisoners made public on the international scene. Second, how was the number of imprisoned in all the overcrowded provincial jails calculated at the end of 1939, considering the numerous large prisons and improvised smaller jails all over the country?

Furthermore, there was a totally chaotic penal situation in which thousands of prisoners were shuffled back and forth from one prison to another. What about the more than 23,000 women who were imprisoned in 1940, many of them with their children? The aforementioned total number can only be taken as a starting point for determining the total.

Gutmaro Gómez Bravo agrees that there is a marked difference between the official number of imprisoned and the reality, particularly as the official figures only take into account prisoners who were tried and sentenced. Not only were there hundreds of imprisoned who were not sentenced, but there also were thousands of prisoners of war, the imprisoned by the State Security Service, preventive imprisonments and so forth, not forgetting the extra-legal arrests after the continuous raids against clandestine reorganizers and those presumed to be assisting fugitives and guerrillas. He estimated that if one adds the data for the actual victims of the severe deprivation of their physical liberty held in the multitude of Francoist penal complexes – prisons and concentration camps – the true number of imprisoned in 1939 comes closer to one million.[iii]

Added to the validity of the official figure at the end of 1939/beginning of 1940, is that the Francoist Ministry of Justice's report does not include 90,000 who had been sentenced to Workers Battalions, 47,000 who were 'conscripted' into the Disciplinary Battalions of Worker Soldiers and the hundreds in concentration camps. It also appears that the report left out those imprisoned in countless improvised jails (convents, castles, manor houses of all kinds), as well as prisoners of the State whose dossiers continue to be kept under lock and key.[iv]

Ángel B. Sanz cited the official figures in 1945 and they were repeated by Halliday Sutherland in London in 1948: 170,719 for 1939; 233,373 for 1940; and 159,329 for 1941.[v]

What suffering there must have resulted from Franco's mass imprisonments. According to a report by Tomás de Boada, Count of Marsal and President of the National Council of Saint Paul for Prisoners and Convicts, from 1944 to 1948, MORE THAN ONE MILLION families had to contend with having one or more of its members in prison or out on parole and with having to care for young children and/or disabled relatives.

[iii] Gutmaro Gómez Bravo, "El desarollo penitenciario en el primer franquismo (1939-1945), *Hispania Nova*, number 6, 2006.

[iv] Ibid, *I Congresso de Victimas del Franquismo*, Rivas Vaciamadrid, Madrid, April 20-22 2012.

[v] "Angel B. Sanz, *De Re Penitenciaria*, Talleres Penitenciarios de Alcalá de Henares, Madrid, 1945, p. 181. Figures reproduced by Halliday Sutherland, *Spanish Journey*, Hollis and Carter, London, 1948, p. 47.

Location of Principle Prisons for Women
under Franco

1. Seville

2. Oviedo

3. Durango

4. Saturraran

5. Amorebieta

6. Zarragoza

7. Les Corts

8. Segovia

9. Guadalajara

10. VENTAS

11. Palma de Mallorca

12. Valencia

13. Alcala de Henares

14. Malaga

15. Melilla

Under Franco's Law, once any one of those babies reached the age of 3 years, the Social Welfare Services stepped in and took the child away from his mother and he was put into care, sometimes for several years, until she was paroled, if ever. Some of these children were adopted out, their names changed and records destroyed. It is estimated that in 1975, when Franco died, some 30,000 adults in Spain had no idea who their parents were, who were their relatives or even from where they came.

I

FRANCOIST PRISONS: EPICENTRE OF THE REPRESSION. CORDOVAN GENOCIDE 1941 – FRANCO's AUSCHWITZ. OTHER ASPECTS OF THE MULTI-REPRESSION.

MASS DEPRIVATION OF PHYSICAL LIBERTY: Conditional freedom, provincial jails, mass transfer to Cordoba prisons.
DESCENT INTO THE BLUE HEL: Cordova Provincial Prison: administrative structure, depths of the penitentiary world; conditional release, classification of prisoners, National Parole Board.
SLAVE LABOUR: 1. Workers battalions. 2. Re-educational camps. 3. Devastated regions. 4. Paramilitary labour camps. 5. Prison workshops.

Franco's prisons, the epicentre of the repression

Most authors agree that the Francoist prison world was the linchpin and backbone of Francoist repression, dedicated to exterminating recalcitrants (disaffected of political significance) and re-educating the reclaimable (disaffected with little or no political significance), that is, the majority of the population who would be the object of the most ferocious ideological repression with a view to forcing National Catholic thought upon them. Raphael Lemkin describes the transplantation of beliefs as a core feature of genocide as an attempt to rip out the defeated's personal beliefs and impose the ideology of the victors.

Many authors consider that the Francoist repression was also a type of class justice.[1] Likewise, as the extreme subjectivity that pervaded and disrupted the Francoist prison world, a product of the ambiguity of Francoist legislation, As Suárez claimed: "The laws, in addition to being terrible, were sufficiently ambiguous to ensure that they would be applied with all conceivable subjectivity. Some imprisoned were sentenced to longer prison terms than others only because their father or mother, or uncle, held the same beliefs." In his White Paper, Suárez also pointed to the idea of 'class' as a means of creating a domesticated labour force from the retrievable, until not a single trace of their past activism or traditional class awareness remained.

1

The question of the effect of the lack of definition on the strict application of the legislation to penal punishment is equally important. It is known that everything depended on the so-called theory of 'reverse justice' used to eliminate or imprison all those who remained loyal to the legal Government. The umbrella crime of 'military rebellion' that Francoists cited with monotonous regularity when punishing half of the Spanish population, was defined and regulated under the terms of the 1890 Code of Military Justice (not amended until July 17 1945). In their rage to persecute the defeated, the military oppressors used little imagination when it came to defining appropriate charges for an indictment. There could not be nothing more absurd than this lack of legislative definition.

Franco began by rescinding the Republican penal legislation with Decree of November 22 1936 and replacing it with the pre-Republican Penitentiary Regulations of November 13 1930. New Prison Service Regulations were not introduced until 1948 by which time the greatest part of the penitentiary disaster was over. During the war, military commanders published a whole series of all kinds of rules and regulations, the *bandos de guerra*, or wartime decrees.

Looking forward, the government created the System for Redeeming Sentences Through Work, October 7 1938, a hypocritical and exploitive invention by the Jesuit José Augusto Pérez del Pulgar. Although Victoria Kent did away with prison chaplains August 1931, Franco brought them back by Decree October 5 1938.

Despite the apparent legislative ambiguity when it came to suppressing the Regime's opponents, Franco approved a number of complementary laws in support of Francoist authoritarian aspirations: Law of Political Responsibility, February 9 1939; Law Against Freemasonry and Communism, March 1 1940; Law for the Security of the State, March 29 1941, as well as other regulations that dealt more generically with the penitentiaries such as the Decree creating the Probation Service May 22 1943, and the 1946 Regulations for Prison Work, introduced long after the 'terrible years'.

Although the study of the regulatory framework for the Francoist prisons has become fashionable – and there is no doubt that this is a positive subject of research - why should this research be done to the exclusion of other essential study such as those aimed at retrieving the facts of the Francoist prison world at that time. Curiously, in Spain, when something becomes historiographically 'fashionable', it is always accompanied by an anathema for and the proscription of everything that has been done before, including that which still remains to be done or is pending. In this case, all that occurred inside the prisons, how badly the prisoners were treated and how they died. This subject is so studiously ignored that there is still only an extremely limited amount of information regarding the monstrous mortality rate in Franco's penal establishments. Consequently, the Francoist Auschwitz of 1941 remains largely ignored by historians and nobody has thought to sink his teeth into this task. Ángela Cenarro, Professor of Modern History at the University of Zaragoza, made a remarkable comment about this:

> "If we stick to simply listing the infrahuman conditions in which thousands of anti-Francoist prisoners spent their days among such misery and desolation, we run the risk of losing our resolve, of failing to contribute anything to the knowledge of the legal and institutional framework on which the operation of the prisons was based."

How can one possibly 'lose one's resolve' in studying the inhumane conditions when almost nobody has studied this matter in any depth, even less so members of Academia, when almost the only information that has come to the public's attention is Tomasa Cuevas' monumental compendium of eyewitness accounts.[2] Why cannot the study of the regulations and the study of the inhumane conditions complement each other? There is no doubt that the exclusionary temperament of the Spanish does its damage. For example, in 1987 Moreno Gómez published an extremely detailed study of the Cordoba city prisons, the first time that anyone spoke openly of the terrible mortality rate in 1941 when 756 inmates from a prison population of fewer than 4,000, died.[3]

At the end of her book, Ángela Cenarro recognizes that the Prison Regulations had no more effect on prisoners than soggy bits of paper they could have been written on and that the daily routine inside the jails had nothing to do either with rehabilitation or re-education. In other words, the regulations went along their merry way along one path whilst the terrible daily routines of the prisoners went along another. Prison directors allowed torture and corruption. Inspectors turned a blind eye. Guards facilitated communications in exchange for gifts. Prison chaplains reigned as lords and masters of the men. That was the real picture, according to her. Moreno Gómez agrees in that the regulations do need to be studied, of course, but we must not waste the large amount of field work done so far by those who dug deep into the Francoist sewers, by flushing it down the drain.

When working on the draft for his first book on victims of the civil war, Moreno Gómez outlined some notable features of the appalling world of Francoist penitentiaries: 1) the overcrowding and its consequences were absolutely never unwanted or ignored by the new totalitarian State; 2) this destructive situation was neither an isolated or occasional occurrence, but universal and systemic; 3) the defeated never foresaw nor expected to be punished through the deprivation of their personal liberty, nor could they come to grips with the logic behind such repressive furore, so much blood and so many tears; 4) the magnitude of the imprisonments set the stage for the project to exclude half of Spain from the New State, the total absence of any desire to integrate the defeated and the absolute priority given to the plans for punishment, revenge, 'cleansing' and the ideological repression of all the progressive-reformist-leftist ideals that were the soul of the II Republic; and 5) that the mass deprivation of personal liberty and punishment was characterized by the victors' unpredictability and randomness, all of which was stoked by the lack of legislative and normative definitions regarding these matters.

The aforementioned White Paper on Francoist prisons described three stages in the Blue Hell of the totalitarian New State's penal complexes, all three of which are in agreement with the Nazi model and practices. The first and most basic, employed all the typical forms of corporal punishment (torture, forced labour, shortage of food, etc.) in prisons, police headquarters, concentration camps and Falangist checas. The victorious Nationalist Army and Political Police had carte blanche to act as they liked in the prisons, to arrest or release prisoners at whim, to arrange for paseos and sacas, interrogations and torture both in the prisons or in purpose-built interrogation centres.

The second stage was directed at the prisoners' inner self, with methods that were even closer to those practised by the Nazis, as Francoists used human behaviour and psychological pressure techniques in order to obtain an individual's total dependence on his tormentor. More than 're-education', as they say this was today, it was ideological repression pure and simple. There is no re-education in crushing an individual's self-esteem to the limit of his endurance. When the tormented individual weakens until in many cases, he becomes uncapable of reacting to the continuous harassment of religion, non-stop patriotic ceremonies, the omnipresent cult of the Caudillo, the praise of 'redeeming' labour and the impact of the propaganda against the 'Godless' or those who were 'anti-Spain'.

Lastly, the third stage consisted in the psychological effects of the entire process: convincing the tormented man of his guilt and managing to get him to accept the truth of the accusations levied against him. Many victims ended up accepting their guilt, as did Juan Simeón Vidarte, the well-known Socialist, when he wrote *Todos fuimos culpables* – We All Were Guilty. Because of the persistent lack of information today, the twisted version of the History of this period continues to have a destructive effect on certain sectors of society. Another example of the victors' use of language as a weapon of mass destruction.

Regarding the aforementioned first stage, that of the typical forms of corporal punishment, this is in agreement with a 1949 British report cited by Gutmaro Gómez, from which the following is an extract:[4]

> "Its archives are based on the Nazi model and ensure a systematic watch over all suspicious enemies of the State... As they are paid extra, the poorly paid police tend to apply increasingly violent methods and to prolong, as much as possible, the isolation of prisoners in order to obtain confessions..."

The same author recalls a statement from the Ministry of the Government, regarding that hyperbolic repressive macro-process, according to which THREE MILLION individuals were already on file in 1944. This leads Moreno Gómez to believe that Gutmaro was mistaken when he said that in March 1948, when the state of war was finally declared over, the repressive system was already fully operational and suffered no substantive changes until the end of the Regime. This was in contradiction with everything that was going on in Spain on those very same dates, that period that since 1987 Moreno Gómez has called the Triennium of Terror (1947-1949), and all its precursor and succeeding actions, the thousands of victims of paseos and the Law of Fugitives in all of Spain, from Asturias to Málaga. It appears that nobody is interested in looking at the repressive barbarity of the totalitarian State at the end of the 1940s.

The first period of mass deprivation of physical liberty. The provincial jails (1939-1940)

> *"One cannot say what justice consists of, if we ignore*
> *the injustices, which is what occurs today.*
> *The memory of the injustice invalidates all those*
> *theories of justice that are currently taught in the*
> *Faculties of Law and Philosophy."*

> Manuel Reyes Mate, La piedra desechada
> (The Deactivated stone), 2013.

One of the first problems facing the victorious horde at the end of the war in 1939, was how to manage its imprisonment of half of the Spanish population. The Army of the Republic, half a million men, captured and disarmed, was imprisoned in the almost two hundred concentration camps that existed all over Spain. The Regime also had to imprison the entire Republican governing elite and a considerable number of civilian Republican Leftists. Never before in the history of this unhappy country had anything like this happened, not even remotely so.

If in the concentration camps the inmates were predominantly ex-military, in the multitude of improvised jails in the majority of the towns and villages in the countryside, the inmates were a mixed batch: military and civil, because ex-soldiers were straying all over the place and, having abandoned their weapons, were making their way back to their home towns where they fell into the clutches of local Fascists, the worst of the lot.

The victors, drunk with victory, just did not know where to put so many people. Undoubtedly, this was one of the most absurd and clumsy mismanagements of victory and defeat ever seen on the face of this Earth. Only an idiot would order putting half of the Spanish population behind bars simply because they were 'disaffected', or imprison an entire Army of half a million men. Such was the mental power of the Caudillo, of the 'consummate Caesar' as Alberto Reig described him; 'the great manipulator' according to Paul Preston; the 'Criminalissimo' as Rafael Sánchez Guerra called him. April 1939 Spain was, quite simply, catastrophe and gaucherie elevated to the nth degree.

Other European post-war scenarios were not managed with the schizophrenia that afflicted post-war Spain. Post-war Germany did not dump all the defeated in the same sack, but it divided them into three groups: major offenders (of which there were only 1,600), Nazi sympathizers and minor offenders. Except for the war criminals who were tried in Nuremburg, no death penalties were handed down, only prison sentences and dismissal. The government soon pardoned the youngest offenders, issued another amnesty Christmas 1947 and in 1948, downgraded major offenders to sympathizers.[5] All this, three years after the end of the Great War, whilst Spain, eight to ten years after the end of its war, was still suffering the effects of the Triennium of Terror (1947-1949) and the Law of Fugitives was still being applied without restraint in every ditch and gutter in the Spanish countryside. Franco's terror, far from being analogous to anything that had happened in Europe, was more comparable to something that might be seen in Ruanda.

Post-war Italy began to introduce sanctions to Fascism in 1944 and June 1946, and one year after the end of the Great War, the government issued an amnesty for all sentences under 5 years and commuted longer sentences. Soon afterwards, only leading Fascists and individuals condemned for major crimes remained behind bars. Whereas in Spain, the Francoist administrative purging of all public services were directed at half of the Spanish population, in Rome, for example, of 394,041 public servants investigated, only 1,590 were fired. If in Europe the tormentors were the new democracies, in Spain, Fascism was the oppressor.

Back in Spain, the Regime began packing 'disaffected' Spaniards, both civil and military defeated, into the most surprising improvised jails, where triumphant fascist thugs lay about them with their fists, clubs and whatever they could get their hands on. Historians who have investigated these jails have written very little regarding this first stage of Francoist mass deprivation of physical liberty. Attracted today by the fashion of primarily studying the penal rules and regulations, researchers have chosen to ignore this terrible first post-war year and a half (1939-1940), when there still were no legislative rules or regulations, only systemic, widespread torture . This was the terrible stage of the improvised country jails that lasted until Fall 1940 when the prison population was removed from the countryside and concentrated in the prisons in the provincial capitals. There is apparently no present-day detailed account that today's generation can read, that faithfully describes the extreme Calvary that the prisoners suffered in the country jails.

At this first stage, Francoism's social base furiously devoted itself, heart and soul, to the New State's task of purging the country from all the 'fiendish Rojos'. A pact of blood bound the Regime's base with its hierarchy to form a carefully fashioned operational triangle that would ensure that all the victors would unite to further their Crusade: to punish and exterminate all the defeated, without the minimum thought for any humanity, clemency or fraternity between Spaniards. No one in the new totalitarian Regime conceived, not even by chance, a single reconstructive project that would assimilate all Spaniards.

The New State looked to the most terrible reprisals for its base. This was the so-called Christian attitude in the midst of the greatest schizophrenia ever seen in Spain, a tripartite association led by the barracks, the Casino and the church vestry. Military projects in Spain, even more so when encouraged by fascism, have always been blood and guts punitive events to the tune of bugles. Today, some may consider that it is politically incorrect to speak of these matters, but that was History.

THE PROVINCIAL JAILS (1939-1940)

Here follows a brief revision of the details of the first stage of the mass deprivation of liberty, primarily, that of the condition of the individual local jails (1939-1940), most of which were improvised, the lack of local conditions, overcrowding and mistreatment of the inmates. (The attending carnage in the province is discussed in greater detail in Volumes 1 and 2.)

In Cordoba Province

In the village of <u>Castro del Río</u>, in the heart of the Cordoba countryside, a great many local workers – most of them anarchists – fled to the Republican zone to fight for the government and at the end, returned to their village looking forward to a time of peace', only to be immediately arrested. When the Municipal Depot became rapidly packed to the rafters with prisoners, the authorities improvised a jail in the Santa María de Scala Coeli Convent, a large building with many cells, patios and thick stone walls, where hundreds would end their days. Prisoners from Baena, Albendín, Valenzuela, Luque and Espejo were transferred here in February 1940. A total 1,500 individuals were held behind bars in this village.

In <u>Belalcázar</u>, in the north of the province, prisoners were crammed into the Divina Pastora School, another improvised jail. As the number of death sentences began to rain upon the inmates, a large number of desperate men organized a great escape August 4 1939. 15 of those condemned to death escaped, 3 died in the attempt and the remainder fled to the hills where they joined the bands of freedom fighters and guerrillas who later played an important role in the post-war history of the district.

In <u>Hinojosa del Duque</u>, an improvised jail was created in the Convent of the Concepcionistas, where prisoners from Hinojosa, Belalcázar, El Viso, Santa Eufemia and some other villages were kept. Another building, an old manor house named Casa del Condesito, was also turned into an improvised jail in the first few days after the end of the war. (Today, it is an inn.) Here, too, desperate prisoners organized a great escape the night of August 31 1940. 20 inmates escaped through a hole in a wall, 5 or 6 failed to get away and their bodies were left to rot on the town streets; the remainder also fled to the hills where many became famous guerrilla leaders.

In <u>Villanueva de Cordoba</u>, the capital of Republican Cordoba province during the war, the usual penitentiary chaos began in the early days of April the year of the Francoist Victory. The town was the headquarters of the Nationalist 63rd Division and it also housed a great number of refugees. Prisoners were packed into the Municipal Depot, the anti-aircraft shelter, Romo's House on Calle Herradores, Pepe Barrón's factory warehouses on Calle Industria, schools and other improvised jails such as La Preturilla, the provisional Guardia Civil barracks, and there still were enough inmates left over to justify setting up an improvised concentration camp in Ángel Diaz's yard, next to the Ramirez Factory. The authorities soon began to send convoy after convoy of prisoners out of town, to Valsequillo and La Granjuela and especially to Castuera concentration camps. The bells of victory were still pealing when the notorious SIPM Lieutenant Leopoldo Mena began 'working' with his Information Committee.

Soon after the end of the war was declared, a large number of prisoners in Villanueva were rounded up in Juan Herrero's home, a large manor house on Calle Conquista: men on the top floor and women on the ground floor. Prisoners from Torrecampo, Pedroche and Adamuz were also sent to Villanueva. At the beginning of June 1939, many of these prisoners were transferred to the Fuente Vieja Schools improvised jail, the site of much torture and executions by firing squads until September 26 1940 when all the imprisoned in the town were marched to the Villanueva train station, on their way to Cordoba capital. There, they joined prisoners from all over the province in inaugurating the New Prison, a kind of Auschwitz without gas chambers, in which 502 died from starvation and deprivations in 1941 alone.

The appendixes in the two previous volumes of this book record a sample of the multiple accounts of the suffering in the town jails (overcrowding, unhealthy conditions, torture) and of inmates' desperate attempts to escape. One such story is that of José García Coleto – El Perica, who managed to escape from the line of prisoners who were being transferred and who vowed to get his revenge on his tormentor – which he finally did in 1940 – only to be caught and killed six months later near Villaviciosa. There is also the tale of a planned escape that came to nothing.

In Bujalance, inmates were packed in the local judiciary party's jail. In Baena, although an even greater number of prisoners filled the so-called Tercia, or Posada, jail next to the barracks and the town hall, the authorities still had to improvise a jail in the Plaza Vieja. Prisoners from Albedín, Luque and Valenzuela were also housed in Baena until February 1940 when all the imprisoned were transferred to the Castro del Río Nunnery in early Fall, and from there, those who had survived the multiple executions, were sent to Cordoba Provincial Prison in the capital, to join all the others from the province. Likewise in Puente Genil, the large number of prisoners far exceeded the capacity of the local jails, which is why one was improvised in the La Alianza Factory warehouses in Molino del Marqués until they, too, were sent to Cordoba.

The drama of the Fuenteobejuna prison world was played out on the ground floor of the City Hall building from 1939 until the beginning of 1940 when the prisoners were transferred to the Peñarroya-Pueblonuevo jail, also located on the ground floor of the City Hall building, together with others in improvised jails such as the Miners' Union building and the Trade School.

As the Municipal Depot in Fernán Núñez soon filled up, a movie theatre in the town centre became an improvised jail, with an average 200 inmates, some of whom came from Montemayor. The number of imprisoned rose rapidly at the end of the war: 440 women, 271 civilian men, 688 ex-soldiers and a great many young people under the age of 21.[6] 1 October

1940, 146 inmates were transferred to Montilla jail and soon afterwards, to the Provincial Prison in Cordoba.

The San Luís Convent School in Montilla became an improvised jail. As the Municipal Depot quickly reached maximum capacity. In 1939, Montilla contributed 646 inmates, 239 from Montilla and the remainder from neighbouring towns, to the total imprisoned in all of Spain. July 1940, 27 prisoners arrived from Lucena – not many, because earlier there had been mass executions in that town and besides, there was a small concentration camp with 305 inmates in the town. In La Rambla, there also was mass imprisonment when at least 583 men of the more than a thousand townspeople who had fled earlier to the Republican zone, returned.[7]

The fact of the matter was that half of the Spanish population was packed into every conceivable prison and jail throughout the country. According to Casimiro Jabonero's testimony, more than 2,000 inmates filled the Cuenca Seminary. In Guadalajara, in addition to the Polígono concentration camp, the provincial prison was filled to the rafters, there was a military prison and the Convent of the French Nuns women's prison. In Alicante, the penitentiary chaos was total as the authorities strove to find room for all the people they were arresting as they attempted to leave the country. Prisoners filled the Campo de Albatera concentration camp, the provincial prison, movie theatres, the House for Spiritual Retreats, and more. The Alicante Reform School for Adults, designed to house 300, held 3,000.

The provincial prison in Albacete filled quickly and so did the improvised San Vicente jail. Juana Doña wrote that 1,000 women were imprisoned in one of those prisons [8]. Other notorious prisons and jails in the province were in Chinchilla, Yeste castle and Hellín jail. The worst of all was the Chinchilla penal complex that had been closed down in 1870 because of the terrible conditions and only reopened by the Francoists.

In Rute, the Municipal Depot was extended to the premises of the Las Palomas anis factory, to house 80 captive members of a Workers' Battalion who had been sent to repair the Carcabuey road. To speak of Rute is to remind us of the suffering in Francoist jails during this first stage of the repression, of the constant and rabid harassment of the defeated, of the lines of prisoners taken daily from the jail to the Guardia Civil barracks where they were forced to sing the Francoist hymn *Cara al Sol*, forced to attend Mass under guard every Sunday, or as in Posadas, of group after group of prisoners marched to the town square and forced to kneel before a cross to the Francoist fallen and pray for the victims of the Left.

In Cordoba capital, the Provincial Prison was traditionally located in the medieval dungeons of the Alcázar de los Reyes Cristianos. These extremely unhealthy installations were the venue for the great genocide of 1936, when some 4,000 were exterminated. The New Prison was built in 1940 near the Asland Factory, in the north of the city, on the road to Pedroches. When the first waves of prisoners were transferred to Cordoba from the province in Fall 1940, the building work was not complete, there were no panes in the windows and the sanitary installations were insufficient for the needs of the first 3,000, soon to total 4,000, inmates. It is therefore not surprising that the genocide in the Cordoba prisons began within a few weeks and that no less than 502 would be exterminated in 1941 alone.

In the rest of the country

The penitentiary world in Madrid was in total chaos, as every conceivable space served as a prison: Santa Engracia (1,000 inmates); Porlier (4,000); Torrijos on Calle Conde de Peñalver (3,000); Duque de Sesto (800), San Antón, a religious school on Calle Hortaleza, (2,000); Yeserías, an asylum for beggars, in Delicias (3,000-5,000); Convento de Comendadoras (1000); Atocha (2,000); Santa Rita (4,000); Conde de Toreno (700), in addition to Barco, Príncipe (near Carabancheles), Jaime Vera (another ancient workhouse for beggars), and Cisne on Calle Martínez Campos, an old convent of Trinitarian nuns that had served as a convalescent hospital during the war. All the Que courts in Madrid were located on the ground floor and the first floor housed more than 300 prisoners, almost all Republican military. There were more prisons (two of them military) for women, namely Ventas (12,000 women), Claudio Coello (1,000), Malasaña, and San Isidro (women who were breast-feeding children).[9]

Also according to Rafaela Sánchez Guerra, imprisoned at the time, if to these numbers we add those who were interned in neighbouring concentration camps, in the Security Services dungeons, in the ten police headquarters in Madrid and the several Falangist checas, we can easily reach a total of 50,000 individuals who were deprived of their liberty in the Spanish capital.

July 1939, the Puerto de Santa Maria, Cádiz, prison housed 5,400 inmates, 2,000 of whom were Basque. According to a report from the National Basque Archives, the situation on that date was deplorable.[10] In the tragic San Simón, Pontevedra, penal complex, 2,176 inmates were packed in inhuman conditions during the immediate post-war period, most of whom were over 60 years old (up to 666 inmates were executed here).[11]

In Amorebieta, 800 women were interned in each room in a monk's school. Women's' prisons in the North were particularly terrible: Santander, Saturrarán, Durango (housing 2,000 women, many with their children), Segovia, and more. The Cuéllar jail in Segovia was especially notorious, as this was an ancient castle dating from the end of the Middle Ages, dungeons and gloomy installations, housing 1,500 inmates. Survivors of the Torrero, Zaragoza, jail continue to talk of their sufferings.

There were three jails in Toledo capital: the provincial prison, the improvised jail and San Bernardo prison. There were many jails in the countryside, but the largest and most overcrowded were Talavera de la Reina and the tragically infamous Ocaña jail (housing 5,000 men and 2,000 women), where 9 inmates were packed into individual cells built for one. In 1940, there were 8,200 prison inmates in the entire province. [12]

Overcrowding was a feature of the Modelo prison in Valencia. Built to house 528 in 1907, up to 15,000 inmates were housed at one time during the post-war. In Jaén, there were 6,000 prisoners in the capital in 1941, when 4,000 were housed in the provincial prison built for 80 inmates in 1930. [13]

The first year and a half of the Francoist penitentiary world (1939-1940) in the local jails, was characterized by an astonishing, extremely humiliating, cruel and inhuman overcrowding. The degree of harassment of the unfortunate defeated reached levels that are difficult to conceive of today. The main terrible feature of that situation was the 'proximity' of the victors and the defeated. In the countryside, the tormenters lived near the victims who were no strangers to them, whom they met regularly with their henchmen when it was time for the defeated to make their daily declarations to the authorities at the barracks or the prisons. A second, very important feature of the local jails was the facility it gave the victors to retaliate for presumed slights during the Republic, both personal and in the form of complaints against employers, labour conflicts, strikes, everything they saw as the 'revolution', as in their minds, all labour unrest was 'revolution'.

The local setting was perfect for anyone who had an ancient quarrel that rankled. Matias Romero, for example, describes the terrible beating that his brother, Crisóstomo Romero Badía, received at the hands of a group of Falangists. Among these, Pedro 'El Barbero' was revenging himself for the fact that during a strike, a group of men in which Crisóstomo accompanied Alfonso Ibáñez Tamaral, had forced him to close his barbershop. They tossed him head first like a ping-pong ball against the blood-splattered walls of the office [sic. in the La Preturilla barracks], until he lost consciousness.

Accordingly, during the first year and a half after the war, the New State began its avowed intention to cleanse all of Spain of even the most insignificant syndicalist ideals or activism, both past and present, and this could only be successfully achieved in those places where the defeated were well known, that is, in their home towns. Although the constant, violent attacks on the defeated was slightly more controlled when they occurred in the major provincial prisons, in the country, the absence of any legislation, rules or regulations of any sort meant that the rule of daily beatings and uncontrolled violence was the norm. When the returnees, returned to their home towns, they ran the constant risk of being lynched by unruly victorious mobs.

Although there are several academic studies of the situation in the large city prisons, most authors have paid little or no attention to the horror of the country jails in this first post-war period. In the countryside, more so than in the provincial capitals, the inmates suffered what Moreno Gómez calls *retaliatory torture*. Local tormentors' favourite 'sport' was the visitors they brought to the jails, day and night: Falangists, pimps for the New State, spoiled brat Señoritos who amused themselves by pistol-whipping, lashing, throwing chairs and other objects and otherwise humiliating the inmates. Added to this, there was the *judicial torture* that was applied when prisoners went to make their declarations to the authorities, and the *law enforcement torture*, bloody affairs that took place in police headquarters in the cities such as Madrid, and in the Guardia Civil barracks in the countryside and local Falangist headquarters, where so many left their lives.

In APPENDIX I, Matias Romero provides some additional personal details regarding the retaliatory torture that the victors applied at random in the country jails, out of pure and simple repressive fury, day after day, night after night. The cruelty of the repression in the provincial capitals was nothing compared to that which occurred in the countryside where the victors revelled in thrashing the defeated.

Miguel Hernández's prison diary and letters[14] reveal that it was in Orihuela, his home town where he was imprisoned for three months, from September to November in 1939, that he received the worst treatment. He expresses his despair for the mistreatment he received from the intolerant, clerical and hateful townspeople whom he compares to those that Gabriel Miró depicted in his painting 'Our Father Saint Daniel and the Leprous Bishop'.

The degree of sadism that the local tormentors applied on a regular basis was never matched in the central provincial prisons. Already described in some detail in the previous volumes, is the barbarous treatment meted in towns and villages such as Montilla, Fernán Núñez, Villanueva de Cordoba and elsewhere in the Cordoba countryside, but these methods were applied throughout Spain. Nightly visits of drunken Falangists are documented in towns of Toledo province, such as in Aldeanueva de San Bartolomé where one of those who suffered was Jesús Gómez Recio-Quincoces, the Republican Mayor, who successfully escaped from the jail and became a famous guerrilla fighter. Also in Quintanar de la Orden, where they crushed the prisoners' feet so that they could not run away, as they did to José Manzanero whose wounds took three months to heal.

At this first stage, the Francoist repression was intentionally directed at the visibility of the punishment, to further punish and terrorize the general population. It was the almost daily show of Rojos, of the Godless, the anti-Spain prisoners, expunging their guilt, of lines of prisoners paraded through the towns, men and women with shaven heads, humiliated, their clothes in tatters, signs of the constant starvation and torture they were subjected to etched on their faces.

At this stage, the State spent the very bare minimum share of its budget on feeding its prisoners, whose sustenance was left to their families. Every day, relatives went to the jails to take them their breakfasts in milk cans and jugs and their meals in lunch boxes, baskets and woven cloth bags. Despite their social exclusion and abject poverty, these families wrought miracles to take some food to their imprisoned kin which is how they survived the first year and a half of their incarceration, but all this ceased with the mass transfer of prisoners to the central prisons in Cordoba capital. This circumstance alone may explain, but only in a very minor way, the 1941 Francoist Auschwitz in every prison in Spain. Such an astonishing disaster that nobody has yet studied it in any detail.

Mass transfers to Cordoba capital prisons and to Burgos – Summer-Fall 1940

This section begins with the great march of prisoners from the rural jails in the entire province to the central prisons in Cordoba capital at the end of the Summer and beginning of the Fall 1940. One might presume that the Machiavellian Regime was satisfied that it had done enough with its first stage of penitentiary repression to ensure that it had attained the desired effect on the population as a whole – that is, an uncontested awareness of the terror, punishment and executions that awaited the disaffected. It could now proceed with the second stage, a more systemic prison hell in the New State's large provincial prisons, those that could now be called the Regime's great penal complexes (Burgos, Puerta de Santa María, Alcalá de Henares, Ocaña, Carabanchel, and so forth).

Enormous convoys and never-ending lines of prisoners made their way to Cordoba capital in a spectacle of humiliation and punishment with which the Regime bombarded the defeated. Great troupes of prisoners were marched daily along the streets of Cordoba capital, from the railway station to the prison, a multitude of men tied to each other by wires, knapsacks over their shoulders, the mark of torture on their faces, gazing blankly over the panorama of a world that was totally hostile to them. Although it is true that many people commiserated with them in silence, the shamelessness of the excited victors expressed itself as insults of all kinds. Hysterical society ladies, flippant young Señoritos, jocular wealthy members of the Circulo de la Amistad and frenzied Falangists, lined the route taken by the prisoners and transformed it into an authentic *via crucis*.

As described in Volume 2 regarding Cordoba province, the greater number of trials were carried out in the countryside in the immediate post-war. When at the beginning of Fall 1940, the majority of prisoners were transferred to the provincial capital, they were weighed down by the fact that almost all had already been sentenced to death. (Only a minority would be tried and sentenced in the capital in 1941 and 1942.) Behind them, in their hometowns, they left many companions who still faced the firing squads: 167 in Castro del Río, 209 in Pozoblanco, 102 in Villanueva de Cordoba, 88 in Peñarroya, 67 in Hinojosa, etc., etc. although the last legal executions had been carried out in many of the towns and villages during the Summer. The last shots were fired in June in Belmez, Puente Genil, Peñarroya an Pedro Abad. In this last village, they left a pregnant woman who had been sentenced to death, 37-year-old Josefa Ortega Egea whom they would execute October 3, a few days after giving birth.

September 1940 witnessed the last legal executions in Bujalance, Castro del Río, Honojosa, Montilla, Montoro, Pozoblanco and Villanueva de Cordoba. All these prisoners would now be dispatched during the great wave of executions in Cordoba capital in 1941.

There now follow some description of the manner by which the prisoners were transferred from Villanueva de Cordoba to the capital. September 26 was the date set for this transfer and it would be done with considerable military pomp and circumstance (soldiers, Guardias Civiles, municipal policemen, Falangists with revolvers tucked under their belts, etc.) down the city streets, effectively cutting off any access roads. A huge chain of prisoners, tied to each other, their meagre belongings over their shoulders, was brought from the Fuente Vieja square where the Schools served as an improvised jail. Relatives of the prisoners, especially children, pushed against the crowd on the street corners, trying to make themselves seen, under continuous insults and slaps from the policemen. There were more than 400 men, not only natives of Villanueva, but also from Pedroche, Torrecampo and Adamuz. Another cordon of 50 women was taken from Juan Herrero's House on Calle Conquista.

As they walked, every prisoner tried to see if he could spot his relatives and especially his children, and call out words of farewell. Within the city limits, it was difficult because of the large number of military, but as soon as they moved towards and into the avenue that led to the railway station where they were packed into a passenger train, it was all a frantic waving of hands, tragic calls of farewell from the prisoners to their relatives and from the relatives to the prisoners. Witnesses to the events of that day tell how, as the train started off and for quite some time afterwards, relatives, women and children ran alongside the train, through the fields, hoping for a last glimpse of their husband, father, brother, son, as long as the carriages were still in sight.

That night, the prisoners spent a terrible night in improvised shelters in Peñarroya-Pueblonuevo and the next day, September 27, they arrived in Cordoba where they inaugurated the unfinished building of the New Provincial Prison. Of those who arrived from Villanueva de Cordoba, 35 soon faced the firing squads in the capital and at least another 23 would starve to death in prison. Around the same dates, another large convoy of more than 600 men arrived from Pozoblanco and neighbouring towns (there had been 990 in 1939 but 209 had meanwhile been executed); in the capital, they shot another 10 and 8 died from hunger. There were two more large convoys to Cordoba capital, one from Hinojosa (with prisoners from Belalcázar and Santa Eufemia) and one from Peñarroya (with prisoners from Fuenteobejuna, Belmez, and other towns); from Hinojosa, 20 were shot in the capital and another 23 starved to death; from Belalcázar, 18 were shot; from Belmez, the most notable is that 16 died from hunger; from Fuenteobejuna, 19 also starved to death in prison; from Peñarroya, 24 more.

As to the prisoners from Montoro, in addition to the 61 who were executed earlier in the town, 40 were executed soon after they arrived in Cordoba and another 25 died from hunger in prison. From Adamuz, in addition to those executed in Villanueva, 20 were executed in Cordoba and 22 died from hunger.

In the countryside, in Puente Genil and all the towns and villages in the so-called Red Belt around the capital, the imprisoned in the local jails were transferred to Cordoba city on the same dates in September and October. Fernán Núñez had already sent a group of 146 prisoners by truck and tied to each other with wire, to the improvised Montilla jail, where they were packed in the San Luis Convent School jail. When the time came to send the prisoners to Cordoba, those who had not been previously sentenced to death were sent to Puerto de Santa Maria. Those sentenced to death and the prisoners from Montilla, with Manel 'El Perla' Sánchez Ruiz the Republican Mayor at the head of the group, were sent to Cordoba between October 17 and 19.

A mixed group of prisoners formed the large convoy that left Castro del Río and also included the prisoners from Baena, approximately 1,500 who had been held since February 1940 in the Scala Coeli Convent improvised jail. 167 prisoners were executed in Castro and the remainder sent off to the Provincial Prison tied to each other, in several groups of trucks. 18 were executed in Cordoba and 7 starved to death in prison. Another large convoy left Bujalance. 55 prisoners were executed before it left; 13 more in the capital and 13 later starved to death.

All this was a feature of the Cordoba genocide. Three or four days after the arrival of the first wave of prisoners from the countryside, the authorities began to send part of those who had already been sentenced to death to prison in Burgos, where they were to spend the winter. As Eutimio Martín describes it,[15] the prisoners were transferred by train, crowded into closed cattle wagons with a bit of straw on the floor, similar to those used by the Nazis to take Jews to the concentration camps. The trip to Burgos, with one stop in Cáceres, took three days, during which they gave the prisoners nothing to eat or drink. Unlike Hitler who charged the Jews for their trip, under Franco, the ride was free. However, as soon as the prisoners arrived in Burgos, they were stripped of all their belongings, including tobacco. The similarities between Franco's New State and Nazi Germany were much more factual than people believe.

Once in Burgos, the bitterly cold winter weather made life intolerable for the inmates; they died not just from hunger but also from the cold. As Diógenes Cabrera wrote: "There are only two seasons in Burgos: Winter and the season for travelling by train." [16] His and other personal testimonies agree with Eutimio Martín's comment regarding the role of the weather as a means of extermination, that Franco created a unique Auschwitz of his own where the weather, because of the particular physical weakness of the imprisoned, played the same sinister role as the gas chambers.

The great return trip to Cordoba capital began during 1941, in the so-called 'trains of death'; as soon as a sufficient number of approved death sentences were obtained, a trip was arranged.

Diógenes Díaz Cabrera, Freemason and ex-Consul for Venezuela in La Palma, an excellent witness of what happened in the Canary Islands, published an impressive description of his transfer from Madrid to Burgos a couple of years later:

> "At the end of October 1942 [from Porlier, Madrid] we were rousted from our cells at 3 a.m. and taken outside where we were forced to stand in formation for more than three hours until a Guardia Civil Captain arrived with a large number of guardias carrying machine guns… Marching to order, backpacks slung over our shoulders, surrounded by Guardias Civiles,

soldiers, requetés and Falangists armed to the teeth, we were led to the Madrid railway station. On the street corners, we could see prisoners' wives and mothers weeping and waving handkerchiefs from a distance; they were not allowed to approach us.

The enormous convoy in which we were packed, our feet tied together with wire, left at the sound of a bugle. This was the most painful trip of all those I was taken on… We were forbidden to speak… The train travelled maddingly slowly… We arrived in Burgos at 3 a.m. November 3- the trip took 4 days . All of our feet were horribly swollen, our whole body ached, we were extremely drowsy and numb from the freezing cold.

They tossed us like bales of hay onto trucks and took us from the railway station to the prison. Our backpacks remained at the station and we were placed in damp, cold cells like ice-boxes. Totally exhausted, we lay on the floor and tried to sleep, but it was impossible. The floor was just too cold…. The second night, we had not yet been given our backpacks and we were desperate from the lack of sleep because of the cold… I said [to Antonio Cepero]: ' I cannot stand this any longer. I am from a warm place and I have to ask the Director of this damned prison to help me if he wants to keep me from freezing to death.' Our backpacks were finally delivered on the 5th but we were not allowed to get them until the 6th. Thus, three nights in a row in Burgos Prison without backpacks, without blankets, without anything, plus the 4 days of the trip – 8 days of absolute exhaustion.

Such were the transfers, the worst being the one to Burgos, symbol of Eternal Spain, and these were the shame of the 'penitentiary tourism'."

Moreno Gómez received reports of another great convoy of Cordovan prisoners who were not sentenced to death but were sent to the Labacolla Penal Camp near Santiago de Compostela. One of those who suffered that misfortune, Antonio Ruíz-Fernández, native of Espiel, wrote that at the end of the war he was a sergeant in a machine gun unit, taken prisoner and sent to Labacolla air field next to Santiago de Compostela and the 28th Disciplinary Battalion, to work with a pick and shovel. Of the 5,000 disaffected with Francoism who went there from Cordoba capital and province, few of them returned with their lives. It was a pure Inquisition.[17] Casimiro Jabonero, a native of Cuenca, mentioned earlier, arrived at this camp via Madrid-Ponferrada-Santiago April 28 1939, travelling in the usual cattle-cars. Another testimony from Cordoba province, Pedro Gómez González, native of Villaralto, worked out his sentence in the 28th Disciplinary Worker Soldiers Battalion,[18] details of which will be discussed later when we address the matter of Franco's slave labour.

Descent into the circle of the blue hell

"Whoever denies Auschwitz is precisely the person who is willing to repeat it." (Primo Levi). There are two deaths in every crime: the physical and the hermeneutic. The assassin does not only kill, but he also strives to conceal it and to do so, nothing is more effective than depriving it of all meaning, that is, to make it appear insignificant. This concealment of the moral and political meaning of the crime is proof that the enemy is still on the loose. The historian trained in the school of Walter Benjamin, must know it and be prepared to face this."

Manuel Reyes Mate, La piedra desechada
(The Deactivated stone), 2013

José Saramago said that "We are the memory that we retain and the responsibility that we shoulder. Without memory we do not exist and without responsibility, perhaps we do not deserve to do so."

Our scourge today is the erroneous belief in denying History. Those who deny it today and those who persist in sweetening the facts of the terrible Francoist repression, who today pollute the environment like toadstools, are causing irreparable damage to the truth of what happened.

Negationism, as defined by Stanton, is the last stage of genocide with which it is complicit and, as such, gives rise to major problems. The main one being how to determine just who are those responsible for the negationist phenomenon and what are their deep-rooted intentions as it does not appear amongst those who are nostalgic for the dictatorship, but amongst influential members of society and a great many academics. It would be disastrous to find the ulterior motive, not in scientific revelations but in the underlying political ideologies of today and in the terrible effects of postmodern light thought.

Without a doubt, the "Spanish Case" has not enjoyed any historical luck or justice. All the attention has been directed at the "Jewish Case". Neither in Europe nor elsewhere (except for worthy Hispanic scholars) will you find the most elementary knowledge of exactly what Francoism did within Spanish borders, against the cemetery walls, within the prisons and jails, inside the barracks and police headquarters, in rural and urban areas. The criminality of the "Spanish Case" is buried amidst one or another of these, consigned to the most deceitful oblivion.

Given the above and fully aware that the thematic labyrinth is extremely complex, we are only able to glimpse the reality of Francoist prisons, that is, just what happened inside them, through the evidence given by survivors and provided in the diaries of those who experienced that tragic world.

1. Cordova Provincial Prison in 1941– Franco's Auschwitz

Cordoba Provincial Prisons usually held an average 4,000 inmates (one thousand in the old prison, the Alcázar, and the remainder in the New Prison). In July 1939 when only the old prison was operational, it was packed with 1,500 inmates. In the countryside, the provincial jails were equally overcrowded. At the end of 1940, prisoners began to be brought to the as yet unfinished building of the New Prison in the north of the city. This improvised jail was not officially inaugurated until 14 July 1944, by which time the great manslaughter of 1941 was over. 400 inmates were employed in finishing the building work, under the Regime's original invention of the program that allowed prisoners to redeem their sentences through work. The old jail, the one located in the Alcázar, was emptied of its five hundred inmates and closed at the end of Winter 1942.

Cordoba Provincial Prison in 1941 was an authentic Auschwitz, as were all of Franco's large prisons that year. It was the venue for an extraordinary extermination, no matter how many still deny that it ever occurred, despite the early information that Moreno Gómez first published in 1987 regarding the situation in Cordoba and the facts that are contained herein. What is certain, is that what occurred in these prisons was neither ignored nor unwanted by the leaders of the Regime who freely consented to this crime against humanity in 1941, the same year that an equal extermination was occurring in the Nazi concentration camps.[19] In the Cordoba capital Provincial Prison, the mortality rate among inmates during the 1940s for a penal population of 3,000-4,000, was 756 inmates, 502 of whom died in 1941 alone.

Table 1 – Inmate Mortality from hunger and deprivation in Cordoba Provincial Prison in the 1940s for a prison population of 3,000 – 4,000

1939	15
1940	30
1941	502
1943	22
1944	5
1945	4
1946	13
1947	7
1948	10
1949	33
1950	30
TOTAL	**756**

Source: Cordoba capital Civil Registry and Provincial Prison Chapel Record Book only.

The reasons for such a scandalous mortality are difficult to determine. For one thing, this was not limited to Cordoba province and was widespread all over Spain, yet practically nothing has been written about the events of 1941 in Cordoba capital. Also, although this was the year of the great penal manslaughter countrywide, it was not quite the same in every province. For example, in Coto, Gijón, prison, the great manslaughter was in 1938, after Asturias fell to the Nationalists in October 1937; in the case of the prisons in Catalonia, the manslaughter was widespread over time, from 1939 to 1942, inclusive; and in Navarra, the greater manslaughter occurred in 1942 in San Crstóbal Fort. [20]

2. Fascist Administration of Cordoba

The Prison Staff

In 1939, the <u>Director</u> of the Provincial Prison in Cordoba in the immediate post-war period, was Miguel Villarrubia y Garcia-Chico, who died soon afterwards in Málaga at the beginning of 1940. From 1940 onwards, during the days of the Cordovan genocide, the tragically notorious Director was Don Enrique Díaz de Lemaire who lost his position March 1941 in the wake of arguments between corrupt officials. The new Director, Juan José Escobar Sánchez, an equally fierce exterminator and every much as corrupt as his predecessor, took up his post April 1941. The manslaughter of inmates continued throughout the year, only dwindling at the beginning of 1942. Escobar remained in this position until February 1943 when, after he was transferred to Barcelona, he was replaced by Fernando Garcia González.

During those tragic days, the Sub-Director was Ramón García Lavella. Rafael Herreros was the Director of the Women's Section, assisted by the infamous and greatly feared Doña Dolores. Conchita Costa was another such assistant mentioned by witnesses. The Chaplain General was Rev. P. Garcia, S.J., frequently accompanied by the parish priest from El Salvador Church, José Torres Molina. Health Care was entrusted to a quaint physician, Don Celso Ortíz Megias, under the Provincial Director of Health, Dr. César Sebastián. The Director General for Health in the country was Dr. Palanca.

The Prison Manager, who ended up being prosecuted, was Manuel Hernández Vox. The Purveyor of Supplies was Rafael Bejarano, who owned a butcher shop on Calleja Marqués de Boil. The Caterer was a so-called Don Francisco.

All three stole as much as they could, whilst the inmates were served a lethal diet of nothing more than a dirty broth of rotten turnips, according to the magnificent testimony of Dr. Joaquin Sama Naharro[21], an inmate at the time, one of the most articulate individuals it has been Moreno Gómez' good fortune to assist him in his research.[i] Dr. Sana strongly condemned the cohort of merciless Prison Officers who specialized in beating that multitude of living skeletons. Those who today still can testify to this, refer particularly to Enrique de la Cerda, Antonio Justo, Manuel 'Y Pico', Andrés 'El Boxeador', a so-called 'Don Ángel', a temporary 2nd Lieutenant, and others such as 'El Teleras' and 'El Negro Desperdicios'. These were guards who stood in the halls and doorways, throwing out a beating or two as the lines of inmates walked past. One such guard who was especially feared was Ángel 'El Dientudo' Baena and his assistant Segundo Rojas, who tortured the inmates in the punishment cells and kept them for days on end on a diet of bread and water.

The Regime's governing authorities in Cordoba

During those days of genocidal extermination, Manuel Sarazá Murcia, Mayor since 27 November 1939, was succeeded by Antonio Torres Trigueros

---

[i] Joaquin Sama Naharro, M.D. Interviewed by Moreno Gómez in Córdoba, 8 July 1983, a day-long Q&A session during which he eloquently answered this historians' questions and expressed his deep-rooted belief in the Republic and profound anti-Francoist convictions. This was totally contradictory to an interview his son later published in a Cordoba newspaper, in which he said he father belonged to neither the left nor of the right. Obviously, like many father-son relationships, the son had a minimal understanding of his father and his ideals.

on November 5 1941. Rafael Jiménez Ruíz was appointed Mayor the following year. The Presidency of the Municipal Assembly was held for a long time by Enrique Salinas Anchelerga,[ii] whose brother Ángel was murdered by Falangists in 1936, and who took over from the great Nationalist conspirator, Eduardo Quero.

Joaquín Cárdenas Llavaneras, an Artillery Commander, held the position of <u>Civil Governor</u>. He was replaced October 10 1941 by a long-standing Falangist and retired Army officer, Rogelio Vignote, another of the great conspirators of 1936, who died on the job September 16 1942, a few days before his general factotum, the aforementioned Eduardo Quero. Vignote was succeeded by Ramón Risueño Catalán, from Granada.[iii] <u>Military Governor</u> General Francisco Formoso Blanco served from November 1939 to 1941 when he was replaced by Colonel Antonio Pérez Torrealba who in turn was replaced February 26 1941 by General Saturnino González Badía.

In 1941, the <u>Director of the Provincial Falange</u> was Jesús Aguilar, a well-known Falangist from Puente Genil. Fernando Fernández continued as Falange Secretary for Cordoba until he was replaced in mid-September 1941 by Manuel González Ruíz-Ripoll.

[ii] Enrique Salinas Anchelenga, a member of the high Cordovan bourgeoisie, had a son who was captured by the maquis in 1945 and held for a month in the Villaviciosa mountains, until his father paid a 75,000 peseta ransom. A relative of his, José Miguel Salinas, was a PSOE deputy to Parliament around 1980. When Moreno Gómez approached him with some questions regarding the civil war, he shouted, in a threatening manner: "Don't you ever again dare talk to me about this subject." The *Córdoba* newspaper society column ironically published a report of his luxurious jet-set wedding in the famous Círculo de la Amistad, known in the past as the 'Casino of the Rich' and since then, José Miguel Salinas' name has disappeared from public notice.

[iii] Ramón Risueño was well thought of by the general public who spoke of him as the 'good man of the Regime', in the midst of all this tragedy and outrage. The *Cordobés* newspaper of January 16 1943 published an article describing his efforts to ensure that rationed goods would be fairly distributed to inmates and how he would sometimes show up at a queue for goods to make sure they were being properly distributed. He even collected beggars from the street and had them clothed and fed, telling them that it was all being paid for by the Civil Governor. He did his best to keep a lid on prices and to prosecute several tradesmen without scruples. Unfortunately, this period of Christian charity soon ended as the Cordoba right-wing took over and removed him from office. It was a time of fascism, not of charitable acts.

3. Descent into the depths of the corrupt penitentiary world

Having described the administrative world of Fascist Cordoba in 1941, we shall now travel to the depths of the corrupt penitentiary world in Cordoba capital, as seen through the eyes Dr. Sama Naharro, the Republican physician from Madrid whose journey through the Francoist prison world brought him to Cordoba, where he settled down after his release from jail. Dr. Sama was first transferred from the Scala Coeli Convent improvised jail prison in Madrid to Castro del Río in October 1940, after the majority of provincial prison inmates had already been transferred from the rural jails to Cordoba capital.

> "It took us two weeks to get to Castro del Río from Madrid. Only seven of our party were common criminals and I would entertain them with stories. After we arrived, we spent five days without any food. The Director of the jail, a nattily-dressed Army officer, call us and told us that he had run out of funds. 'If there were more than 25 of you' he said, 'I could get some outside catering for you, but as you are fewer.... you're going to find it pretty difficult.' At long last, they brought in a group of individuals they had arrested on a farm, a whole family. Together, we added up to the minimum 25 inmates the Director needed to have food brought in from outside."

The following November, Dr. Sana was transferred to the Provincial Prison in Cordoba:

> "When they took me to Cordoba, I weighed 45 kilos [99 lbs.]. When I entered the patio in the old prison, it looked like something out of a novel by Cervantes: misery, lice, filth. Everyone was packed tight. There was a single urinal in the patio and long lines of inmates waiting to use it. I was dumbfounded: everyone was mixed together – political prisoners and common criminals. Nevertheless, we were still fed somewhat. I had arrived with a sleeping mat on my back and a suitcase, tied to my companion in line. When I saw that scene, the inmates de-lousing themselves, I asked myself: 'to where have I sunk?' It was so overcrowded, that each one of us was allotted two and a half floor tiles; we had to act together when we wanted to turn around. There were dramatic anecdotes. One day, I was told: 'Don Joaquim, there is one who is very ill.' I came closer and the man was ice cold. 'Yes, we knew that, but we did not want to wake you.' We had been sleeping next to a dead man.
>
> The prison doctor was a Don Celso Ortíz, whom they called Don Ciezo; the famous Director was Don Enrique. We soon were fed turnips only. People's faces would swell a little, under their eyelids, and Don Celso

24

would diagnose 'albuminia'. He prescribed a milk diet but the milk was watered down. They didn't last three days. I told Don Celso that he should find out what they were suffering from and I asked him if he ordered blood and urine tests. 'No. I don't do those things. Forget it.' In effect, the oedema was a sign of starvation. The person would get diarrhoea and the end result came quickly. There was no such thing as medicine. For Don Celso, everything was a case of 'albuminia' for which he prescribed milk, but the orderly who came in from outside, a so-called Paco or Francisco, watered down the milk and took the sugar home.

The young prison officers were very disrespectful towards the older ones whose jobs they wanted so that they could share in the hoarding. The prison caterer, Rafael Bejarano, owned a butcher's shop on Calleja Marqués de Boil. According to Bejarano, the prison Director stole everything he could. Both these men were later prosecuted. The prison Governor turned a blind eye to what was going on and he also took his share. The Director of the women's' prison, which was in a next door pavilion, the infamous Doña Dolores, was also implicated in the thieving.

During the 'battle of the turnips', as the inmates called our diet, diarrhoea was the last stage of a colitis caused by the lack of food. The meal lists were falsified. They apparently described varied menus when the reality was that the only thing we were given was a watery turnip soup. Don Celso was fully aware of this as he signed the falsified menus. Still, he sent separate, secret lists to the Governor, informing him that the prisoners were not being fed the regulation meals. It was his signature on these secret lists that later saved Don Celso from prosecution. He would tell me: 'Sana, keep out of this. What happens is that the officers are divided: the young ones want to steal and so do the old ones, and they don't want anybody else involved.'

I tried to bring some dignity to the removal of the dead. At first, they were just dragged out. I made a stretcher and placed the dead man on one of the benches in the patio from where they were removed with a bit of dignity, as some of them had relatives present. I also organized what they called 'the potato cellar', where those who were very far gone and the highly contagious were kept aside. Everyone knew that anyone who was taken there would not return. It was located at the end of a corridor so that they would not die in front of the rest.

Epidemic typhus is transmitted by the body louse when it stings the host. The doctor who replaced Dr. Celso – who was fired for negligence – was a so-called Pedrajas who stubbornly insisted that there was no typhus in the prison. So much so, that one prisoner who had all the symptoms of this disease was released and allowed to spread it to others in the town.

Our meals improved with the addition of beans and black carrots (the Nazarene broth) and the number of cases of typhus dropped. The prison Governor, the Director, and the Head of the Women's Prison and Rafael Bejarano were all fired, but not the milkman nor the nurse. A special military judge was appointed for their trial. The Governor was sentenced to 30 years and the Director to 20 years and both were imprisoned in Puerto de Santa Maria. However, they appealed their sentences, which were reduced, and the following year they were free and back in the same jobs, with back-pay and all kinds of other benefits."

There are several assumptions that one might make after reading Dr. Sams' written eye-witness testimony. One, that because it was a physician who diagnosed the cause of the inmates' sufferings, his conclusions should be taken as sound. Second, that the diagnosis of the extermination cannot be exclusively based on the prison officers' corruption but instead of on the perverse nature of the entire system, as this same extermination was occurring all over Spain in 1941. Third, that even if one blames the corruption in the prison, punishment was purely a pro forma affair as the sentences were quickly overturned. Fourth, that during the entire decade of the 1940s, the majority of the inmates died of starvation, because almost all those who died in 1941, did so from hunger (499 of the 502 total deaths in 1941.

Another opinion regarding this dark matter of corruption in the Cordoba Provincial Prison is that of a Cordovan attorney, Francisco Poyatos López, whom Moreno Gómez visited in his office at the beginning of the 1980s and who kindly gave him a copy of his book of memories. According to Poyatos, the Governor, the caterer and two prison officers were prosecuted. The court martial was held in Cordoba with great expectations., under the presidency of Colonel Aguilar Galinda, notorious genocide of Fernán Núñez, Commander of an Artillery Regiment. The Prosecutor asked for two death penalties but the sentences were reduced to thirty years in jail, which in those days meant almost nothing.

Poyatos, acting in defence of the Governor, pled his innocence on grounds that the food ration approved by the Directorate General of Prisons, was below 800 calories a day, whilst a minimum number of 1,200 calories is necessary for a totally immobile person. Poyatos also argued that the deaths were not the result of a fraudulent decrease in the rations fed the inmates, but on the fact that the Directorate General of Prisons recklessly approved insufficient rations. He concluded his defence by deriding an allusion to a tale from The Arabian Nights, in that examples should be set when, for example, if a high-ranking official could not be hanged, a lower-level officer would do. The most important was that no crime should go unpunished. [22]

This Cordovan attorney's input is extremely clear: the responsibility for the deaths was not so much that of the corrupt officials, but of the Directorate General of Prisons. In other words, it was the fault of the system because the latter approved food rations that would clearly lead to the extermination of those who were expected to survive on them. More descriptions of the conditions in the prison from several inmates, are recorded in APPENDIX I.

Hunger remains almost the sole topic of discussion amongst all those who survived the Francoist prisons. Hunger was a special repressive instrument of Francoism and of Fascism in general, a tool for the genocide in the prisons, even more than a means of oppressing those who were free. It was a basic principle of European Fascism in the endeavour to bring about the total, material and moral, dispossession of its political opponents, as Ricard Vinyes wrote. Everything was a ploy to bring about the ideological and moral destruction of the individual. It was institutionalized poverty, hunger and destitution. According to Vinyes, this element of the State's dispossession or moral and material plundering represents the universal point of contact with the great Fascist systems of political reclusion. There is no way that one can deny this institutionalization of hunger in Franco's prisons, exactly as practiced in Hitler's prison camps, although the Francoists did not reach the same level of perfection as the Germans in the 'art' of extermination.[23]

4. The typhus epidemic

It seemed that the Four Horsemen of the Apocalypse – war, hunger, disease and death – were riding roughshod over the entire country as, in addition to the hunger, there was the typhus epidemic. In effect, the 1941 typhus epidemic was not limited to the prisons as it had spread to the general population as a result of shortages and misery of all kinds. The Regime always insisted in minimizing the problem and in covering up the data as much as possible. However, in the Francoist prisons especially, overcrowding, unhealthy conditions and the ever-present parasites provided the ideal breeding ground for the spread of the epidemic.

The authorities in Cordoba waited far too long before admitting that epidemic typhus was free in the city. May 25 1941, the *Azul* newspaper first published a report of 16 cases of epidemic typhus in the city. In the meantime, nothing was said about the epidemic that, together with hunger and anaemia, was decimating the prison inmates. The new Prison Director, Juan José Escobar, made some half-hearted attempts to control the epidemic but without much success and it was only in January 1942 that we hear of a campaign against typhus in the city. Civil Governor Rogelio Vignote, presided over a public meeting of the Provincial Board of Health January 9, when the Provincial Director of Health, César Sebastián, informed the meeting that a new mobile disinfection unit with showers and a gas chamber with hydrocyanic acid. Had been installed in the prison. Inmates' communication with anyone from the outside was suspended, as was sending clothes out to be washed, all of which had a negative impact on inmates' survival. Measures for quarantining the ill were increased and court martials were stopped for the time being, the only positive effect of the situation.

The *ABC* newspaper in Seville published a rather euphemistic article November 19 1941 regarding the typhus epidemic, in which it stated that during the 1940-41 Winter, 1,097 victims died from typhus nationwide and 8,000 were affected. The article was accompanied by a map, in which we note that the provinces that were most affected were Madrid, Seville and Malaga, followed in second place by all of Andalusia and all Southern Spain, that is, from Madrid South. The provincial prisons were pointed to as the centres of the infection. In the article, the newspaper hinted that there were practically no cases of typhus in the North of the country other than a small focus near Vítoria, in the Nanclares de Oca prison camp. Cordoba is not mentioned in the newspaper article that does, however, say that those infected ranged from between twenty and fifty years of age, not so coincidentally the age range of the prison inmates. The index of longevity for Spain, during those ill-fated days fell like a stone due to the lack of food and health care and all sorts of suffering.

Large periods of malnutrition explain to a great extent, the high incidence of typhus after March 1941, when it was at its height in the Cordoba Prison. This so alarmed the Regime that it attempted to cover it up by instructing the registry offices to issue death certificates for other reasons, such as avitaminosis, starvation, cachexia and so forth, anything but typhus, even though many more were dying from hunger than from this disease. APPENDIX II.

The first signs that the typhus epidemic was coming under control in the Cordoba prison were noted in February 1942, when the official death rate from the disease began to fall from an average of 40 a month to about a dozen, even though the majority were still starving to death. Whereas in 1941 the death rate rose to 502 cases, in 1942 in dropped to 85. In 1946, the 'year of hunger', 13 inmates died, only to rise again to an average of 30 victims per year after 1948.

Undoubtedly, the great prison disaster in Cordoba occurred in 1941, the worst months being March and April with an average of almost 100 deaths per month. There was no typhus then; starvation and basic privations were the cause. An examination of the towns and villages of origin of the greatest number of dead were those that were at a distance from the capital, therefore making it even more difficult for relatives of the inmates to bring them food: Peñarroya 24 victims; Montoro 25; Villanueva de Cordoba 23; Hinojosa 23;

Villaviciosa 22; Adamuz 19; Fuenteobejuna 19; Belmez 16; Villanueva del Rey 14; Dos Torres 13; Pedroche 11; El Viso 10; Baena 13; Bujalance 13; Puente Genil 10; and so forth. Of special note, the fact that the majority of dead inmates came from outside the province, a total 150, who were even less likely to receive any outside help.

Also noteworthy is the highest mortality rate for inmates who were natives of mountain towns and villages, who felt the full weight of the post-war repression and who had been arrested in greater numbers than in the countryside. The fact is that even though the oppressor had already implemented a considerable part of its genocide program in the countryside in 1936, in 1941 it was the proximity or distance of an inmate's relatives that were determinant to the mortality rate in the prison.

Table 2. Number of inmates at death in Cordoba capital prisons by age group during the period under study								
Infants	-20 years	20-29 years	30-39 years	+40 years	+50 years	+70 years	1941 Total	Period Total
		17%	17%	26%	26.8%			
		112	113	151	176		**502**	
Also died during Spring 1941 but not included in -20 and +70 age groups above								
5	20					12		**539**

The age of the inmates was another key factor. For the period under study, inmates older than 50 years led the number of those who died (26.8%, a total of 176). They were followed by inmates older than 40 years (26%, a total of 151). The remaining two groups, 20-29 years, 30-39 years, were equal with 17% of the whole (112 and 113 victims, respectively). Although younger inmates appeared more resistant to the effects of the privations and hunger, it was not always so. During the acute stage of the extermination – Spring 1941 – victims aged 20-29 years died in greater numbers that those older than 30 years. There were 20 victims under 20 years and 5 infants who had accompanied their mothers in jail. Lastly, there were 12 victims among elderly inmates, more than 70 years old.

Hence, the impressive disaster in Cordoba Provincial Prison that we can truly call the Francoist Auschwitz of 1941 and that Moreno Gómez will further show was repeated in a similar vein in the rest of Spain. Meanwhile, we note an example of the great exercises in hypocrisy and cynicism that a Francoism without scruples delighted in displaying, a grotesque poster that the 'magnanimous Caudillo' ordered displayed in his 'beneficent' prisons, to his shame forever:

> Should you visit penal complexes in other countries and should you compare their systems to ours, I can assure you without fearing of being mistaken, that you will not find as fair, as Catholic and as humane a system as the one created by our Movement for our inmates.
>
> *Francisco Franco, Madrid, 17 July 1944.*

This section on the Cordovan genocide closes with the exceptional testimony of an illustrious Cordovan Republican, Rafael Sánchez Guerra, who was interned in several Francoist prison complexes in Spain (Madrid, Cuéllar, Algeciras, Cordoba, Puerta and Santa María, and more) until his 'penitentiary tourism' brought him to Cordoba Prison in 1941:[24]

"...The next morning, Don Ramón Carreras Pons, ex-Member of Parliament for Cordoba, the most eminent inmate in all the prison population, having heard of my arrival, invited me to have a bit of coffee and to accompany him on a visit to all the sections of the prison.

The penal regime in Cordoba was an 'open air' regime, by which, all the inmates were cruelly forced to spend at least nine hours a day, in a row, in the patio, unless they were sent on some other business. It is there that they went after they were first released from their cells in the morning; there that they were served a meal at half past noon; there they remained after they were called to prayers.

There they had to remain sitting on the ground or walk about to keep from dying from the cold. The patio, occupied by about one thousand five hundred inmates (in the old prison), was really impressive: it was an authentic mass reduced to the most iron discipline.

Don Ramón Carreras Pons, after having been detained for several months, had been absolved by the Courts of Justice, but the Governor of the Province, a man who was 'more Papist than the Pope', refused to accept the judge's decision and arbitrarily kept him interned, so that his new period of captivity might be indefinitely prolonged.

As this case of Carreras, I knew of others. In Falangist Spain, sometimes, tyranny was exercised at the margin of the laws, and at other times, without the minimal appearance of justice."

THE 1941 FRANCOIST AUSCHWITZ
IN THE REST OF SPAIN

> *"The unalterable characteristics of the great oppressive political systems do not rest on the number of imprisoned or killed, neither in the extermination procedures, but in the denial of the crime against humanity; whether it is to rub it out or to cover it up by means of an appropriately mystifying language that contributed to trivialize the vulnerability of human rights which, under Francoism, was the language of the Christian Church. There can be no doubt that the feature common to the great punitive Fascist systems is, essentially, the removal of all trace of the crime."*

Ricard Vinyes, in *Una inmensa prisión*

Extermination through hunger and deprivation in Francoist prisons, especially in 1941, was not by any means limited to Cordoba; it was practised throughout the rest of Spain, in prisons to which tens of thousands of natives of Andalusia had been sent. No discussion of the Cordoba genocide would be complete without a description of Franco's Nazi-like methods of extermination of the disaffected throughout the country. This topic, however, is barely addressed by historians who today appear solely dedicated to studying the rules and regulations governing the prison world.

Moreno Gomes begins by providing a description of the sadly infamous Puerto de Santa María prison in Cádiz in 1941 where Rafael Sánchez Guerra was sent straight from Cordoba:

> "The terrible spectre of hunger had already cast its sinister shadow on Puerto Prison. The inmates, despite the personal efforts of the Prison Director to find food, were starving to death. Avitaminosis, a disease that was unknown in our country until Franco decided to create a great Spain, caused enormous harm to the poorer classes of society in Andalusia and was responsible for daily deaths in the Central prison, in which I was incarcerated.
>
> I was stunned by the appalling problem of providing food for the inmates in Alcázar de San Juan and in Cordoba prisons. Whereas in the first of these, I once saw two oranges and half a dozen chestnuts shared out for the noonday meal, in Puerto prison, as there was a total lack of bread, the situation was more acute and more tragic.
>
> The several prison infirmaries were packed with young men whose swollen faces were a clear symptom of the disease, impoverished, skeletal, presenting no organic disease but physically unable to stand up. It was a rare day that we did not line up, sad and silent, in the large patio, to witness them carry out the remains of two, three or four cellmates in rough

wooden boxes, those who had found such a painful means of 'recovering their freedom'.

Seventy-eight inmates starved to death in March 1941, a huge number that amazed us all. Such was the desperate desire for food of some of the inmates, that each patio had to appoint an inmate to keep watch over the garbage cans to prevent others from poisoning themselves with the waste and filth that were thrown in them. Orange peels, often trodden upon and dirty, were absolutely devoured by the starving men."

Manuel Martínez Cordero discovered a 'confidential' report dated July 1939 in the Archives of Basque Nationalism and the Sabino Arana Foundation, entitled: "Report on the Basque prisoners confined in the Puerto de Santa Maria penal complex".[25] At the end of the civil war, some 4,000 Basque prisoners held in Euskadi and Santoña prisons, were dispersed amongst other Francoist prison in the country. Of these, 2,000 arrived in Puerto de Santa María, which brought the total number of inmates to 5,400 in a space designed for 800 internees. The information contained in the report, referring to 1939, provides important, terrifying information, of the overwhelming situation of those thousands of men. According to the report, presumably submitted by Basque authors:

"The general impression of the data that we are presenting cannot be more deplorable and once again, it confirms the truth of the matter that has already been repeatedly presented regarding the current penal regime in Francoist Spain, which because of its inhumane characteristics exceeds, in its cruel reality, anything that the most partial and unfavourable opinion can imagine. For Francoism, the prisoner has lost his condition of being human and he is treated like an animal. We do not have to make an effort to stress the cruelty, the uncivil and bloody sense that presides over the treatment to which our prisoners in Puerto de Santa María are subjected to."

The authors of the report explain that the prison complex is an installation that is open to the Atlantic Ocean and, therefore, subject to blustering winds year-round, especially the east wind during the Summer. The sanitary installations were also disastrous, few and badly placed as there were only two shower rooms, with 57 keys shared by 5,400 inmates.

Inmates were packed body to body, mouth to mouth, so that there was a profusion of diseases of the respiratory tract, in addition to tuberculosis and pre-tuberculosis. Because of the lack of space in the infirmary, inmates suffering from any of these lived cheek-by-jowl with all the others. There also was a special kind of influenza that attacked many inmates and left them as weak as if they were recovering from an attack of typhoid fever. This type of influenza, sometimes pulmonary, sometimes intestinal, often caused body temperatures above 40ºC (104ºF) that left the patient totally prostrate.

Water was scarce and poorly distributed. Add to this an unbelievable profusion of bed bugs, lice, fleas and flies, especially on extraordinarily filthy blankets and mattresses, none of which could be washed because of the lack of water, somewhere to wash, boil or even dry these, it not surprising that nobody escaped suffering some kind of dermatitis, at least once. All these weaknesses were mainly due to the lack of individual physical reserves and to bad food. Added to this, hunger and privations easily explain the resulting extermination.

The prison infirmary consisted of three main wards: one for patients with tuberculosis, one for general medicine and surgical treatment, and a special ward for the chronically ill. The most serious problem was that of patients with tuberculosis who lived with the rest of the inmates. It was Basque physicians, also prisoners, who managed to keep them separate. During Summer 1939, the only quarantined tubercular patients were the 44 who fit in the ward, that is, the most serious cases. There was a very long waiting list for a space in this ward.

There were 17 beds for patients in the ward for the chronically ill. There was no room for any more and remember, there were approximately 5,400 inmates at the time. According to the aforementioned report, the beds on the wards were little more than table-tops about 50cm from the ground. There were no sheets, blankets, pillows or anything else. If a patient wanted any of these 'luxuries', someone from outside the prison had to buy them in the town and bring them in for him.

Based on the Basque report and the problem of the insanitary conditions in the prison, there can be only one conclusion: *the care that the official prison doctors gave the inmates was either negligible or non-existent* and that the health care problem was left to any inmates who were physicians to do what they could for their fellow prisoners, at least at the beginning. Eventually, an authoritarian and despotic prison doctor who not only did not give a damn about the inmates' health arrived and he began to make arbitrary decisions such as refusing to sign vouchers for the purchase of medicines. Consequently, if the problem of feeding the inmates was serious, no less serious was the problem of medication for the ill. So much so, that aspirin, streptomycin, luminal, etc., bandages and all kinds of sterile, and sometimes unsterilized, equipment, were only available in limited quantities and for very short periods of time.

The absolute truth of this is confirmed in Miguel Hernández' diary. Terminally ill with tuberculosis, he was only able to receive treatment on the days that his wife visited him in prison and brought bandages and compresses for him. In a February 1942 letter that he wrote her from Alicante prison,[26] he begs her to send him three or four kilos of cotton and gauze, with the utmost urgency, without which he will not receive any treatment that day. He tells her that the infirmary has run out of everything and that the day before they had to resort to rags to treat him as best they could, which was not at all right. Obviously, the New State had made no provision for the care of the ill. Was this intentional or by omission?

Also, according to the Basque report, more than 2,000 inmates a month were seen in the infirmary for general consultations. Most of the complaints were related to the digestive tract and the skin and a whole series of afflictions related to the hardships. The few surgical interventions were for abdominal hernias, appendicectomies, epidermitis fimica, etc. No less than 1,943 cases of pulmonary or heart complaints were treated in 1939. Of those admitted to the tuberculosis ward, only three were released. Of all the complaints seen to in the general consultation in the first year, most (40%) were bronchial, mainly involving tuberculosis.

As regards the mortality rate, the report refers not to the entire prison population of 5,400, but only to the 2,000 Basque inmates, of whom 43 died during the first ten months of their stay in Puerto Santa Maria, that is 1939 and early 1940. There is no available information regarding the 1941 genocide, nor what happened to the entire prison population.

The Basque report deplores the thoughtless and disrespectful behaviour of the prison chaplains and it names two Jesuits, Rev. P. Gutiérrez Silva and Rev. Arjona. The clergymen's negligence was such that the dead were buried in plain, unlined wooden caskets without the presence of a priest and no religious ceremony, something that rang foul of the Basque people's strong Catholic beliefs. An example of this belief was a whip-round amongst prisoners who did not have any food to eat, to purchase a statue of Our Lady of Mercy. As to the chaplains' behaviour, in accordance with the regulations of the Regime, the amazed report states:

> "We have been reliably informed of the existence of secret instructions from Prison Headquarters to prison chaplains, instructing them that, as they are engaged in carrying out their sacred mission, should they find an inmate who is innocent of what he was wrongly condemned by the Courts Martial, instead of taking note of his complaints and transmitting them to the Prison Director, they should attempt to discourage these inmates from complaining and encourage them to accept their situation as atonement for all the sins they may have ever committed against God, and to abstain once and for all from bothering the Prison Headquarters."

There are still very few studies of the other great Francoist penitentiary establishments. Two teachers from the Almendralejo School, Badajoz, Manuel Rubio Díaz and Silvestre Gómez Zafra, who visited Moreno Gómez in Villanueva de Cordoba in 1987, later published a very interesting study of their village where there were two prisons: La Colonia and the Almacén de la Hiz, which they very kindly dedicated to him 24 August 1987 in thanks for his support and collaboration.

One of the eye-witnesses they interviewed told them that in La Colonia, where he was interned, the inmates were divided into twelve prison gangs. Hundreds of them were crammed into the prison and they slept on the floor on blankets their family brought them when they could; in winter, it was much, much worse. Anyone who was unable to receive some food from his family did not last long. With only a ladle of white beans, what did they expect? Their witness was transferred to a Seville prison in May 1941 but his brother José, who remained in La Colonia, was tried and executed a few days afterwards. [27]

In their study, Díaz and Zafra include an enormous list of 333 inmates executed following numerous sacas, mostly in 1941. In addition to these, no less than 144 inmates starved to death in the sixteen months between July 1940 and November 1941.

It is not easy to explain how it was possible for 144 individuals from a single village to die from hunger and hardships during 16 months' imprisonment under Franco. It is extremely galling that, still today, when such a tragedy is brought to the attention of individuals who consider themselves members of the intelligentsia and who despise as much as they ignore the facts, insist that there was no extermination, nor eradication, just re-education.

There were many holocausts in Franco's jails where men fell like flies, but one that can be truly called an Auschwitz was the Penal Colony on the Island of San Simón, off the Pontevedra, Galicia, coast. This prison was set aside as a kind of scrap yard for extremely elderly men considered decrepit with age, specializing in the internment of elderly men from the South of Spain.[28] Diego San José de la Torre, in his memoires, describes the drama of prisoners from the South of Spain who were transferred to prisons in the North of the country. He writes that the majority of the individuals 'invoiced' to the most humid and coldest regions were elderly peasants from Andalusia who were so poor that they only had the clothes they were wearing and who were leaving the land where they were born, never to return."[29]

In May 1941, when autocratic Miguel Cuadrillero was appointed Director, the hunger in San Simón reached such a level that the prison became a slaughter-house. More than 300 inmates died in less than three months of that terrible year. As Diego San José reports, the Director horse-traded with contractors and suppliers and those who were responsible for the canteen. He would buy the cheapest cereals and vegetables and rotten fish. The mortality was so great during that Summer, that the stench from the cadavers that were stacked in a warehouse on the seafront waiting for caskets that were not being supplied by the local carpenters because they were not being paid, alarmed the villagers of neighbouring Redondela. The 1941 mortality rate did not spare a neighbouring penitentiary, the Camposancos concentration camp, where 70 inmates starved to death and another 100 were executed.

Amoedo-Gil, in their study of San Simón prison[30], calculated that there were 666 prisoners in the prison, of whom 161 (24.2%), of a total 2,176 inmates, were from Andalusia. Given the specialized nature of this penal complex, it is not surprising that over half of the men who died were aged over 60. In conclusion, these authors stress that the excessive mortality of the period cannot be considered as exceptional, typical of only this or that prison establishment, as many of those who blame the prison director claim. On the contrary, 1941 must be seen as a tragic year during which this was the norm in prisons all over Spain. Basically, they say, Spanish Fascism was no more than a crude, would-be farcical imitation of Italian Fascism or German Nazism, more appropriate to a satanic music hall. There lies the difference. All that happened during the Spanish civil war was nothing more than a try-out, or a rehearsal if you prefer, of the wave of terror which Nazism would later unleash over all of Europe.

Eutimio Martín García came to almost identical conclusions as Amoedo-Gil regarding the extermination program and the Hispano-Nazi similarity, with which Moreno Gómez agrees. After establishing a resemblance between the Francoist repressive methods and those of the Nazis, *mutatis mutandis*, knowing that the German barbarity shall never be surpassed in all the world and that any future attempts would be more or less bungling, albeit equally deadly, copies, Eutimio says the following regarding the San Simón penal colony:[31]

> "On the island of San Simón, Francoism devised an Auschwitz of its own creation, where the harsh climate, due to the particular physiological weakness of the inmates, would play the same sinister role as the gas chambers. It rains day and night, for months at a time. The rainstorms that whip the island are frequently accompanied by gusts of wind so powerful that they can bring down the strongest trees by the dozen."

Eutimio Martín points to similarities with Nazism, not only when it came to the extermination (it was never a case of total extermination in Spain, nor even in Mauthausen) but also when it came to the method of transferring prisoners in cattle wagons on trains, day after day, without any food or water. In Spain, that is also how prisoners were transferred in closed carriages, in never-ending, exhausting journeys, from one prison to another.

As to the Francoist desire to exterminate its opponents, Eutimio points to National Catholicism's deliberate intention to exterminate (or at least decimate) the defeated by starving them, something that became clearly apparent the moment the Republican Army surrendered. Every concentration or transfer of prisoners always lasted several days during which prisoners were not fed. In the prison, an inmate's ability to survive depended on his ability to receive food from outside. Officially, the Directorate General for Security set the daily ration at a maximum 800 calories, a murderous ration given that the minimum intake for survival when inactive was 1,200 calories, according to Dr. Sama. In other words, when one speaks of extermination in the prisons, much was carefully planned and very little improvised or left to chance.

There is data from the Military Prison Hospital in Guernica, established between 1938 and 1940 in the Augustine College building as a penitentiary for prisoners and also as headquarters of a Battalion of Workers from Devastated Zones. Designed as a 650-bed hospital, 265 sick prisoners (almost half) from all over Spain (8 from Cordoba) died from disease from June 1938 to May 1940, mostly from tuberculosis, typhus and typhoid, the result of privations of all kinds.[32]

<u>Cordovans who died in Guernica Military Prison Hospital</u>

Andrés Blanco Castro (Villafranca), Francisco Cantarero Castillo (Bujalance), Ramón Ferrer López (Peñarroya), Manuel López Castillejos (Alcaracejos), Jesús Molina Villaga (Villanueva), Eusebio Murillo Ortiz (Fuenteobejuna), Juan Muro Acedo (Pueblonuevo) y Antonio Rojas Ruiz (Cordoba capital). Buried in the extension of the Zallo Cemetery.

As to other prison establishments in Spain, Eutimio Martín reports that in El Dueso prison in Santoña, Cantabria, with a capacity of 3,000, 53 inmates died from starvation on a single day – 9 January 1941.

A study by José María García Márquez provides reliable data on the mortality rate in Seville prisons of 786 victims, most of them during the 1940-1942 period of extermination, of which 500 in the Provincial Prison and the remainder in several concentration camps. The most scandalous of these was the Las Arnas concentration camp where 144 of its 300 inmates died from starvation during the tragic 1940-1942 Triennium. Even more shocking is the fact that this camp was especially created for the imprisonment of 'beggars', in those days, anyone from the thousands and thousands who were starving because they had been reduced to extreme poverty.[33]

For the first time, in all the studies of the civil war, we are told that a concentration camp was destined for 'beggars', half of whom would be 'exterminated'. This brings us to reflect on other aspects of the Francoist repression that are similar to the III Reich and add to the description of the genocide in Franco's Spain. We are continuously told that there was no 'technical genocide', but this is clearly doubtful because the totalitarian New State did not tolerate, in any form whatsoever, the poor, beggars, the impoverished rabble nor shirtless individuals who wore *alpargatas*[iv]. The truth is, we still have much more to learn about Francoism.

García Márquez provides significant evidentiary insight regarding the degree of neglect and total lack of interest with which Falangists impassively observed the great national scandal of prison mortality. Actually, it was the Regime, wishing to turn a blind eye to that which was happening in the prisons, that abolished the *compulsory inspections* required under Articles 684 and 685 of the Code of Military Justice.

When June 22 1937 the Military Governor of Cádiz informed the Inspector of Prisons that there had been no inspection of the prisons as required, the Inspector replied June 30 that "in accordance with Decree 88 from the National Defence Junta of September 18 1936, all regulation prison inspections were deferred *sine die*." Right from the beginning, the Regime was well aware of exactly what was happening in the prisons but it preferred not to hear of it.

As to the hypocaloric diet mentioned earlier, Moreno Gómez agrees entirely with García Márquez when he says that the great mortality in Francoist prisons could be directly attributed to the Regime that knew full well that its policy for feeding inmates was causing the death of thousands of prisoners all over the country. To deny the evidence of this is an exercise in unscientific and unethical frivolity. Obviously, victorious Francoists did not give two hoots for what was going on in the prisons; the Rojos simply did not deserve to live. If they died in prisons, the Regime would save bullets. Admitting that the death of three or four inmates in a prison during one year might be the norm, there can be only one name to describe the scandalous mortality rate death from starvation in post-war Francoist penitentiaries: a *crime against humanity and extermination*, regardless of what negationists want to call it.

[iv] Rope sandals, the typical footwear of country people and the height of fashion worldwide today.

The following table gives some figures for the extremely little amount of data currently available regarding Franco's prison holocaust. More than 6,000 dead in a dozen prisons, all but no data for major prisons such as Puerto de Santa Maria, Málaga, Hellin, Chinchilla, Cuéllar, Segovia, Madrid, Ventas, Alcalá de Henares, Burgos, Palencia, Santurrarán, Amorebieta, Santander, El Dueso, Santoña, Zaragoza and so many more. How many more thousands actually died?

3. Sample prison mortality from starvation across Spain in the 1940s

Location of penal establishment	Died from starvation
Cordoba capital	756
Seville	786
Almendralejo (Badajoz)	144
4 Pueblos de La Serena	90
San Simón (Pontevedra)	666
Oviedo	251
Gijón	84
Guernica	265
San Cristobal (Navarra)	328
Catalonia	648
Castellón	112
Valencia	813
Alicante	240
Toledo	680
Cáceres	150
TOTAL	**6,013**

In conclusion, Franco's crafty, underhand extermination policy, negligent by action and omission, was a colossal, scandalous phenomenon in the prison world that we might call the Four Horsemen of the Penal Apocalypse: 1) Mass imprisonment and large-scale overcrowding, with lethal effects of their own; 2) Official starvation diet, that is, planned hunger pure and simple, excused as the greed of corrupt prison employees; 3) Almost total lack of health care and medical assistance, where not even aspirins or bandages for dressing wounds were available; 4) Climate as a weapon of mass destruction, where prisoners from warm Southern Spain were sent to the cold, damp jails of the North where the inmates dropped like flies, especially the weak and elderly as in San Simón, or in the Artic conditions of Burgos prison in winter. Few historians have drawn attention to this particular feature of the Regime's perversity.

OTHER ASPECTS OF THE MULTI-REPRESSION

"The Historic Memory still continues to be dominated by the victors; it remains the memory of the victors. In Spain, nobody comes out to protest because the Church has initiated the beatification of members of the clergy... Nobody protests in favour of the Basque priests who were executed by Francoism, nor because there is no 'beatification' of the other dead. People appear to think that this is normal, they accept it... This is, however, an indication, an aftertaste of the absolute domination that the victors have had over the memory of the people, they who have imposed their memory and their interpretation of the civil war. Today, there are books that tell that it was not always so, but in the collective memory of the population, it is still the victors' memory that prevails."

Jorge Semprún, *Los caminos de la memoria.*

Those who have little knowledge of this topic believe that Franco's reprieves and pardons at the beginning of the 1940s were a philanthropic gesture by a magnanimous, honourable and benevolent Caudillo. Nothing could be further from the truth. It was not a question of magnanimity but of getting rid of, as it were, of the chaos of half a million prisoners-of-war interned in concentration camps and prisons of all kinds, all over Spain. A chaos for which there were no infrastructures, no penitentiaries, no budget. After the first post-war year, when all kinds of persons faced the firing squads regardless of their political importance, or lack of it, Francoism had no choice but to begin releasing prisoners, from the bottom to the top, timidly beginning with the lesser sentences in 1940.

This marked the first application of the Francoist theory for classifying prisoners that it divided into two categories: the confirmed disaffected (politically significant) and the recoverable (of no political significance). Nonetheless, this was not an exact classification as prisoners were often classified at random as many of no political significance ended up being executed or starving to death in prison. There is another factor to bear in mind also, that until the end of 1941, as in the III Reich, extermination as a measure predominated and overcrowding was intentionally used as a method for exterminating the unwanted. This is why, both in Nazi camps and in Franco's prisons, 1941 was the year with the highest mortality when little attention was paid to the lives of the imprisoned.

Conditional release from prison, classification of prisoners, National Parole Board

Beginning in 1941, both in Spain and in the Nazi concentration camps, the regimes started to implement their "magnificent plan" for using prisoners for forced labour, which led to some improvement in their living conditions. Furthermore, the slow decrease in the number of inmates gradually contributed to prisoners' survival. Thus, the appearance of all kinds of so-called humanitarian and charitable programs that had nothing whatsoever to do with the earlier punishment, extermination, submission and educational measures. No matter how hypocritical or cynical its propaganda, the victorious New State intended to resort to the new programs to squash all ideas of trade unionism and republicanism, once and forever. Reprieves (and the commutation of sentences) were mechanisms to 'rid itself of some penal ballast'[34], never benevolent measures, no matter what the Regime said it its propaganda.

Thus, we see the onset of a wave of reprieves (until 1945 they were not called 'reprieves' but instead 'extraordinary measures of conditional freedom') as a means of alleviating the penal chaos and its insupportable budget. Drop by drop, beginning with inmates condemned to lesser sentences, prisoners who had been 'cleansed of their dissolutionary ideas' and old grievances as evidenced by their 'good behaviour' and who had demonstrated their submission to the New State and acceptance of its principles, were gradually released on probation.

They were reminded that this was 'conditional freedom' and as such, they and their families, were subject to the supervision of the local authorities and their movements restricted. The released prisoner was obliged to make regular visits to the Guardia Civil headquarters to sign in, which frequently implied a beating from the victors. As far as benevolent measures were concerned, not a single one. To make matters worse, as the released inmates were always subject to the hostility of their Francoist neighbours, they and their families lived in a social vacuum, despised, marginalized and excluded from all kinds of activities. Sometimes it was better to remain in prison than to have been released and forced to live amid the pack of fanatic victors, the constant singing of *Cara al sol* and the fascist salute.

April 5 1940 marked the first release on probation of prisoners older than 60 who had been condemned on the grounds of Marxist rebellion, had served at least a fourth of their sentence and exhibited impeccable behaviour.[35]

June 4 1940, probation was granted to those "condemned by Military Courts to sentences from six years and one day to twelve years and who have served at least one half of their sentence, have exhibited exemplary behaviour, and obtained a favourable report from the local authorities and the Falange." The latter requirement made it almost impossible for an inmate to be released in this manner given the great amount of local hatred of the defeated in those days. In order to lessen any opposition from the local Falange, the Regime provided an alternative in the form of "probation in exile". Whichever way you look at it, this was an additional punishment that was applied in Spain after the 1919 repression of the Bolshevik triennium in Andalusia. Besides, all totalitarian regimes exile individuals as a standard repressive measure.

October 1 1940, release on probation was granted to those sentenced by a Military Court to serve twelve years and one day. Considering that the majority of the inmates were condemned to thirty years in prison or given the death penalty, these lesser sentences had very little impact from a numbers viewpoint.

October 16 1942, release on probation was granted to those "sentenced on the grounds of Marxist rebellion to up to 14 years and eight months.

March 13 1943, the 1942 law was amended to apply to those "sentenced to no more than twenty years in prison". The insignificant impact of all these laws is shown by the fact that, in this case, only 1,087 inmates were released (311 in exile and 776 on parole).

September 29 1943, release on probation was granted to those sentenced on the grounds of Marxist rebellion and were at least 70 years old, regardless of the length of their sentences. Their dossiers were amended when an appeal had been denied because of an unfavourable report from the local authorities, with the indication 'Approved by the recently created *Servicio de Libertad Vigilada*'.[v]

17 November 1943, release on probation was granted to those sentenced to twenty years and one day and in the case of those sentenced to longer periods, "on health grounds, extraordinary behaviour and other outstanding accomplishments". This covered all those considered "recoverable" in which the ideological repression was successful, abjured their principles and accepted, without question, the National Catholicism platform. Again, these were not "benevolent" measures, even though they were promoted as such (especially in view of the adverse scenario that was emerging as it appeared that the Axis might not win World War II). They were the result of the unavoidable pressure of the chaotic and costly situation of the Francoist prisons.

These release measures were, to a great extent, also motivated by the sluggishness and lack of effective release operations of the Redemption of Sentences through Work Board, which is why the Regime had to resort to

---

[v]   Probation Service, basically, National Parole Board.

additional parole measures. Even so, these measures did little to resolve the Regime's problem.

From the beginning of 1940 to mid-1941, only 28,787 of the 300,000 inmates of Franco's prisons at the beginning of 1940, were released under probation.[36], [vi] In 1942, 29,353 were released.[37] By then, this 'benevolent measure' was available to anyone who managed to survive death from starvation during the great prison famine of the previous year.

This brings us to the mythical "total pardon" decreed by the Regime October 9 1945, which had nothing of the "total" to it. There is so much misinformation regarding this matter that it has led to considerable confusion. The October 9 1945 Decree for Total Pardon, does not refer to the total number of the condemned, but, as indicated in the Introduction, to a total or full, pardon for all sentences for crimes of military rebellion, against the internal security of the State or public order, committed *before* April 1 1939. In other words, war crimes, *not* to the multitude of arrests for post-war 'crimes', crimes relating to clandestine activities and association, to the persecution of fugitives and their supporters, and so forth.."

The Introduction to the Decree contains a great piece of propaganda directed at World War II's victorious allies, in that it affirms that "90 percent of all those who were condemned for their activities during the Communist Revolution have been arrested". Continuing in a conciliatory manner, the Regime speaks of the normalization of life in Spain, with reference to those Spaniards who fled the country. Still, it will escape nobody's attention that the Regime classifies the prisoners as either black or white sheep, because when it speaks of "normalization" it distinguishes between "those who fought because they were conned by the political fervour and those who led and incited the masses." This is an important distinction as it separates the "mass of criminals" into two groups: those were tricked into fighting (the deceived) and those who led and incited them (the deceivers).[38]

Item 1 of the Decree stresses that a pardon will be granted "in all cases where it is shown that the delinquent never participated in acts of cruelty, death, rape, desecration, larceny and other deeds that because of their nature are abhorrent to all honest men". Other individuals were disqualified from benefitting, such as Masons, Franco's nightmare, for whom he would never contemplate any kind of reprieve. Clearly, the door remained open to all kinds of repressive pretexts.

[vi]   Domingos Rodríguez Teijeiro in *El Régimen de Franco*, (Franco's Regime). Alianza, Madrid, 1988, p. 240, points out that Stanley G. Payne exaggerated when he spoke of 40,000 prison inmates were released on probation during this period.

Item 2 states that the "reprieve will be granted upon the request of the condemned" whenever the information is favourable.

Item 3 proposes a curious extension of the reprieve to "those who are still insurgent on the condition that they turn themselves in within one month" (in other words, fugitives who have fled to the hills or are in hiding elsewhere). This was a trick to capture them. There also is a message for those who had gone into exile - "individuals who are living outside Spain and who return within a maximum of six months."

Item 6 qualifies the terms of the reprieve that "shall not be granted to accessory sentences and shall be considered null and void in the event of a repeat offense."

Anyone who still believes that the Total Pardon of 1945 opened the prison doors wide and freed all the imprisoned, is living in cloud cuckoo land.

José Manuel Sabín has reported on the consequences of the 1945 reprieve in Toledo. There were no such reprieves in the jails of the capital as these were mainly inmates with short-term sentences. Some inmates in the major prisons of Ocaña and Talavera de la Reina did, however, benefit by the new regimes, as 35 inmates had been reprieved by the end of 1945 and considerably more, 523 reprieves, in 1946. Sabín says that one had to wait until 1964 when, as part of the celebration of twenty years of peace, all prison inmates jailed under the terms of the 1945 Decree who benefitted from the extinction of the accessory sentences exclusion, were reprieved and their criminal records were destroyed.[39]

Classification of Prisoners

The Committees for the Classification of Prisoners, created by Decree 9 January 1940, were another of the Regime's useful inventions for keeping wrapped up, and well wrapped up, at a time when no less than 300,000 individuals were imprisoned all over Spain. Again, this was no new mechanism for releasing inmates nor a charitable measure, as some claim, but a means of organizing and classifying prisoners in an attempt to bring penitentiary chaos under control.

Under this Decree, inmates were divided into four large groups:
A. For whom the reason for and the authority who ordered the prisoner's arrest are unknown.
B. Arrested by the Government.
C. Tried by emergency summary courts.
D. Under 16 years of age

The classification of young men of military age who had been in the Republican zone during the war and whom Franco was now conscripting, was much more simple. The lists of young men eligible for the draft in each township were examined by the local army enlistment boards, one by one and year by year, to determine their status:

- *Desafectos*: having been involved in politics, supporters of the Left or the Republic (more than 90% of all). Sent to the Disciplinary Worker Soldiers Battalions
- *Encartados:* already tried and either on their way to jail or already sentenced. If the sentence was a light one, also released to a Workers Battalion.
- *Indiferentes:* with no leftist tendencies, drafted into the Nationalist Army.

The processing of all prisoners was somewhat straight-forward, depending on which group classification they belonged to.

Class A: Information was taken out on these, somewhat similar to the earlier requests for certified good conduct declarations, and if the resulting report was favourable, they were released from prison.

Class B: These were detained for a further maximum 30 days and unless otherwise retained by the authorities, were released.

Class C: These prisoners were the meat of the Francoist repression; they were the cannon fodder for the court martials and the firing squads. In these cases, the Examining Magistrates were told to speed up their deliberations.

Class D: Surprisingly, eight months after the Nationalist victory there still were minors in the prisons - either teenagers or children. The latter were infants who remained with their mothers in the women's prisons. This group of inmates was put under the supervision of the Child Protection Services.

The Regime clearly had a plan for the hundreds of thousands of prison inmates and detainees, consisting of every class of society: elderly people over 70 years of age, 60 year-olds, younger men from all walks of life, women, teenagers and infants. Something totally beyond comprehension today.

The National Parole Board

The <u>Servicio de Libertad Vigilada</u>, or National Parole Board, created by Decree May 22 1943, was another New State invention with which to control the movements and activities of prisoners who were released on probation. Accordingly, those who were released remained under the constant watch of the victors, never truly free. Tagged as criminals, they were excluded and marginalized within their communities.

Established under the aegis of the Directorate General for Prisons, the National Parole Board was mandated to 'maintain an effective supervision of both the released prisoner's activities and channel them along safe paths of conduct, particularly their politico-social behaviour.' It was as if, once the prisoner was released, the seed of National Catholicism that had been sown in prison were to fall on fallow ground or fail to germinate.

The fundamental principles of the Movement and of National Catholicism were also directed at ensuring the submissive and converted change in any prisoner on parole who exchanged permanent incarceration for a life of submission and silence. The Regime's official line was that the Release on Parole program had the social duty to 'find work [for the ex-convicts] and to ensure that they were accepted by society without any misgivings.' What a blatant lie! The reality was totally different: it was the pure and simple strict control of the released inmates, within and without the penitentiary. Neither the Nazis or the Italian Fascists wielded such a hard and long-standing control over their political opponents.

Each town set up its Parole Board, consisting of three members: the Mayor, the local Commander of the Guardia Civil and a representative of the Falange. For the first time, the clergy was not represented on such a body as it would have been in the past. These Parole Boards could oppose the conditional release of a prisoner, something that often occurred given the enduring vindictive fanaticism locally. In such a case, the prisoner might still be released on probation but he would be exiled, or deported, to a town at least 250 kms distant from his place of residence. Sabin's research has shown that of all those released on probation, 25% were exiled locally. Francoists presumed that the internal exile or deportation of local disaffected was an effective weapon against local trade unions whose organizations were thus dismantled forever. (This measure was also applied to the families of individuals who were in the maquis during the persecution of the guerrillas.)

Most importantly, we must keep in mind the difference between the longstanding penitentiary regulations as compared to the real penal hell that the disaffected had to suffer. The following is an explicit example of how vindictive a Parole Board could actually be and often was.

Manuela de la Cruz Cabrera, from Almadén, Ciudad Real, was a young 16-year-old when war began. She studied typing and was an active member of the JSU and the UGT but not otherwise particularly involved in politics. May 2 1939, like so many others, Manuela was arrested and taken to Almadén prison but she was not tried until October 1940 when she was charged with '…during the Marxist rule she belonged to the group of antifascist women,

46

she applauded the Red cause and insulted the National Army, making propaganda in the press and in meetings… and she generated arrests…', all of which was highly unlikely for a young person of her age. She was condemned to six years and one day for 'promoting rebellion'. Had her activities been truly punishable, she would have been guaranteed a 30-year sentence. Six-year sentences were those given to people who were totally neutral.

April 18 1941 Manuela was transferred to the Ciudad Real Prison for Women. Soon afterwards, procedures began for her to Conditional Release on Probation, for which she applied for 'permission' from the Almadén Parole Board. May 1 1941, Justo Sánchez Aparicio, the Mayor and one of the members of the Parole Board, sent the following report to the Directorate General of Prisons:

> "It this this Municipality's firm opinion that this person must not be set free and let alone, agree to her returning to live here as she will resume her obsession with slandering the National Cause as she did before."

Meanwhile, the Directorate General of Prisons who wanted to get rid of those who had been condemned to lesser sentences in order to alleviate the chaos, resubmitted her application, in which the Mayor redoubled his opinion regarding the young woman, whom he said was:

> "…totally incorrigible as it seems that she was born a Roja and she decided to continue to be one; such imbecile behaviour on her part could be excused on its own, if it were not to cause such harm."

Young Manuela was finally released on parole but she was exiled to Madrid, where she went to live with an aunt. In June 1942 she obtained permission to live in Almadén but she was so ostracized that she moved to Puertollano. She finally obtained a full release in May 1945. A few months later, it so happened that two of the guerrillas in the hills killed an Army Sergeant and in the following encounter, two guerrillas were killed. It was the Regime's custom, whenever something happened in the mountains, to cast a web in the region, not especially to catch any accomplices, but in most cases, as an excuse to terrorize members of the Left and ex-convicts on parole.

Manuela was arrested by the Guardia Civil in the middle of July 1946 and charged with complicity with the rebels in the mountains, which was untrue. She was sent to the Ciudad Real provincial prison, charged under Military Justice authorities who dispatched her to Madrid to be tried by the Special Court Against Crimes of Espionage and Communism.

The last we hear of Manuela de la Cruz Cabrera, she had been confined in Ventas women's prison since August 1946. Thus ended 'conditional freedom'.[40]

The Regime continued its demagogic and cynical propaganda campaign in favour of the National Parole Board, full of lies about counselling and protecting those who were released on parole. The reality was that this was no more than supervision and control, repression, marginalization and exclusion. Theoretically the parolee had to sign in at police headquarters every fifteen days, but not always. Frequently, it was not just the parolee but all the members of his family – wife and adolescent children – who had to sign in. In the evening, all the parolees were required to gather at the gates of the barracks, sign in again, sing *Cara al Sol* and suffer further humiliations; several were also regularly chosen at random to receive a beating.

Although there clearly was nothing paternalistic nor protective about the parole regime, there are still quite a few scholars who, in their enthusiasm for the new prison regulations, still believe that these New State regulations had anything to do with the reality of the situation. APPENDIX I records Ernesto Cabellero's description of how he had to appear at the Villanueva de Cordoba barracks every evening to accompany his mother had been released on probation (and because his father was still fighting the guerrillas in the mountains).

There can be no lingering doubts as to the false and cynical root of the 'conditional freedom' system in Franco's Spain.

THE EXPLOITATION OF PRISONERS AS SLAVE LABOUR

> *"Without memory, following generations will not, obviously, have any idea of what happened. Furthermore, without memory it is as if there never was any injustice and the world could proceed as if no barbarities had ever been committed... We have to erase the traces of the crime, not with a crude negationism, but by depriving the crime of any meaning. Western culture has been a masterful creator of the invisible crime."*

> Manuel Reyes Mate, La piedra desechada
> (The Deactivated stone), 2013

Three can be considered the number of Francoism's great barbaric acts during the post-war period: the mass deprivation of personal liberty of more than half a million Spaniards; the new wave of executions of 40,000 victims of reprisals (added to the 100,000 already executed the previous three years); and lastly, the monumental phenomenon of widespread forced labour applied to hundreds of thousands of prisoners, forced to work as a punishment and exploited as a means of economic management by both the State and by corrupt private companies.

The forced labour phenomenon began with the Regime's usual subtle rhetoric, when June 1 1937 the official Government Bulletin published Decree 281 of May 28 1937, by which the imprisoned are granted the 'right to work'. In reality, this was no such 'right' but a 'requirement'.

Furthermore, Article 3 decrees that the imprisoned shall be considered 'military personnel, thereby subject to the Code of Military Justice and the June 27 1929 Geneva Convention.' This reference to the Geneva Convention is as surprising as it is cynical, considering that the Francoists never ceased resorting to the summary executions of prisoners whenever they felt like it. What is clear, is that these references to International Law were cheap rhetoric for the consumption of the democratic governments of the day. The aforementioned decree also established the amount of the measly daily wage paid to each slave: 2 pesetas a day (the standard wage was 10 pesetas), from which 1.5 pesetas would be withheld for food and lodging, which means that each 'worker' actually received a daily wage of 0.5 pesetas, paid at the end of each week.

The exploitation was scandalously evident and, as one would expect, immediately triggered the greed of the great private enterprises, as well as the public ones. Of course, the Church also wished to have a slice of this cake. Thousands and thousands of men who should have been at home taking care of their homes and families, enjoying a modest, happy and productive life in their home towns as part of society, lost their future and all personal aspirations, no matter how humble, including sharing the love of their young lives. All of this was destroyed by the barbaric acts of an upper class that was stupefied by the repression, by the influence of European Fascism and by the greed of their class, as they partook in the frenetic management of the Nationalist victory that had been left in the hands of the Barracks, the Casino and the Church vestry.

1. Slave labour camps or Disciplinary Workers Battalions

Whilst the Regime's great idea of exploiting the prisoners was taking shape and as Rev. Pérez del Pulgar was preparing the Holy Water, the Workers Battalions were being set up, in the middle of the war. January 1 1939 there already were 119 such Battalions with 87,589 worker prisoners, engaged in many tasks behind the lines and housed in campsites under deplorable conditions.

Thousands and thousands of prisoners, some who had not been tried and others who were already sentenced to 'light' sentences of a maximum 12 years, were required to enrol in a Workers Battalion if they wished to be conditionally released after they were considered to be duly repentant and willing to accept a two-fold ransom for their freedom: "physical redemption through work, as a recluse, and a 'spiritual redemption' through positive acts", in other words, the full acceptance of the Catholic doctrine as certified after examination by the chaplain and the prison Parole Board.

This was nothing else other than applying the ancient Inquisitorial mechanism of forcing prisoners to abjure their beliefs as a means of instilling National Catholicism. For three centuries, the Catholic Church in Spain looked to the Inquisition as the means to punish dissidents (torture and pyre) and during post-war National Catholic Spain, under the *purgandus est populus* motto, to eradicate all heretic ideas, namely Republicanism, syndicalism, democracy and secularity.

During the war, after the Francoist had begun blowing off steam by eliminating *in situ*, political commissars or skilled individuals, at will, the imprisoned were sorted by the so-called Classification Committee that would class them in one of four groups we already know:

A. Supporters or favourable to the Movement
B. Insignificant disaffected with no responsibilities
C. Disaffected with political or military connotation
D. Suspicious individuals or common criminals

Based on the above, prisoners classed C and D (and some B) were handed over to the Military Examining Magistrates to be tried by court martial, the outcome of which was extremely gloomy. The remainder were sent to concentration camps or to Workers Battalions to wait for their release documents to arrive.

The Workers Battalions (later, Worker Soldiers Battalions) were comprised of prisoners or young men of military age held in concentration camp and classed as disaffected, They were sent directly from the concentration or prison camps to the Battalions, reaching the enormous number of 100,000 slave labourers in 1940.

These were men who had no taste of freedom after the war; in the majority of cases, they had never been found guilty of anything because they were never tried. They were punished on the basis of political criteria, simply because they were opposed to the victorious fascists. Hence, the double purpose of the Battalions: 1) to provide cheap or free labour; 2) as an instrument of physical and ideological repression. Punishment, humiliation and submission, by means of miserable living conditions and an iron discipline, to ensure they learnt the lesson of exactly what their marginal role was in the New Spain.

This 'appetizing' scenario of a mass of cheap, slave labour was now influenced by another divine Francoist invention. The Redemption of Sentences through Work Regime, Ministerial Order of October 7 1938, was the brain child of Jesuit Reverend Pérez del Pulgar (and some say, the magnanimous brain of the Caudillo), as a continuum of the May 28 1937 Decree's philosophy regarding prisoners' right to work. The Council for Redemption of Sentences through Work was appointed December 15 1938, effective January 1 1939. The number of prisoners who turned to this Regime was insignificant: 4.5% in 1939 and 6.6% in December 1940 (18,781 prisoners of a total 380,000 imprisoned nationwide). In Cordoba, only 600 of a total 4,000 applied.

The Workers Battalions were the first forced labour modality during the war and the immediate post-war period. The highest number of these slave workers was recorded in 1939-1940, at the end of the first year: 90,000 (34,143 in 1937; 40,690 in 1938). A gradual change to a new designation appeared during 1940 (new name, same thing) when they were renamed: Disciplinary Battalions of Worker Soldiers (BDST) as they focused not so much on prisoners of war or concentration camp inmates, but more especially on the young men of military age that the local Army Recruitment Cs had classified as disaffected, with some leftist tendencies. If a worker had already been sentenced, his file was marked BDST1.

Thus, in addition to being a source of slave labour, the battalions were now also responsible for punishments, purges and repressive discipline.

Table 4. Number of slave labourers in the Disciplinary Battalions[41]
[Both Workers Battalions & Disciplinary Soldier Workers Battalions]

1937	34,143
1938	40,600
1939 & 1940	90,000
1941	47,000
1942	46,380
1943	4,800

The two names for these Battalions were used interchangeably and mostly the usual reference was just to Workers Battalions. All of Spain was full of these centres of slave labour. Still, when mention is made of great public works carried out by this means, one notes that Franco clearly preferred to centres in the Centre-North of Spain, especially the North.

Andalusia appeared to be somewhat forgotten in Franco and his henchmen's plans. The most famous public work slave labour construction was the *Canal of the Prisoners* in Seville, on the lower reaches of the River Guadalquivir, at Los Merinales. Also built with slave labour, the Torre del Águila Seville reservoir[vii] and the Algeciras-Bobadilla railway between Cádiz and Málaga.

Cordoba Province was assigned Workers Battalion No. 130. One company was billeted near Espiel and another in Peñarroya-Pueblonuevo, where the battalion Commander lived. In all these battalions, where the workers were housed in very poor housing and feeding conditions, almost like concentration camps, special emphasis was given to the spiritual education of the Rojos. The task of morally disinfecting and re-educating the workers was entrusted mainly to the Jesuits who spearheaded National Catholicism. Workers Battalion 130 was placed in the hands of José Luís Díez, S.J.

Pedro Gómez González, from <u>Villaralto in Cordoba</u>[viii], was sent to Workers Battalion No. 28, Company 4, in La Bacolla, near Santiago de Compostela, where they were put to work building an airfield. His description of the situation there is reproduced in APPENDIX I.[42]

It was not just the New State that took advantage of this colossal exploitation of labour, but also and surprisingly so, numerous private enterprises all over the country. Great public works of today were built by those who preyed on the slave labour. The Cordoba Civil Registry Office contains records of quite a few deaths in Workers Battalions, undoubtedly victims of the inhuman living conditions, as well as some who were shot on the spot as they attempted to escape. The Official Bulletin for Cordoba published Wanted Ads for deserters from these Battalions and, when they were caught, details of the courts martial who tried them, stressing the grave consequences of their acts. This happened to Miguel Caballero who, having been sent to the Los Barrios Workers Battalion in Cádiz, escaped but was turned in by a fellow countryman. He was sent before a court martial which he managed to survive by miracle.[43]

During 1939, the Year of Victory, thousands and thousands of Republican prisoners were distributed among all the concentration camps and Workers Battalions, the length and breadth of the country. Cordovans,

---

[vii] Magdalena Gorrell Jaén's cousin, Antonio Jaén Romero, the young Commander of the Cordoba Volunteer Militia founded by his uncle, Antonio Jaén Morente, spent many years as a slave labourer on both these public works before he obtained his freedom.

[viii] The first mention, in this section, of a Cordovan town or village as the hometown of a slave labour prisoner is underlined, to highlight the effect of this program in this particular province.

for example, could be found everywhere. Jesús Maria Romero, from La Rambla, published a book containing more than 500 statements from those who returned to their home towns, with details of the Workers Battalions to which they had been sent:[44]

> Workers Battalions Nos. 41 and 116 – Zaragoza
> Workers Battalion No. 51 – Teruel
> Workers Battalion No. 179 – Ceuta
> Workers Battalion No. 152 – Palencia
> Workers Battalion No. 26 – Medina del Campo
> Workers Battalion No. 91 – Oviedo
> Workers Battalion No. 24 – Melilla
> Workers Battalion No. 159 – Salamanca
> Workers Battalion in Reus, to name but a few.

During in the first months of the victory, prisoners were not only continuously shunted from one concentration camp to another, but also between camps and Workers Battalions. As Casimiro Jabonero told Moreno Gómez, in April 1939, the government began sending convoys of inmates from the more than 2,000 prisoners packed in the Seminary and La Serrería prisons in Cuenca, to concentration camps and Workers Battalions. April 25, a shipment of 900 left La Bacolla, La Coruña, followed by another convoy to a concentration camp in Madrid that also housed a Workers Battalion.[45] In Cordoba May 21 1940, 12 inmates from Carcabuey were sent to the Rota Workers Battalion in Cádiz.

Prisoners were treated like so much cattle as they went from one concentration camp or Workers Battalion, to another and back before they were released. In his study of Montilla, a fellow historian, Arcángel Bedmar, records several such cases. Antonio Arroyo was first sent to Number 92 Disciplinary Battalion of Worker Soldiers, then from one to another battalion, going through Bilbao, Palencia and North Africa until he was able to return to Montilla in 1943. José Gómez Márquez, aged 19, was sent from Padul, Granada, concentration camp to Cádiz Workers Battalion No. 6 in December 1941, then to Workers Battalions in Cherta, Tarragona, and Logroño. He only returned to Montilla in 1945 after serving in the Francoist armed forces. Antonio Alcaide went from the La Bacolla Workers Battalion where he remained for a year and a half, then to a roadworks in Algeciras, until, after doing his military service in the Canary Islands, he returned to Montilla in 1944.

Living conditions for the prisoners in the Workers Battalions were inhuman, particularly when it came to the manner by which the guards, mostly professional soldiers many of whom had served in the African Legion, disciplined the inmates. Cristóbal Carrier Díaz, from the village of Santa Cruz, Montillo, was sent to the Cherta, Tarragona, Disciplinary Battalion of Worker Soldiers, where Sergeant Aurelio Azcona Zabalza forced the men to run with sacks of sand tied to their backs, after which he would lash them with a whip in a hut. Another Montillano, Miguel García Ruíz spoke of the hunger he suffered when he was interned in Rentería Disciplinary Battalion No. 51, where they were only fed boiled cabbage. When he complained, he was punished by having to run with sacks of earth tied to his back, a type of torture typical of Foreign Legion punishment. Another form of torture was to make the inmates walk past a companion who was punished, slapping him as they went by. Francisco Carmona Priego, interned in the Cerro Muriano, Cordoba, Disciplinary Battalion of Worker Soldiers, saw a sergeant break a prisoner's back with blows from a pickaxe handle. This particularly brutal punishment is also mentioned by another historian, Antonio D. López, when he relates the testimony of Manuel Esperilla, from Castuera, Badajoz, that he saw just how many beatings with sticks a person could endure, as the handles of the pickaxes broke a guy's ribs.[46]

Young men from every town in Spain, ex-soldiers of the Republican Army, were swallowed up by the mass imprisonment whirlwind: camps, prisons, workers battalions, exploitation of slave labour, a gigantic oppressive scene that almost nobody today can comprehend. Every town's history reflected a Dantesque picture, inside and outside Spain. Arcángel Bedmar studied this in depth in the village of Rute. Brothers Francisco and Pedro Caballero Tirado died as members of the French Resistance. Pablo Baena served his sentence in the Cherta, Tarragona, Workers Battalion, as did Manuel Jiménez and Gabriel Porras. Bernabé Montes, Gregorio Puerto and Francisco Viso worked as slave labourers on the building of the *Canal of the Prisoners*, Dos Hermanas, Seville. Siméon Rojas worked out his sentence in a Workers Battalion in Tetuan, Algeria.

And so on, in every Spanish town and village. Below, a sample from Baena [47] of 172 natives of this town who were exploited as slave labour:

Workers Battalion No. 3, Melilla	36
Workers Battalion No. 8, Los Pastores, Algeciras	34
Workers Battalion No. 26, Labacolla	19
Workers Battalion No. 29, Labacolla	12
Workers Battalion No. 33, Tetuan, Morocco	6

A few more Workers Battalions

Workers Battalions 6 & 58, Los Barrios, Cádiz	Workers Battalions 17 & 116, Zaragoza
Workers Battalion 42, Oyartzun, Guipúzcoa	Workers Battalions 12 &140, Barcelona
Workers Battalions 9, 55 & 211, San Roque	Workers Battalion 32, Tarifa, Cádiz
Workers Battalion 145, Tetuan, Morocco	Workers Battalion 152, Palencia
Workers Battalion 33, Ceuta	Workers Battalion 125, Manresa
Workers Battalions 54 & 124, Algeciras	Workers Battalion 21, Astorga
Workers Battalions 53 & 155, Madrid	Workers Battalion 51, Teruel
Workers Battalion 130, Peñarroya	Workers Battalion 212, Morocco
Workers Battalion 151, Alsasua	Workers Battalion 128, Navarra
Workers Battalion 63, Camprodón	Workers Battalion 23, Arañones, Huesca
Workers Battalion 178, Serós, Lérida	Workers Battalion 166, Sam Blas, Teruel
Workers Battalion 64, Maya, Navarra	Workers Battalion 15, Torroella de Montgri

J. F. Luque Moreno's catalogue of 55 forced labour inmates from Montemayor is interesting in that the name of the camp varies as either BDST (Disciplinary Battalion of Worker Soldiers) or BT (Workers Battalions):

BDST No. 8, Los Pastores, Algeciras ………………...	17
BDST No. 29, Labacolla, Santiago de Compostela ……	14
BDST No. 51, Oyarzun, Guipúzcoa ……………………..	12
BDST No. 3, Melilla ………………………………….	8
BT, Cherta, Tarragona …………………...…………….....	4

There were more, dispersed one at a time in other camps, in 20 other Workers Battalions all over Spain, several in Morocco, as well as Ceuta and Melilla. The men from Montemayor, classified as disaffected without any other crime, lost several years of freedom as slave labourers in the Workers Battalions and/or doing military service, only regaining their freedom in 1944 and 1945.

One cannot help but be impressed with the way that the Regime dispersed so many thousands upon thousands of men from every town and village in Spain, among Workers Battalions and Disciplinary Worker Soldiers Battalions all over the country. Just take the example of a small village in Cordoba province, Fuente Palmera, for which Alberto González Sojo reports on 48 men and how many were dispersed, as follows:

Others from Fuente Palmera were the only prisoners from that town in other Workers Battalions, such as BDST No. 214, Tifasor, Mieilla; BDST No. 108, Zaragoza; BDST No. 162, Gerona; BDST No. 55, Tarifa; BDST No. 50, Cordoba; BDST No. 212, Bab-Tazza, Morocco; BDST Nos. 5 & 213, Melilla; BDST No. 13, Ceuta; BDST No. 2, Santiago de Compostela; BDST No. 35, Palma de Mallorca; Dos Hermanas, Seville, Penal Colony; Alberche Prison; Vega de Pas Penal Detachment, and so forth.

Mortality in the Workers Battalions was high and frequent. Luque mentions five deaths for Montemayor: Manuel López Sánchez, in the Algeciras Battalion, died 'from eating poisonous roots'; Miguel Moral Nadales, Battalion No. 29, Labacolla, from where he was released already moribund, only to die as soon as he got home; Juan Moreno Gómez, same as the previous one, from Battalion No. 8, Los Pastores, Algeciras; Antonio Galán Sillero, Battalion No. 13, Larache; and María Navarro Bernal, a Montemayor matron, who died after she was released from a disease she contracted in jail.

After considering all the above, one's attention is drawn to a very interesting feature: the great majority of all the prisoners from Cordovan towns regarding whom the above data refers to, were doing forced labour in 1942.

There are various conclusions we can draw from this: 1) After 1942, Francoism preferred to increase its income from slave labour, rather than let prisoners die in prison; 2) That the drop in the number of prison inmates noted from 1941 onwards, is an ambiguous bit of data because many inmates, especially those condemned to minor and intermediate sentences, were being released from jail, not to freedom on the streets, but to servitude in Workers Battalions, Disciplinary Battalions of Worker Soldiers, Penal Colonies, etc.; 3. The 'official' number of prison inmates that are published and the only ones that are taken into account are totally useless, considering that a great many inmates were only 'released' to become slave workers.

The migratory/deportation movement in Franco's Spain was awesome. It is impossible, today, to understand how it was possible for the victors to turn Spain upside down in this manner. How was it possible for the Regime to manage the victory in such an absurd and irrational manner? Could it be that the only possible answer is that only the Regime's barracks mentality can help explain such bestiality and savagery, all raised to the maximum degree by the influence of European Fascism and its cult of radical violence.

Seen from another angle, it is worth pointing out that young men of military age, classified as such by their local army enlistment boards, were not only first sent to Disciplinary Battalions of Worker Soldiers, then also to Africa to a Regular Army Regiment, where they would be subjected to an extremely harsh disciplinary and punitive treatment. This is something that Moreno Gómez has not seen mentioned in any study, but that was confirmed to him by several eye-witnesses, such as Manuel Bustos, one of those young men.

> "In 1942, I was one of 16 young men of military age from <u>Villanueva de Cordoba</u> who was examined by the local enlistment board and declared to be disaffected. All 16 of us were sent to the IVth Regiment, 4th Company, whose barracks were in Alcázarquivir. The senior officers were all veterans of the civil war who boasted of the abuses and excesses they had committed in Spain. Some regular soldiers had already been promoted as officers. They had as confidents, affected or Falangist Spaniards.
>
> The discipline was so strict that that one day, when a recruit arrived late for the roll call, he was spread out on the ground and given 'half a beating', or 50 lashes, 25 on one side and 25 on the other.
>
> Eurgenio "El Ramo" also came with us from Villanueva, despite the fact that he was disabled, for the only reason that his family were leftists; they beat him to death one day. I also remember a bugler from Ciudad Real who when on leave, stole some sheets to sell and make some money. Unfortunately, he was caught and beaten; he died the next day.
>
> The disciplinary terror declined when the Americans landed in Casablanca. They lined us up along the River Luco, to defend our position from attack, but there was a general desertion: more than 200 of us went over to the Americans."[48]

If the Francoist prison nether world, inhabited by hundreds of thousands of men and women, many accompanied by their children, is a clear case of genocide, no less so is the nightmarish scenario of the thousands of slave labourers interned in Disciplinary Workers Battalions all over Spain. The general situation in the prisons and Battalions was so astounding, it appears impossible that so many atrocities could have been committed in a country like Spain, a nation that was celebrated for its enlightened culture.

Tragically, the above was the product of a Regime created by the union of a hawkish, loud-mouthed and pedantic Spanish military class whose mind-set remained bound by its experience in Africa, and a no less manic, Inquisitorial National Catholic clergy whose minds were liberally seasoned with the savagery exported by Nazi Germany. There could be no other consequence than a human catastrophe.

No wonder that there are those who still today would like to conceal, cover-up and silence the events of the post-war period, because crimes against humanity are so beyond belief that any acknowledgement of these is capable of shaming the most callous scoundrel.

Historians' field work done on the Workers Battalions in the Basque province of Navarre, has provided some references and testimonials regarding the "slaves of Francoism" in Valle del Roncal, Erronari, and Zaritzu, where some 2,000 slaves worked on building the Igal-Vidangoz (Igari-Bidangoze) highway in the Pyrenees of Navarre, interned in Workers Battalions Nos. 106 and 127, later transformed in 1940 into Disciplinary Battalions of Worker Soldiers Nos. 6 and 38. This slave labour came from many places in Spain, especially Andalusia, Asturias and Vizcaya. Of these, 245 came from Vizcaya, 211 from Granada, 165 from Jaén, 126 from Asturias and 78 from Cordoba and elsewhere.

The Franco Regime designated Navarre as a zone of preferred action as part of what it called the 'Plan for the Defence of the Pyrenees'. Under this program, more than 10,000 slaves were employed on a great many public works through the province: roads, railways and others. Improvised housing in terrible conditions was found in schools (from which they removed the children) and ramshackle huts. In the Vale del Roncal battalions, there was "nothing but hunger, cold and beatings", according to Fernando Mendiola and Edurne Beaumont's magnificent documentary.[49]

As one of those interviewed in the documentary said: "As I worked, I did nothing else but think: Am I going to spend the rest of my life here? I would sit down and think... I spent 6 years in Roncal". To these years, the younger survivors had to do an additional 3 years' military service. In all, the lost youth of an entire generation.

As elsewhere, the living conditions in Roncal were horrendous, particularly in terms the hunger everyone suffered. In addition to the meagre rations, the prison officers stole as much as they could and sell it. The inmates felt sorry from those whose families lived far away and could not send them anything: "Those poor Andalusians", they would say. "As they did not receive anything, there was nothing for them to eat…" One day, there was no dinner. "We were called to attention and the sergeant told us: "Considering that there is no dinner tonight, you can stand easy." As to food packages from home, "It took fifteen days to one month for a package to reach us; when it arrived, the contents were rotten."

The working conditions were primeval. "There were no machines of any kind. Everything had to be done by hand, with a pick and shovel… We were practically barefoot and our feet were cut by the stones… They later gave us some new boots, but one of us who had received a new pair from home, decided to sell the new ones. He was caught doing so and they beat him to death." A frequent punishment was to strip the slaves naked and make them stand in the cold all night. "They tied a large stone with wires to the backs of others and made them run around the parade ground."

The documentary also refers to the Regiment's chaplains. "The priest was a bad one. He was a Francoist. He was really awful! He would tell us that we were evil and that we were redeeming our sins through work. We had to listen to all this garbage and keep quiet… We were the bad ones."

The worst treatment was reserved for any inmates who tried to escape, a crime for which the punishment was death. One of the eye-witnesses in the documentary said that "There was a fellow from Catalonia who spoke to nobody; one day he escaped but he was turned in by a companion who had planned to escape with him. The snow was a metre deep. The sergeant ordered his men that "when you find him, kill him." They discovered him in a mountain refuge and there he died. Later, they brought his body in on a stretcher." We worked in groups and if one of tried to escape, they shot all the others and their families had to suffer the consequences."

Another tragic incident, also the subject of another Mendiola and Beaumont documentary,[50] was the case of Cecilio Gallego García, a 24-year-old who belonged to a family from Dom Benito, Badajoz, all of whom had been very active members of the PCE. July 25 1939 a convoy of forced labour workers for the Roncal works arrived at the same Workers Battalion we have been speaking of, Number 127, 3rd Company.

October 23 1939 Cecilio decided to escape but he was caught and shot on the spot. In 2009, one of his brothers went through hell and high water to obtain permission to dig up his grave in Roncal public cemetery and take Cecilio's remains back to his hometown to be buried. Cecilio's remains were duly taken back to Don Benito in February 2010 . The family was denied a formal wake in the *Casa de la Cultura* because of the opposition of the PP

Mayor. "If he had been a Falangist, they would have welcomed his remains with open arms," lamented his ninety-year-old brother.

Escapes from the Workers Battalions (or Labour Camps as the people also called them) were quite frequent and a number of successful escapees joined groups of other fugitives in the mountains. A number of famous native Cordovan guerrilla leaders came from these groups, such as: Francisco 'El Gafas' Expósito who turned himself in in Andújar, Jaén, at the beginning of 1944, together with 'Aragonés', both of whom had escaped from the Anguiano, Logroño, Labour Camp and were leaders of part of the II Guerrilla Group in Ciudad Real. The famous Sebastián 'Chichango' Moya from Albacete, escaped from a Disciplinary Battalion of Worker Soldiers in Santoña, Santander. Emilio 'Escobero' Pérez, of the Albacete maquis, escaped from a Labour Camp in Belchite, Zaragoza. Felipe 'El Castaño' Moya, from Pozoblanco, fled to the hills from a Disciplinary Battalion in Galicia. Another famous guerrilla, Francisco 'Veneno' Blancas, from Adamuz, escaped from the Toledo Penal Colony in the Fall 1944. He was known as 'the last guerrilla from La Mancha'.

One of the more remarkable escapes, which became famous after the publication of his memoires, was that of Albino Garrido[51] from the Castuera concentration camp, March 4 1940, when he was about to be executed. He was one of a group of 5 who, except for one who was shot by the Guardia Civil, managed to make it safely to France March 22.

2.   Re-education Camps

The Re-education Camps, directly managed by the Council for the Redemption of Sentences, were another form of forced labour, one that was most directly associated with private enterprises. These consisted of larger or smaller groups of individuals condemned to less than twelve years and one day (and some whose higher sentences had already been commuted), who were allocated by the Council to public companies, to private enterprises or to Church-owned companies. To be sent to one of these was considered somewhat of a privilege as the labourers worked under a semi-free regime, although they had to return to prison for the night. Communists and Masons, for which there was no possible redemption, were banned from these camps.

Theoretically, a prisoner was paid a daily wage of 14 pesetas but in actual fact, he only received half that amount. His family, if he had one, received 3 pesetas. 1.40 pesetas went to pay for food and housing and the remaining 9.60 pesetas were withheld for taxes. This was a pot of gold business for the New State, as it also was for the Regime's emblematic construction companies, similar to the cheap labour arrangement that enriched the great private companies during the III Reich.

In 1940, there already were 70 re-education camps with 5,155 slaves working on several projects, most of them in the Centre-North of Spain. At the end of 1943, there were 92 Re-education Camps in Spain with a total 11,554 slave workers.[52] There were practically none in Cordoba province.

The Hato Blanco Re-education Camp was located in Ciudad Real, in the Port of Niefla, almost on the border with Cordoba. From there, 50 slave labourers allocated to the A. Carretero company organized a mass escape June 29 1943, most of whom went to join the groups of fugitives in the mountains. Other well-known construction work carried out by workers from these camps were: Hermanos Nicolás Gómez, Madrid; Vich Cathedral, Bishopry of Vich; Valle de Los Caídos, Banús, San Román and Huarte & Cia.; Pozo de Fondón, Asturias, Duro-Felguera; Alberche reservoir, Talavera de la Reina; New Prison, Cordoba, with 120 workers; Valdemanco, Madrid, Sociedad Marcor (from which the guerrilla stole a large quantity of dynamite in 1947, which in turn led to a court martial that ended tragically with torture and executions). At the end of 1943, there were 92 Re-education Camps in Spain housing a total 11,554 slave workers.[53]

3. Devastated Regions

Work in regions devastated by the war was another way of putting convicts to work, very similar to that of the Disciplinary Detachments. Also controlled by the Council for the Redemption of Sentences, the inmates were individuals condemned to lesser sentences, or at the prisoner's request. Again, this was also forbidden to communists and Masons. The work that was to be done were public works or work that the State requested from the Council, with a view to rebuilding installations or centres of population that had been damaged during the war. "Let them rebuild that which they destroyed" was the motto, as if the defeated were responsible for the destruction, not those who caused the war and fought it with the assistance of the destructive machinery provided by Rome and Berlin.

A Ministry of the Interior March 25 1938 Decree assigned responsibility for this reconstruction to the Directorate General for Devastated Regions, for which it would use convict labour, although the work would not start until after the war was over. By the end of 1940, 2,034 slave workers were working in Teruel, Belchite, Potes and Oviedo. According to José Manuel Sabín, Ministerial Notice of 1943 reported that 4,075 convict labourers were deployed in Figueres, Guernica, and other locations.

4. Paramilitary Labour Camp

The Regime's most important post-war 'redemption and exploitation' invention was the Paramilitary Labour Camps, under Law of September 8 1939, with a view to providing a systemic organization of the slave labour as part of the New State's growing programme of public works. Actually, this was just another version of the Regime's program for punishing and cleansing the defeated whose penance was work, although in practice it was the State and the great private construction companies who were especially engaged in hydraulic works, who would benefit.

As those in power always use rhetoric to cover their shameful intents, in this case the explanation was that the Government had to "compensate the increase amounts" that it was spending on prisons. (Just who told the Government to put half a million Spaniards behind bars...?) The militarization of the service (organized in Battalions and companies, under the command of the military). was justified on the grounds that as these convicts were working in areas far from any jails, they required strict discipline.

8 such camps were created between 1939 and 1957 (at the end, common criminals were also sent to these labour camps). Slave labour from Camps 1 and 6 worked on the famous canal on the Lower Guadalquivir River, the Canal of the Prisoners, at Dos Hermanas, Seville; Camp 2 was assigned to the Montijo Canal, Badajoz. Many Catalan prisoners worked here, some of whom had been condemned to 30 years in prison (157), others to 20 years (22), and the majority who were serving 6 years, until 1946.[54]

From August 1940 to September 1946, 2,826 slave workers from Camp 3 worked on the Bajo Alberche canal, Talavera de la Reina, Toledo. This camp was divided into three sections: San Román, Real de San Vicente and La Sal. Camp 4 was assigned to the construction of the Rosarito canal in Añovar de Tajo, Toledo, on the right bank of the River Tiétar. Camp 5 was sent to the work on the new Infantry Academy. Camp 7 was engaged in several works for the National Colonization Institute in Aragon and Catalonia. Camp 8 worked on the mining railway from Samper de Calanda to Teruel.

There was another such camp on Formentera Island regarding which practically nothing is known other that the living and working conditions were so bad that in 1941 and 1942, 58 convicts starved to death (avitaminosis, weakness and lack of nutrition are the causes of death given in the records), most of them from the province of Badajoz. To Moreno Gómez' knowledge, so far no study has been made of this extermination.

The most notorious of the Paramilitary Labour Camps was the one put to work on the construction of the Canal of the Prisoners in Dos Hermanas,

Seville. January 20 1940, the first batch of workers for the canal arrived from the La Corchuela, Dos Hermanas, camp. The canal was designed to cross the entire province of Seville, from its border with Cordoba to its border with Cádiz, a distance of 158 kms, and it would take from 1940 to 1962 to complete. Although the initial work was done with slave labour, free market workers were hired to put the finishing touches on this megalomaniac project for the sole benefit of the local landowners. The first workers came from Camps 1 and 6 and after 1946, only from Camp 1.

As the work progressed further from the La Corchuela base, three nearer camps were created in 1945: La Corchuela, El Arenoso and Los Merinales, the latter of which was the most notorious. The prisoners came from all over Spain and when released, found themselves living conditional freedom in exile at great distances from their hometowns. As their families had to travel far to visit them, many settled in the area. At first they lived in shacks in a number of peculiar shantytowns on the flood plain and as time went by, they built permanent houses. These are the origin of today's popular neighbourhoods on the outskirts of Dos Hermanos and Seville, such as Torreblanca, Bellavista and Valdezorras. In this respect, the Regime's policy of deporting the disaffected workers as another means of ensuring the dispersal and the deep-rooted destruction of the Spanish labour movement, was successful.

The award-winning *Prisoners of Silence* 2009 Spanish television documentary[55] presents a collection of accounts that clearly illustrate the dark world of the *Canal Prisoners*, extracts of a few of which follow, others are reproduced in APPENDIX I.

- "After waking, we were lined up in rows of 3 persons each, surrounded by soldiers, and marched to the canal works. If you wanted coffee in the morning, you first had to sing *Cara al sol;* the same at noon and in the evening before you got your soup."

- "During Holy Week, a van would arrive with four or five priests to take confessions and give sermons. Many prisoners did not listen to them, which infuriated the priests who complained to the commander who then ordered beatings. Attendance at mass was compulsory."

- One day when I was at work, two apprentice priests came to see me: "We have come to get the boy and take him to the children's home, because as your father is in prison... I replied: "My father may be in prison, but I am free and I have the balls to care for my son; and if I go to look for you, you come to me. My son is going nowhere..."

One is struck by the imposition of religion by force and the daily humiliation of requiring the inmates to sing the victors' hymns. Moreno Gómez already stressed that one of the distinguishing features of genocide, as Lemkin states, is the imposition of the oppressor's ideology and the demolition of the oppressed's beliefs. Equally important and deserving consideration were the inmates' complaints regarding the enormous difficulty they had in communicating with their families, particularly in view of the Regime's underhand attempts to take control of their children.

This description of the desperate situation of Francoist prisoners is best summed up by what two ex-prisoners who were interviewed in the documentary had to say:

> "It was not one day: it was many years without seeing our families, without seeing anybody, which is why some were not quite right in their heads when they were released. Others were forever marked by their experience, because all of this remains engraved forever on our hearts." "I have been kicked out of many places because I was a Rojo. One cannot speak of anything. We have to shut up. People are still afraid. Franco died and we were released to walk the streets as free people… If you do not speak of something, you erase it; you rub it out…"

5. Prison Workshops and Special Assignments

This discussion of the monumental phenomenon of Francoist exploitation of prison labour, ends with the Prison Workshops, a form of free labour within the prisons. The first workshops were created by Order of April 30 1939, in the Alcalá de Henares prison. Some of the first items produced by this Graphic Arts and Carpentry Workshop included furniture for the Social Welfare organization, pews for churches and 15,000 crucifixes for schools. The management and exploration of these workshops was also the responsibility of the Redemption of Sentences Council. Soon, every large prison created its own workshops: Burgos, El Dueso, Gijón, Guadalajara, Ocaña, San Miguel de los Reyes, Yeserías, Barcelona, Cordoba, to name but a few.

Lastly, there was another means by which prisoners could work to reduce their sentences: Special Assignments. These were reserved for inmates who had a record for good conduct; that is, absolutely no communists, Masons, adulterers, individuals who had not married in the Church, who blasphemed, etc. Special assignments could be work in the prison kitchen, bakery, storehouse, barber shop, school, infirmary, cleaning, offices, etc. It is believed that these inmates represented a wide range of other professions: craftsmen, doctors, university graduates, construction workers, bricklayers and so forth. Inmates could also use their experience to work, when available, to reduce their sentences as plumbers, electricians and masons and as 'assistants' to the chaplains (altar boys), to the teacher and in the infirmary. Women were allowed to work as seamstresses, embroiderers or other 'feminine crafts', the product of which was put on exhibit whenever the Director, the Mother Superior or the Bishop visited the prison. "Everything was neatly wrapped up and tied tight."

Endnotes for Chapter I

1   Ángel Suárez /Collective 36, *Libro blanco sobre las cárceles franquistas* (White paper on Francoist prisons). Planeta, Barcelona, 2012, p. 14. (Ist Edition, Ruedo Ibérico, 1976).

2   Tomasa Cuevas Gutiérrez. *Testimonios de mujeres en las cárceles franquistas* (Witness accounts of women in Francoist prisons), Instituto de Estudios Altoaragoneses, Diputación, Huesca, 2004.

3   Francisco Moreno Gómez, *Córdoba en la posguerra (La represión y la guerrilla, 1939-1950)*, (Post-war Córdoba – Repression and guerrilla, 1939-1950). Fco. Baena, Córdoba, 1987.

4   Gutmaro Gómez Bravo, "El desarollo penitenciario en el primer franquismo (1939-1945), *Hispania Nova*, number 6, 2006.

5   Margalida Capellá i Roig. *"Represión política y derecho internacional. Una perspective comparada (1936-2006)"* (Political repression and international law. A comparative approach (1936-2006).) in *La memoria histórica en perspectiva jurídica (1936/2006)* (Historic memory from the legal viewpoint – 1936/2006) by Margalida Capellá and David Ginard, Documenta Balear, Palma de Mallorca, 2009, pp. 161 et al.

6   Arcángel Bedmar. *La capiña roja. La repesión franquista en Fernán Núñez (1936-1943).*(The red countryside. The Francoist repression in Fernán Núñez (1936-1943). Juan de Mairena, Lucena, Córdoba, 2003, p. 71.

7   Ibid. *Los puños y las pistolas. La represión en Montilla (1936-1944).* (Fists and revolvers. The repression in Montilla (1936-1944). Ayuntamiento, Montilla, 2009, p. 106.

8   Jesús Mª Romero Ruíz. *Que el 20 de febrero de 1936, cuando los sucesos del jardín* (It happened in the garden 20 February 1936). Ayuntamiento, La Rambla, 2010.

9   Juana Doña. *Desde la noche y la niebla (mujeres en las cárceles franquistas)* (From the night and the fog. Women in Franchoist jails)., La Torre, Madrid, 1978.

10   National Basque Archives and Sabino Arana Foundation. *Informe sobre presos vascos en el Penal del Puerto de Santa María.* (Report on Basque prisoners in the Puerto Santa Maria penal complex). Manuel Martínez Cuadrado, in *El Penal de El Puerto de Santa María, 1886-1981* (Puerto Santa María Penitentiaries 1886-1981). Cádiz, 2004, pp. 150 et al.

11   Gonzalo Amoedo López and Roberto Gil Moure. *Episodios del terror durante la guerra civil na provincia de Pontevedra. A illa de San Simón.* (Episodes of the terror during the civil war in the province of Pontevedra. San Simón island). Serais, Vigo, 2007, p. 66.

12   José Manuel Sabín. *Prisión y muerte en la España de posguerra* (Prison and death in postwar Spain). Anaya, Madrid, 1990.

13   L. M. Sánchez Tostado. *Historia de las prisiones en la provincia de Jaén. 500 años de confinamiento, presidios, cárceles y mazmorras.*(History of the penitentiaries in the province of Jaén. 500 years of confinements, imprisonments, jails and dungeons). Jaén, 1997.

14 Miguel Hernández. III *Prosas. Correspondencia* (III. Prose. Correspondence), Espasa-Calpe, Madrid, 1991, p. 2569; and *Cartas escritas en la prisión de Orihuela, entre septiembre y octubre de 1939)* Letters written in the Orihuela jail between September and October 1939).

15 Etimio Martin Garcia. *"El turismo penitenciario franquista"* (Franco penitentiary Tourism), in *Historia 16*, number 239, 1996, pp. 19-25.

16 Diógenes Cabrera. *Once cárceles y un destierro* (Eleven jails and one exile), Santa Cruz de Tenerife, 1980, p. 102.

17 Antonio Ruiz-Fernández. Typed letter dated 15 June 1985, sent to the author by his daughter Isabel Ruiz on 19 April 2013.

18 Pedro Gómez González. Interviewed by the author in Vallaralto, Córdoba, 16 December 1986.

19 Ángel del Río et al. *Andaluces en los campos de Mauthausen* (Andalusians in the Mauthausen camps). Junta de Andalucia, 2006.

20 José Manuel Sabin. *Prisión y muerte en la España de posguerra.* (Prison and death in post-war Spain). Anaya-Mario Muchnik, Madrid, 1996, pp. 229 et al.

21 Joaquin Sama Naharro, M.D. Interviewed by Moreno Gómez in Córdoba, 8 July 1983

22 Francisco Poyatos López. *Recuerdos de un hombre de toga* (Memories of a man with a robe), op. cit., pp. 146 et al.

23 Ricard Vinyes. "El universo penitenciario durante el franquismo" (The prison universe during Francoism). In *Una inmensa prisión* (An immense prison). Crítica, Barcelona, 2003.

24 Rafael Sanchez Guerra, *Mis prisione* (My Prisons), Claridad, Buenos Aires, 1946, p. 187.

25 Manuel Martínez Cordero. *El Penal de El Puerto de Santa María, 1886-1981* (The Puerto de Santa Maria Prison Complex, 1886-1981). Cádiz, 2004, pp.149 et al.

26 Miguel Hernández. Undated letter number 309 in the *Epistolario* (Collection of letters). Espasa-Calpe, p. 2719.

27 Manuel Rubio Díaz y Silverio Gómez Zafra*, Almendralejo (1930-1941). Doce años intensos.* (Almendralejo (1930-1941). Twelve intense years.) and *Los Santos de Maimona*, Badajoz, 1987, p. 355.

28 Gonzalo Amoedo López y Roberto Gil Moure, *Episodios de terror durante la guerra civil na provincia de Pontevedra. A illa de San Simón*, Xerais, Vigo, 2007.

29 Diego San José de la Torre, *De cárcel en cárcel*, Do Castro, La Coruña, 1988, p. 159.

30 Gonzalo Amoedo López and Roberto Gil Moure, *Espisodios de terror durante la guerra civil na provincia de Pontevedra. A illa de San Simón* (Episodes of terror during the civil war in the province of Pontevedra. The island of San Simón), Vigo, 2007. In Moreno Gómez' opinion, one of the finest academic studies of Franco's penitentiary world published today.

31 Eutimio Martín García, "El turismo penitenciario franquista" (Francoist Penitentiary Tourism), *Historia 16*, numbrer 239, March 1996, pp. 19-25.

32 José Ángel Etxaniz Oriñez and Vicente del Palacio Sánchez, "Dossier. Morir

en Gernika-Lumo" (Dossier. Dying in Gernika-Lumo), *Aldaba* magazine, issue 122, April-May 2003.

[33] José Maria Garcia Márquez, *Las víctimas de la represión militar en la provincia de Sevilla (1936-1963)* (The victims of the military repression in the province of Seville 1936-1963). Aconcagua, Sevilla, p. 174.

[34] Felicitous expression by Mirtz Núñez, *La gran represión*. (The Great Repression), op. cit. p. 207.

[35] José Manuel Sabin Rodriguez, *La dictadura franquista (1936-1975). Textos y documentos* (The Francoist dictatorship 1936-1975. Texts and documents). Akal, 1997, pp. 406 et al. Also, Domingo Rodriguez Teijeiro. "Excarcelación, libertad condicional e instrumentos de control poscarcelario en la inmediata posguerra (1939-1945)" (Prison release, release on probation and post-penal control in the immediate post-war period (1939-1945). University of Vigo.

[36] *Redención*, 28 June 1941.

[37] *Redención,* 16 January 1943.

[38] Mirta Núñez Diaz-Balart et al.. *La gran represión. Los Años de plomo del franquismo* (The great repression. The dark years of Francoism). Madrid, Flor del Viento, 2009.

[39] José Manuel Sabín, *Prisión y muerte en la España de posguerra* (Prison and death in postwar Spain). Anaya-Mario Muchnik, Madrid, 1996, pp. 212-213.

[40] Ángel Hernández Sobrino. <<La joven Manuela>> ("Young Manuela"). Article kindly given to Moreno Gómez by the author, April 2013.

[41] Fernando Mendiola Gonzalo and Edurne Beaumont Esandi (Associación Memoriaren Bideak). "Batallones Disciplinarios de Soldados Trabajadoares. Castigo político, trabajos forzados y cautividad" (Disciplinary Battalions of Soldier Workers. Political punishment, forced labour and captivity). In *Revista de Historia Actual*, number 2, 2004, and in the documentary *Desafectos, Esclavos de Franco en el Pirineo* (Disaffected, Slaves of Franco in the Pyrenees), 2007.

[42] Pedro Gómez González. Letter to Moreno Gómez from Córdoba, 16 December 1986.

[43] Testimony of Miguel Caballero Vacas, Madrid, September 1979.

[44] José Mª Romero Ruiz, *Recuperación de la memoria histórica de* La *Rambla* (Recovery of the Historic Memory of La Rambla). Ayuntamiento, La Rambla, Córdoba, 2010.

[45] Casimiro Jabonero. *Diário del soldado republicano Casimiro Jabonero. Campo de prisioneros de Lavacolla. Prisión de Santiago de Compostela, 1939-1940* (Diary of Casimiro Jabonero, a Republican soldier. Lavacolla concentration camp. Santiago de Compostela Prison - *1939-1940*). Ed. Víctor Manuel Santidrián Arias, Ayuntamiento, Santiago de Compostela, 2004.

[46] [l] Antonio D. López Rodríguez. *Cruz, bandera y Caudillo. El campo de concentraión de Castuera* (Cross, flag and Caudillo. Castuera concentration camp). Badajoz, Ceder-La Serenam, 2006.

[47] Arcángel Bedmar, *Baena Roja y Negra. Guerra civil y represión, 1936-1943.* (Baena, Red and Black. Civil war and repression, 1936-1943).Juan de Mairena, Lucena, Córdoba, 2008, pp. 215 et al.

48 Manuel Bustos. Interview with Moreno Gómez, Villanueva de Córdoba, 23 June 2002.

49 Fernando Mendiola and Edurne Beaumont . *Desafectos...* . op. cit.

50 *Ibid. 827 kms. sin retorno* (827 kms, one-way). Creative Commons, Iruñea, 2010. Documentary.

51 Albino Garrido, *Una larga marcha. De la represión franquista a los campos de refugiados en Francia.* (A long walk. From the Francoist repression to the refugee camps in France). Milenio, Lérida, 2013, pp. 85 et al.

52 1944 Report from the Ministry of Justice.

53 1944 Report from the Ministry of Justice.

54 Francisco Ruiz Acevedo. *Memòria Antifranquista del Baix Llobregat. El genocidio franquista en Extremadura* (Anti-Francoist Written Report on the Baix Llobregat. The Francoist genocide in Extremadura). Number. 12, 2012, p. 109.

55 Mariano Agudo Y Eduardo Montero. Directors. *Presos del Silencio* (Prisoners of Silence). Documentary produced by La Zanfoña Producciones, Canal Sur T.V. March 2009. Uploaded by Intermedia at: http://www.kaosenlared.net/noticia/presos-silencio-documental-fortaleza-historica

56 Tomasa Cuevas Gutiérrez. *Testimonios de mujeres en las cárceles franquistas.* (Testimonials of women in Franco's prisons). Instituto de Estudios Altoaragoneses, Huesca, 2004 (1st Edition, Casa de Campo, Madrid, 1982).

57 Basque TV documentary. *Prohibido recordar* (No Remembering). Tentazioa Rec, Moztu, Pais Vasco, 2010.Do

58 Gonzalo Amoedo López y Roberto Gil Moure, *Episodios de terror durante a Guerra Civil na provincia de Pontevedra. A illa de San Simón,* Xerais, Vigo, 2007, p. 85.

59 Sr. Prado Girón, nephew of the famous guerrilla from Léon, Manolo Girón. Testimonial in the Catalan television documentary *Los niños perdidos del franquismo* (Francoisms lost children). Montse Armengou & Ricard Belis. 2002.

60 Diego San José. *De cárcel en cárcel* (From jail to jail). Do Castro, La Coruña, 1988.

61 Julián Casanova in *La Iglesia de Franco* (Franco's church). Critica-Bolsillo, Barcelona, 2005, p. 299.

62 José Merino Campos. Interviewed by Moreno Gómez in Córdoba, 22 February 1981.

63 Melquesídez Rodríguez Chaos, *24 años en la cárcel,* Forma, Madrid, 1977, pp. 162 and 97.

64 Manuel Espejo. Interviewed by Moreno Gómez in Madrid January 1984.

65 María Salvo i Iborra. *Interviú* magazine, 17 October 2005. Also testimonials from previously referenced work by Ricard Vinyes, Tomasa Cuevas, Fernando Hernández Holgado and an email from the Andalucia CGT 29 October 2005.

66 Carlos Fonseca. *Trece Rosas Rojas* (Thirteen Roja Roses). Temas de Hoy, Mardid, 2005.

67 *Memoria que eleva al Caudillo de España y a su Gobierno el Patronato Central para la Redención de Penas por el Trabajo, de 1943.* (Memorandum from the Caudillo of Spain and his Government regarding the National Council for the

Redemption of Sentences Through Work., 1943). Madrid.1944.

68 Text transcribed from the *Presos del Silencio* (Prisoners of Silence) documentary by Mariano Agudo and Eduardo Montero. Intermedia Producciones, Seville, 2005.

69 Francisco Moreno Gómez. "La represión en la posguerra" (Postwar repression) in *Víctimas de la guerra civil* (Victims of the civil war). Temas de Hoy, Madrid, 1999, p. 286.

70 Preliminary report of the UN Working Group on Enforced or Involuntary Disappearances after a visit to Madrid, Spain, 30 September 2013.

71 *Prohibido recordar* (Forbidden to Remember). Basque television documentary by Josu Martinez and Txsaber Larreategi, de la ETB, Tentazioa Rec, Basque Country, 2010.

72 *Los niños perdidos del franquismo* (The lost children of Francoism). Catalan television documentary by Montse Armengou and Ricard Belis. Televisió de Catalunya, 2002.

73 Juan Vallejo. *La locura y su memoria histórica.* (Madness and its Historic Memory). Ediciones Atlantis, Madrid, 2013.

74 A. Rodriguez Arias. Interviewed in the documentary *Esa Memoria* (That Memory) by Dominique Gautier and Jean Ortiz, Creav Atlantique, France, April 2011.

75 Montse Armengou and Ricard Belis, The Lost Children of Francoism, op. cit.

76 Interview in Günter Schwaigaer's documentary, *Santa Cruz, por ejemplo* (Holy Cross, for example), Austria, 2005.

77 Mónica Orduño Prada, *El Auxilio Social (1936-1940). La etapa fundacional* (The Social Welfare Program – The foundation). Escuela Libre Editorial, Madrid, 1996.

78 Ángela Cenarro Lagunas, <<Historia y memoria del Auxilio Social de la Falange>> (History and memory of the Falange's Social Welfare Program). *Pliegos de Yuste,* issues 11-12, 2010.

79 *Azul* newspaper, Córdoba, 18 October 1940.

80 *Córdoba* newspaper, 30 October 1941. With the following headlines: 'Social Welfare obeys. Intense social, moral and religious reconstruction. 6,000 christened. 150,000 first communions. 2,000 marriages legalized.'

81 *Córdoba* newspaper, 3 November 1942.

82 Azul newspaper, Córdoba, 24 January 1941. "Campaign against begging in Córdoba. City Hall creates a Municipal Winter Soup Kitchen with a sum of 50,000 pesetas. The Falange will collaborate with all its means."

83 *Azul* newspaper, Córdoba, 17 March 1942.

84 *Córdoba* newspaper of 23 April 1942 published a very complete list of all those assisted in the Soup Kitchens.

85 Minutes of the Meetings of the Villanueva de Córdoba Municipality dated 28-8-39; 31-12-40; 28-1-41; 25-2-41; 16-12-41; and 18-3-1947.

86 Interview with Moreno Gómez on the occasion of a Historic Memory Conference, Seville, 24 November 2012.

87 Ernesto Caballero Castillo, testimonial from one of those boys.

88   *Azul* newspaper, Córdoba, 13 December 1941.

89   There is an ancient publication on this matter with several authors: *Crónica del Patronato Nacional de San Pablo* (Chronicles of the National Council of Saint Paul). Ministry of Justice, Madrid, 1951, 379 pp.

90   Mirta Núñez, op. cit.

II

WOMEN IN FRANCO'S PRISONS
EYE-WITNESS DESCRIPTIONS OF THE BLUE
HELL OF THE PENITENTIARY: 1. Toxic overcrowding.
2. Systemic torture. 3. Humiliations.
4. Hunger. 5.Transfers of inmates. 6. Health care.

IDEOLOGICAL REPRESSION IN THE HANDS OF
THE CHURCH: 1. Prison chaplains.2. the Church as an
overseer and manager of slave labour programs.
SUBJUGATION OF CHILDHOOD:
kidnapping, segregation, brainwashing
1947-1949 TRIENNIUM OF TERROR. FINAL COMMENTS.

"You had to live this to believe it. Even though we say it, even though
we talk of it, those who have never been in jail will ever understand what that
was like.
Those who have been outside may have some idea, but you have to have
lived in the prison environment, else you presumes that you made friends and
that your life was full and happy. Your companions were called, you said your
good-byes and the next day you knew that they were no longer alive. That is
something that one only really knows when one has been in jail."

Tomasa Cuevas,
Eye-witness Accounts of Women in Franco's Prisons
1ˢᵗ edition, Madrid, 1982

It is estimated that between 40,000 and 50,000 women, about 10%
of the total post-war prison population, were imprisoned during the hardest
times in the 1940s. In reality, many more women were punished but an
exact tally is difficult because of the mass imprisonment of both sexes and
the constant comings and goings from the one prison to another. In order
to obtain a clear picture of what was going on in the Francoist penal hell, we
need more than academic studies of the penal regulations. We need the direct
eye-witness accounts of those who were imprisoned such as Tomasa Cuevas'
outstanding account, *Testimonios de mujeres en las cárceles franquistas* [Eye-
witness Accounts of Women in Franco's prisons][1] and four or five other such

reports. Shocking as these accounts are, they let us see what differences we can find between Mauthausen, Auschwitz and the Francoist prisons.

Tomasa Cuevas' book is a monumental compendium of declarations from women who were incarcerated under Franco, a type of Spanish *Diary of Ann Frank* written by many authors. The *Diary of Ann Frank* has been thoroughly examined and researched over the years since it was published: this written testament to what women endured in Francoist prisons deserves no less consideration.

As Moreno Gómez reproduces these women's words with extracts from Tomasa's book, this section of Chapter II goes directly to the heart of the matter. The reader is warned that unless he, or she, is able to approach their descriptions from a more dispassionate academic viewpoint, he may find it so distressing that he might prefer to skip this section and go on to the next one, the Role of the Church.

1.   Toxic overcrowding

Salvadora Luque, imprisoned in Illana, Guadalajara, described how they were crushed together, men on one side, women on the other, like a bunch of grapes. The silk factory had been turned into an improvised jail. When they loaded the women onto the truck to transfer them, the crowd wanted to lynch them, calling them murderers, whores, Rojas, etc. (page 97)

Flor Cernuda was taken from Lillo jail in Toledo, December 28 1939, and transferred to Ocaña prison, where they put her with eight other women in a cell built for one. As they got in, they had to stand with their arms on their sides and they could not move. Never one to keep quiet, she called out to the guard and told him that there were too many people in the cell. 'Too many?' he asked. He went into the corridor and called to another guard: 'We shall see. Bring in two more.' Instead of nine, there were now eleven women, without any light, without water, without anything. She seemed to remember that during the three months when she was interned in Ocaña prison, they were only taken out into the patio two or three times. (page 153)

According to Rosasio la Dinamitera, seven hundred inmates were packed in a single room in Durango. (p. 178)

Another witness, (p. 275), spoke of Ventas Prison in Madrid where, added to everything else, there was overcrowding, a lack of living conditions, not a single moment of privacy, the total lack of mental stimulus, an absence of human kindness. There were twelve women in each cell. All vestiges of the previous purpose of the rooms had been removed: the building had been transformed into a gigantic warehouse, a storehouse of women. There was a lack of food and water – equipped with a kitchen designed to prepare meals for a maximum five hundred inmates, it was impossible for the prison to feed the thousands of prisoners twice a day.

Antonia Garcia also described Ventas Prison which housed eleven thousand women in a prison designed for five hundred. Naturally, all the toilets blocked up, pipes broke and there was no water to wash clothes in and as there were so many inmates, they were only permitted to receive one food package every fortnight. The women were covered in body lice and despondent. Added to these conditions was the fact that the inmates were impoverished, that they had eaten badly during the war, and their families were too poor to send them any food. (p. 322).

Antonia continues to describe the Dantesque scenario (p. 326):

"The first day that I was put in the room, the time came for roll-call. When it was over, everyone threw herself on the floor to grab a bit of space for the night. I fell against a wall and I remained in that position all night. The next day, my legs were terribly swollen and I had a terrifying image of the kind of life that was waiting for me. In the morning, it was like a painting of Bedlam. Some women were de-lousing their bodies; those who had scabies, scratched themselves. My first reaction was that they were turning us into animals. You could not shower. You went to the toilet and it was filled to the brim with faeces.

There was no way that we could live like this. Several of us began to talk to the other women and say that we should take turns with the showers. That we should arrange to sleep in shifts so that each would have more space on the floor, that each group should sleep in three-hour turns. That we somehow had to get better conditions for the children."

2. Systemic torture

The half of Spain that was imprisoned by the totalitarian New State was frequently subjected to the torment of torture, a form of repression that in Spain dates back to the Inquisition. Now, however, the new and improved techniques introduced by Fascism, produced an improved, equally toxic, prisoner management cocktail.

Tomasa Cuevas, herself a prisoner, continues with the testimonials as she reports that in 1945, she was again arrested together with the man who became her companion and husband, Miguel Núñez. His spine was seriously damaged due to the beatings and mistreatment that he received from Commissar Polo in Barcelona during endless interrogations, a lesion that he still suffers from to this day. (p. 13)

    Blasa Roja refers to Guadalajara prison as she remembers the moans and groans from the beatings given the inmates. She states that she will never forget what they did to an inmate called "El Chinés", a bonny young man with black hair when he was arrested who was so badly beaten, so martyrized, that eight days later his hair had turned white. (p. 77) Everyone was deeply affected when Juan Raposo was beaten to death in Guadalajara and she could not forget the way they beat the man, his screams, the way they murdered him: "He was killed like Jesus Christ, tied to the iron prison doors and whipped". (p. 78)

    Nieves Waldemar, also from Guadalajara, opened her heart to Tomasa Cuevas:

> "What can I say? All six of us, brothers and sisters, were in jail One of my brothers was sentenced to death, although he never harmed anybody. Another sister spent ten years in jail: first for five years, after which she was released then rearrested and sent to Gobernación jail in Madrid, for three months' punishment: a beating in the morning and another in the afternoon. She was so badly injured that she lost her mind and for the next ten years, did nothing else but sit listlessly in a chair, taken care of by her husband. (p.94)

    Another witness in the same jail described how that they would often spend hour after hour, with their nerves on edge, hearing the guards beating the men and the men's screams. These were moments that they could not avoid suffering and crying out with rage... (p.94)

    Carmen Machado, from Madrid, told what happened at Police Headquarters at Calle Jorge Juan number 5, under the torturer Aureliano Fontela. The entire time that she was there was a nightmare because of the horrific beatings. One case, specifically that of a Youth Leader from the Cuatro Caminos neighbourhood, was so mistreated that they set a bed up for him under the stairs. During the day, a doctor was sent to treat him and at night, they would take him out again for some more beatings. He was later executed. (p. 129)

    Flor Cernuda from Quintanar de la Orden, a Durango inmate, described a young girl from Ciudad Real, María Fernanda, who slowly became totally disabled and unable to walk after they broke her back during a beating. (p. 155)

    Pilar Calvo, from Talavera de la Reina recalled how her husband, Julián López, from Santa Olalla, suffered after he was arrested in Madrid until he was executed in Ocaña prison where he was terribly badly treated. They attached electric wires to his private parts and did many more terrible things he did not deserve, but he had been an active supporter of the Communist Party and had served in the 5th Cavalry Regiment. (p. 160)

Mari Carmen Cuesta, member of the JSU in Madrid, was a friend and survivor of the famous *Thirteen Roses*. Like those women, she was taken to the Calle Jorge Juan Police Headquarters where she was interrogated every fifteen minutes, night and day, so she could not sleep. As soon as she started to fall asleep, they woke her up. Three or four days later, they first heard terrible, blood-curdling screams as the guards began plunging companions into ice baths and giving them electric shocks. (p. 199)

Agustina Sánchez Sariñena, from Madrid, went through her own private hell. Her mother-in-law was executed July 24 1939, her husband was beaten to death at the Governación jail, and she miscarried after being tortured. When they arrived at the Gobernación they were not allowed to speak.

"They told me: "You bitch, speak and we kill you." The interrogations began and were terrible. Beatings and communion hosts came one after the other, without considering that I was pregnant, and if what they were doing to me hurt a great deal, my suffering was three times worse because they beat my husband and a friend in front of me.

Half conscious, I became aware that they called the doctor and he told the policemen: "Don't interrogate her any more today, leave it for tomorrow, because her mouth is too dry now." I did not know that we need our saliva to talk and what happened to me was that my mouth had gone dry from what I was seeing. I could not even feel my tongue. The next day they took me to some special cells and they really began to beat me hard. They had stopped beating my husband but he was more dead than alive and had begun vomiting blood.

I was left alone in the cell, bleeding copiously, but the foetus was not coming out. I no longer felt the baby move and I was afraid that it was dead, as it was. The doctor came and urged them to transfer me to Ventas Prison as soon as possible. When they came to get me I said I would not leave until I saw my husband. They refused, but when they saw how much in despair I was, they said: "You can see him, but it will be the worse for you". I saw a bundle in a corner that looked like an old man with grey hair. I heard someone call out weakly: "Agus, Agus, it is me." I turned towards him. He was no longer a human being, just a bloody lump who could not move except to hold out his arms. My last hug ever. (pp.236-237)

Returning to Antonia Garcia, she described what she witnessed the day that she was arrested and taken to Calle Núñez de Balboa where she was put in a cell. Sometime afterwards, the door opened, a light was turned on and six or more men brought a woman and a young man in. They began to beat the young man, so much that he began bleeding from his mouth and his nose. The woman cried "My son! My son" and she turned her face to the wall so that she could not see what was happening. Finally, she threw herself against one of the men and scratched his face badly. They shoved her and she fell against the corner of one of the stone benches. As she hit the bench, one of

76

her eyes popped out. I never saw that woman again, not even in the prison. I don't know whether they killed her." (p. 324)

This section concludes with <u>Flor Cernuda</u> from Quintanar, Toledo, who was interned in Lillo prison and whose testimonial is proof that Toledo Falangists were indeed no more than some kind of animals. It also shows how moral damage resulting from mistreatments can ruin a person's life.

"In the end, my father was left alone helpless and there I was in prison, suffering and watching my fellow inmates suffer, women who were treated horrendously as were their husbands. Every alarming and terrifying thing you can possibly imagine. Relatives who came to visit us were made to stand in line and were occasionally beaten with a whip. One day they arrested my mother, a person who would not say two words out loud in order not to offend anyone. According to her death certificate, she died from 'moral debility'. In other words, the doctor recognized that she had not been suffering from any disease; what she had was emotional pain that she could no longer endure. They say that you cannot die from your emotions, but you can. My mother saw so much and this upset her so much that she only lasted a few days." (p.152)

Evidently, the great repression targeted not only individuals of some 'political importance' as it did all sorts of inoffensive country town and village residents. It was the great repression against 'all those who do not think like us'. The Regime mistreated all the disaffected and even those who were indifferent to politics. The sole purpose was to ensure that the terror that upheld the basis of the Regime's power, would permeate every humble working man's and every Republican's home.

3.   Every kind of humiliation

<u>Carmen Machado</u> described that everyone in Ventas Prison was routinely lined up in the patio to sing hymns. If you could avoid it, you did, by trying to hide in some room. There was a prison officer, a tall, good-looking man, who whenever he was on guard went from room to room with a thorny stick, looking for inmates who were or pretended to be sick. Without saying a word, he would poke the thorns against their legs to force them to get up. He was always very watchful when it came to singing the hymns. If he caught a woman who was pretending to sing or just was not singing, he would take her, together with others he had caught *in flagrante*, to the middle of the patio and make them stand with their arms raised in the Nazi salute and sing the hymns over and over again until recreation was over, when he would again poke against their legs with his thorny stick. (p. 134)

Tomasa Cuevas, wrote of Guadalajara where many women in the patio, particularly young women, had arrived with shaven heads. The Guadalajara inmates had a full head of hair. One day, a group of prisoners arrived from a country town and they were all as bald as billiard balls. The Falangists found all this hilarious . Laughing, they said that the law was the law, like it or not: either every woman had a shaven head or they all had a full head of hair… and as you cannot glue hair back on… They called several of us out and, after setting up two inmates who were barbers by profession in a hallway, put them to work shaving our heads. (p.106)

Flor Cernuda told how the Falange in Quintanar de la Orden, Toledo, celebrated the first days of the victory.

> "We were taken to the local jail and the first thing they did was shave our heads and insult us – there was no end to the swear words and invectives they threw at us. 2 or 3 April 1939 in the morning, once our heads had been shaven, they arrived and told us they were taking us to the town square to hear Mass. They said they had intended to burn us at the stake in the square after Mass but the day before a group from the African Harem had come to town and had stopped them. They threatened us with their pistols and rifles to force us to attend Mass; they insulted us at will: both the local priest and the Fascists. Flor also said that when she was in Ocaña after the end of 1939, the humiliations continued. There was an old prison guard, who suffered from tuberculosis, called Don Marcelino, who called out "Come up whores", each time the women were taken from the patio to our cells. (p .153)

Pilar Calvo, from Talavera de la Reina, spoke of humiliations and, especially, the great social vacuum that enveloped the defeated's families. She went to Santa Olalla because her husband had been arrested there. His family told her that she had to leave because there had been so many threats against them, they were terrified of what could happen if she stayed. She left with her infant daughter in her arms. On the way out of town, she met a man who was riding a donkey and he called to her and asked where she was coming from. When she replied, 'from Santa Olalla', he said: he knew who she was: Bicho's wife, a Communist and an evil Roja. He asked her many did she kill. Pilar replied that she had killed nobody, that she had an ideal that she would believe in all her life; she could not deny it, because it was deep in her. He then told her to hand him her daughter; she could ride on the donkey but Pilar would have to walk. Better still, he said he would tie her to the donkey's tail and drag her all the way to the railway station. As he ushered her out of town, he swore incessantly at her and said that they would kill her if she returned. (p. 159)

In Ventas Prison, Agustina Sánchez said that one morning they called all the women to the judges' chambers where they were greeted by a group of young Falangists who shaved the women's eyebrows and their heads. Her eyebrows never grew back, her hair only a bit and some of them, remained bald for the rest of their lives. (p. 228)

4. Hunger as an instrument of submission and extermination

Of all the painful hardships prisoners had to endure in Francoist prisons, hunger was the worst. Pascuala López, from Brihuega, Guadalajara, described what occurred to her the day after her niece Lola was executed, when they were attending Mass. She was too weak to kneel because she was so distressed by what had happened to Lola. One of the nuns, Mother Gertrudis, insisted that she kneel but she could not. Although Pascuala totally lost her appetite after Lola died, she was still so very hungry because they were not given enough to eat – a pot of water with an onion skin floating in it and some days, nothing at all. She might occasionally eat an orange that they old in the Commissary – first the orange, than the orange peel and, because of that, her stomach was a mess.

Blasa Rojo told Tomasa Cuevas that she saw such terrible suffering for eight years. In Amorebieta, she watched women die of hunger. She remembered that those who arrived from Santander, at the same time as Tomasa's group, called them the yellow people as their skins were yellowish from not being allowed out in the patio and because they were dying of hunger. She remembered a casket with the body of a dead prisoner from Asturias in the patio; every day the casket left the prison on a trolley. They removed the casket, took out the body, came back and prepared the casket to receive the next one. (p. 78)

The 2010 Basque television documentary *Prohibido recordar* (Remembering is Forbidden) describes the high mortality of women in Francoist prisons. In Saturarán, there was typhus, scabies, tuberculosis, diphtheria. When the inmates attended Mass, they might hear a thump – a woman had dropped dead. An inmate might be taken to the infirmary and never heard of again. A donkey cart would arrive at the prison and it would be laden with caskets with the bodies of children and adults. [2]

Saturarán was one of the sadly most notorious Francoist women's prisons. Before it was turned into a jail, it had been a beach club. It is there that they imprisoned women who were classified as 'extremely rebellious and dangerous', which was a lie as these were women had done nothing more than exhibit leftist sympathies. More than 2,000 women between 16 and 80 years of age were imprisoned there from 1937 to 1944.[i]

Getting back to Tomasa Cuevas' book, Nieves Waldemar talks of her internment in the Convent of the French Nuns women's prison in Guadalajara. While she was there she became friendly with several inmates, woman who received no help from anyone as they were country people whose families had also been punished and left destitute. The food they fed the inmates was pretty awful: an onion boiled in water and they called that food… (p. 92) Those who were unable to receive any help from outside suffered even more, because all they got was water; they either fell ill or died.

Nieves remembered that one day that they brought the food, a cauldron that they placed on the steps that led down to the patio and from which the inmates were served. Her sister filled her plate, placed it on the stairs and in front of the prison officers who were serving the meal, proceeded to use this 'water', because that is all it was, to wash her face! For some unknown reason, she was not punished for that. Since then, Nieves was operated on four times, because the life they lived in prison was no life at all. In the end, she said it is not a matter of talking or not talking about all this but of shouting out. (p. 95)

Tomasa Cuevas complained that in Guadalahara, hunger chipped away at their bodies and that there were inmates who fainted, they were so weak. The doctors spoke with the prison administrators and told them that the situation could not continue in this way and that they had to allow the inmates to receive food packages otherwise people would start dying. But the administrators could not care less as this is exactly what they wanted. Eventually, the doctors managed to get them to allow food packages for the neediest. In order to qualify for the packages, inmates had to have a medical examination and not all were allowed the packages. The male prisoners were worse off so the women, with the help of several belts they tied together and a satchel, sent them some food through a window. (p. 103)

Tomasa continues to describe her transfer to Durango where she joined other prisoners in the Convent of the French Nuns. They had a hard time as the food was terrible. The building was three stories high and the kitchen was on the ground floor; if they wanted to eat, they had to go down the to the patio with their plate to get their food. It was icy cold and they were served a disgusting mash that stuck to the plate if you turned it upside down; it

---

[i] There is a magnificent book and documentary by Maria González Gorosarri and Eduardo Barinaga entitled *No lloréis; lo que tenéis que hacer es no olvidarnos* (Do not cry. What you must do is never forget us). TTARTTALO, Donostia, 2008. The documentary is entitled *Izarren Argia.*

looked more like carpenter's tar with which to glue their stomachs. The oldest inmates suffered badly. Some broke down, others went five or six days without a bowel movement. Batches of new inmates arrived daily from all over Spain. There just were not enough jails in the country for so many prisoners and many convents were turned into improvised jails.

From Ventas Prison, they sent a batch of youngsters, many of whom were minors. They taught her this song: "People of Spain/we the prisoners are calling you,/this injustice/ cannot continue/ as hunger, a widespread evil, is doing its damage..." (p. 120)

Carmen Machado also had something to say about Durango prison where there was another scourge, avitaminosis: lack of food and little variety. For example, the food in Durango was almost always only rice. Because of this, the women's legs began to be covered with sores full of a watery liquid. They had to set a room aside for the enormous number of women afflicted in this way. There was no food, there was no cleanliness, but of hymns there were plenty and they had to sing them at least twice a day. (p. 134) In 1941, Antoñita Hernández, the most head-strong of their group when it was time for their meal, would collect the orange peels that the Basque women kept for her and she would return with her plate piled high with orange peels. Emilia, their communal mother, would divide them into eleven little piles and each of the women would go into her corner and relish the peels. (p. 135)

The famous Rosario la Dinamitera, described her experience with hunger in Saturrarán prison. This prison had the inconvenience that the sea air opened their appetites and the food was as awful as it was everywhere and there was even less of it. The women were put to work in the kitchen to peel carrots and a nun would stand on a stool to make sure that no woman even attempted to put a tiny piece in her mouth. What kind of religion was that? What kind of Catholicism did they have Spain? Rosario said that as every woman who passed through Saturrarán could confirm the truth of this. (p. 179). Saturrarán was an icy cold prison... the inmates suffered so much from hunger that many women's legs were severely damaged... because all that they were given to eat was some kind of mouldy flour full of bugs." (p. 332)

Agustina Sánchez added some information regarding her stay in Palma de Mallorca prison. The food they gave the inmates was disgusting, nothing more than boiled marrows and, sometimes, a few noodles. (p. 232).

Antonia Garcia also speaks of Palma de Mallorca where she says it was so terribly windy and dusty so that their hair was always covered in a chalky kind of dust. The water for the showers came from a well where the water was so chalky that their bodies were white when they finished washing. They were fed some greens that the nuns cultivated and they were full of ants. You have no idea how bitter those ants tasted. As their families were usually unable to send any food packages, they began to become terribly weak, so much so, that many of them could barely move. It got so bad, that the vertebrae in our bottoms stuck out so much they could not sit. In that prison, you died standing; during every roll call, some would fall down, dead. (p. 330)

Tomasa Cuevas ends with a comment that there was so much hunger in Segovia prison that many young women no longer menstruated. The floor was cemented and not tiled and it was so, so cold that you felt it even more than your hunger. (p. 293)

5. Transfers of inmates, so-called penitentiary tourism

The continuous transfer of prisoners from one jail to another, similar to the practice in Nazi Germany, was another instrument the oppressors used to punish, when not to kill, the unwanted. As Pascuala López, from Brihuega, relates, they were transferred up to four times during the winter, in cattle wagons, because the longer it took for them to complete our journey, the more the guards were paid. They would leave the trains standing in the railway stations for as long as they liked. In some villages, where a train was left standing on the line, the locals would throw some food through the netted window, but elsewhere, they treated the prisoners badly. There was a bit of everything: some liked the prisoners, others did not. (p. 71)

Cecilia Abad, from Guadalajara, describes her penitentiary tourism:

"I was sentenced to twelve years and one day. I spent four years in prison and four years exiled in Zaragoza then in several jails in Guadalajara. I was sent to Ventas Prison. From Ventas, I went to Durango via Burgos where we spent the night. We were put in with all kinds of women and given no food or water. From Burgos, we went back to Durango where I spent six months. The prison was closed down and we were sent to Santander; I was there during the hurricane and the fire, for a year and a half, when they closed that prison and we were sent to Amorebieta. I was finally released from Amorebieta in 1942 and sent home" (p. 83)

Tomasa also describer the first of her trips from prison to prison: Guadalajara, Madrid, Durango, December 28 1939. Only four from every cell were taken, one of them the poor old Letona. The inmates were handcuffed two by two; in one hand they held their little bags and very little in the other hand because they were attached to a companion, and then they were sent into the street. Her father, her mother and her brother were outside, in front of the prison but the Guardia Civil prevented them from speaking to each other. She was marched to the railway station with the other prisoners, where she saw her sister, her brother-in-law and her nephews, but not her father. She

82

was unable to ask about him because the guards would not let us get close to each other. She later found out that her father went home as he could not stand seeing her handcuffed and surrounded by Guardias Civiles. She was not told that actually, he had suffered a stroke. He had reached the end of his strength. Her father died a year later, always asking after her.

A carriage had been set aside for these inmates in Guadalajara station. There were girls from Sierra villages, from her home town, who had only left their hometown to go to prison. They had never seen a train before and had no idea how one worked. When the prisoners arrived in Madrid, at Atocha Station, they were loaded onto a Guardia Civil truck and taken to the North Station. It was terribly cold, there were roadworks all over the place, there were no doors in the waiting rooms and everyone was frozen. They were not allowed to get on to the train for four or five hours as they waited for a group of three hundred and fifty women from Ventas to arrive. (pp. 117-119)

When the prisoners finally arrived at Zumárraga, they had been travelling for three days. As they had been given food for 24 hours and it was already 72 since they had left, they had gone without food for two days. When the residents of this town heard that there a train full of women prisoners, they brought them some food. They arrived in Durango, in the Basque country, having taken four days to get there. The Francoists never gave up their determination to take prisoners from the warm Centre-South of the country to the cold, damp prisons in the North.

6.   The lack of health care

The lack of health care was one of the great shortages in the Francoist penitentiary world and still another lethal tool for decimating what they considered were no more than Rojo rabble. <u>Carmen Machado</u>, from Madrid, who had been travelling from jail to jail since she was 20 years old, as Francoism did with so many other women prisoners whose youth it stole, had an interesting story to tell:

> "There was a very curious case that illustrates just how little they cared for our health and well-being. Just a few days before the Durango prison was closed, we were vaccinated against typhus and just a few days later, sent to Orúe prison. Imagine that although this prison knew that we had already been vaccinated, they repeated the injection as we arrived. As one would expect, many had very high fevers and were frankly very ill. They really cared little for our health." (p. 134)

Flor Cernuda, from Quintanar, Toledo, told Tomasa that she did not remember the exact date when they were told that they were going to be transferred to Durango. Her legs were already bad when they left Ocaña and they had to wait for a long time at North Station until the trains arrived. They were made to walk all over the place, get on a train, get off it, change tracks, so much so that she could not make it, not even sitting down. They had to push her into the carriage with her legs apart and she developed sores on her legs whose scars are still there today… As she could not walk, she was taken into Durango prison on a stretcher. She was not treated because there was nothing with which to treat her. The infection went up her legs, right to her hips; she was terribly ill but there was no medicine chest, no doctor, nobody to treat her sores." (p. 154)

Other situations where there was an absolute lack of hygiene were standard fare. Rosario la Dinamitera described Getafe jail, near Madrid:
> "Worst of all was Getafe and that is where I was sent. In that prison… there were no toilets; all your body functions had to be done in cans, in the three or four rooms, without doors, where we were imprisoned. Once a day only, at 7 a.m., they came and removed the shit cans. There was very little food and what there was, was awful, but worse still, was the lack of hygiene. There were no washbasins, nor running water for us to wash in. We got water in a can of condensed milk, that is, a cupful per person and that had to last us 24 hours. We could not ask for more, not for the elderly nor for the children." (p. 177)

Tomasa Cuevas told of the Ventas Prison for Women in Madrid where medical assistance was totally absent. It was only in 1943 that they appointed a gynaecologist. Until then, the doctors were, heaven know why, practicing dentists. Dr. Delfin Camporredondo who is best forgotten, was the dentist on call in Ventas in 1939. Despite this, there was one exceptional individual, Dr. Juan del Cañizo, a doctor from Segovia, whose name honours all doctors and who remains unforgettable for his self-denial, interest and kind-heartedness. Once the prison hospital was finally set up in Ventas, Dr. Castrillón, a specialist in treating tuberculosis, was another excellent doctor." (p. 277)

Then there is the story of Tomasa's companion Rosita who arrived from Málaga, already sick. She was taken to the hospital in Segovia, a fake tuberculosis treatment sanitorium, where she fell into the hands of an unscrupulous individual. Dr. José Luís Canto, the nephew of a high official in the penitentiary system, who never examined a woman, never even took her pulse. He would make his rounds wearing a hat and overcoat, his hands in his pockets, looking at the skeletons who lay in the beds, with a mixture of revulsion and despise. The only thing that distinguished this hospital from a standard were the very large, bare and icy cold rooms.

More than anything, Rosita was hungry, as we all were, and this young girl's black eyes were terribly sad. She was a tall brunette, with a face that was so pale that it stood out amongst all the other greyish, pale faces. Because she was still under age, she had been condemned to twenty years. Both her parents had been executed: first her father then her mother. Back home, just two young brothers. About to come of age, Rosita was totally helpless, yet another of the Roses who had no youth, victims of the oppression of the barracks, the Casino and the vestry. (p. 286). Tomasa continues with her description of the Segovia prison hospital:

> "There were four large, cold, tacky wards devoid of everything except a few of the patients' meagre belongings . Added to this, the very real illnesses of most of the women, some of whom were considered to be such a nuisance that the staff tacitly hoped that they would hurry up and become even sicker and die once and for all. Of course, this type of patients were nightmares for the hospital administrators [Gusen now comes to mind] who sent them back to where they had come as soon as they could. The prison conditions, the lack of food, the total lack of medical assistance – the doctor was 'allergic' to these women – and the previous lack of all health care for the patient meant that calling this place a "sanitorium" was no less than a bloody joke. Furthermore, the theft of the few 'extras' that had been allocated for the patients was highly profitable for the Sisters of Charity community of nuns who ran the wards. This has been proven because we located the procedure for delivering the food stolen from San Sebastián." (p. 290)

Paz Azati, from Madrid, commented that until 1945, the situation in the prisons was beyond belief in all aspects: hygiene, food, illnesses. All of the inmates were swollen, the doctor would not give them any medicine and there was an illness that the doctor said affected all women in jail and that was they stopped menstruating which led them to swell like balloons… They also suffered from avitaminosis. Then there were problems with the water … The women had to cut our hair because they could not wash it. In spite of all this, it must be said that Spanish women, in the midst of tragedy, surrounded by deaths, executions, beatings, lice, bed bugs, hunger and so much more, nevertheless managed to keep their spirits up and never allowed anyone to debase them, nor has anyone ever done so. (p. 357)

Petra Cuevas, from Orgaz near Madrid, gave birth in jail (New Prison for Mothers, next to the Manzanares) to a daughter who was born without trouble;, weighing 4 Kgs. Sadly, she gave birth in a room in which a little girl had died of whooping cough and it was not surprising that her daughter caught the disease because she was place in the same bed from which they had just removed the sick baby's body and they had not changed the sheets. Lacking medical assistance, the baby worsened every day; she coughed all night. One day she heard that a doctor was coming to examine a child, La Topete's goddaughter. Petra took advantage of this to go to the infirmary unannounced but they closed the infirmary door in her face and refused to speak to her, no matter how much she banged on the door, insisting that the doctor see her daughter. Finally, the ward staff informed her that there was nothing wrong with her daughter and that was what the prison doctor was for. Four or five days later, as the baby got sicker and sicker, Petra returned to the infirmary and told them that there was nothing more that she could do. "Can't you see that the child is dying?" All the prisoners began calling out in protest. The next day, when Petra took her daughter back to the infirmary, they called four doctors in. By the time they arrived, she was already dead. (p. 369)

7.   The general destruction of the family

Francoism placed special emphasis on de-structuring and dismembering the Republican families by breaking them up either in the jails, through exiles, or before the firing squads, all with a view to destroying all the links forged by working men's families and the transmission of their ideals. As we shall see later, this destructive process culminated in snatching the children from their families and bringing them up according to the Regime's philosophy in foster homes, in the hands of the Social Welfare Commission, etc. First, however, there was the appalling treatment of mothers and their children in prison.

It is said that the Regime had a strategy for the wholesale ideological repression of the defeated, but if the truth be told, it was a program for pure and simple unvarnished oppression. This was no kind of 're-education' of disaffected individuals; just new, refined methods for subjugating and repressing those who supported the Republic until no traces were left of their ideals, their family connections or their links with others of their social class. The Regime and the victors knew perfectly well that the most direct and efficient way of de-structuring these families was to arrest and imprison mothers, without whom families would crumble without remedy.

Pascuala López from Brihega, remembers a mother who was executed and her children left uncared-for.

"Many, many of us were sentenced to death. The number of women they took out with the sacas! They killed Señora Antonia, from Yunquera. Did you know her? She had eight children. I remember that she would say: 'Pascuala, killing me, a mother of eight children. They are such criminals! Murderers! They cannot be forgiven. If you sometimes meet one of my little boys, could you wash his shirt?' I never met them, poor little ones. I wonder what happened to them?" (p.71)

You could write a book about how they destroyed <u>Blasa Rojo's</u> life. They destroyed her life but they did not kill her, unlike Paca and Gregoria, who were from the same town, as she describes. You never know, she said, what the last reaction of a defendant will be like, because she saw how brave Señora Paca, from Auñón, was the night that they took her niece, her daughter-in-law and her daughter out to be shot… She was seventy years old when they executed her. Yes, and there was Gregoria who was married to one of the revolutionaries in Auñón; her husband was quite a man. He had been quite a fighter for many years but she was not involved: she just cared for her home and her children. They killed them all that night. Poor Gregoria had three young children, the oldest of whom was only eleven, imagine that, and you could see the poor kids walking, getting rides on the roads. The eldest came and he brought the other younger ones to Guadalajara, begging along the way until they reached the convent of the French Nuns that had been turned into a prison. They up to a window and called out: 'Mamá, mamá!' The poor kids were half barefoot and their noses ran with snot. Gregoria cried that she would kill herself. 'Is there no human being who will take care of my children! Is there nobody who can get them into *La Inclusa*!ⁱⁱ How are my little children? They are going to kill me before I know what is going to happen to them…' After she was executed, the Municipality arranged for her children to enter the hospice." Blasa continued, bemoaning her own misfortune.

"They destroyed the best thing in my life. When Raimundo [Serrado] left, I was twenty-six years old, I was imprisoned and released eight years later, totally devastated, without a home, without clothes, without money… When you have nothing, you bother everybody, even your mother, the poor old lady. I left prison and went to one of my brothers' house, but I saw that I was an inconvenience so I went to another brother's house. The only thing that kept me going was finding out what had happened to my husband; I soon found out that he was living with another woman with whom he had made his life. I was the first communist woman in Guadalajara… during

---

ⁱⁱ *Hospital de La Inclusa.* Hospice for abandoned and orphaned children.

a war, everyone is a communist." (pp.79-80). Tomasa Cuevas added: "War does not only kill. It also destroys homes without killing."

Another prisoner from Guadalajara, Julia Garcia Pariente told how they arrested her mother, her sister and her husband and they all met up in prison. She had another son who was hiding at his grandfather's, Vicentes Montes, but as he was a fascist he made the boy's life impossible, so he left. The poor child asked the nuns in the Inclusa Hospice if he could stay there and they let him in. He stayed there until his mother was released from jail when she took him home with his brother Tomasito who was born in jail." (p. 85)

Tomasa Cuevas used the Diary to help alleviate the pain of her troubles. She recorded how she found out about the many difficulties that her family was enduring, despite the fact that her brother was living with them. His son had died aged 2 and he also lost his wife. He also told her that their father would spend every dawn in front of the cemetery where they carried out the executions. The prisoner officers had frequently told my parents that if they were Catholic, they should pray for me, because one day they would take me out to be shot. So the poor old man spent many months in front of the cemetery, watching the firing squad at work, hiding amongst the bushes outside. His nerves must have been destroyed by these daily spectacles. That was his daily routine: prison, home and the cemetery. He went to the prison because it was there that he felt close to Tomasa even through they couldn't see or talk to each other. Still, he gained some solace by going to the back of the prison that gave onto the fields and sitting down there where he remained until nightfall, when he went home. (p. 112)

She continued talking of her father. The day that she was taken from the jail for her court martial, August 27 1939, they were taken out handcuffed, as you would expect. As only granny Letona and Tomasa were removed from their cell, they were cuffed together. She was such a painful sight, a terribly frail old lady who had done nothing they could accuse her of but they still court-martialled her (she was accused of having fried some eggs for some guerrillas and was condemned to twelve years and one day). When Tomasa walked out of the prison, she saw my father. He was alone and his eyes were shining; he must have cried when he saw her handcuffed and also when he saw the little old lady who was attached to her. Her father walked behind them as far as the building where the court-martial was sitting. (pp. 115-118)

When Tomasa spoke of the Saturrarán prison, located in a Salesian Monastery, she recalled Daniela Picazo, a long-standing communist whose entire family belonged to the Party. Her husband and one of her sons was executed and had no news of her other son who was listed as missing in action –had he died at the end of the war? She and her husband had previously been arrested in 1917 for participating in some strikes in Madrid and Guadalajara. As the authorities had a detailed file on her, Tomasa never understood why they did not execute her as well. (p. 181)

Isabel Huelgas' was another family destroyed by the Regime whilst she languished in Ventas Prison under sentence of death:

Very elderly, weak and febrile, she lay on a makeshift bed, more like a gurney, placed in the corner of a hallway, between the schoolroom (packed with women) and the entrance to the third hallway on the right. She was so ill that everyone hoped, somewhat perversely, that with a bit of luck, she would die before they executed her. During the war, she had lost her husband, a doctor, and her two daughters, from tuberculosis. She presumed that both her sons, Antonio and Joaquim, who had fought on the front, had been taken prisoners-of-war as they were imprisoned in Comendadora. At five o'clock in the morning on a day in Spring, Isabel was called to the office. An ex-prisoner, Pilar Millán Astray, had come to tell her that both her sons had been executed. She was helped back to her corner as she was too weak to make it back on her own and as they lay her on the bed, they noticed that she had died. They removed her body that evening." (p. 281)

Tomasa was released from jail in Segovia on parole and exiled to Barcelona, leaving her roots and family in Madrid and Guadalajara. She said that when she was released, she was concerned about a friend of hers, a member of the JSU, who had also been exiled to Barcelona. 'Young Bene', as she called her, just 19 years old, had spent 5 of those years in jail and had nowhere to go. Her mother was in the Ventas Prison infirmary, sick with tuberculosis, and there she died. Her father and one of her brothers had been executed; another brother had lost a leg during the war and was selling black market tobacco at the steps to the Metro, to make a living. She had another younger sister who was in a children's home. A family of fighters, one more of so many others like it, all over Spain, heavily punished by the victors. (p. 268)

After all that, there is little more than one can say other than this is an extremely painful illustration of Francoism's effective destruction of left-wing supporter families. Moreno Gómez has already spoken of the intent, the punishment and the physical repression of the disaffected and of the ideological repression and radical cut in the chain of transmission of class ideals, all of which the above is an example. The Regime killed the parents or reduced them to penury, so that it could take their children and place them in hospices, foster homes or even put them up for adoption, where it could more easily brainwash their young minds. The Diary continues…

Basque local solidarity with the prisoners

Almost all the reports that we have refer to workers prisons in the Basque Country. Several times, in Tomasa Cuevas' book, we find references to the great disaster of children in women's' prisons (a tragedy that Moreno Gómez addresses in greater detail further ahead). Although no date is given, the following is a testimonial from the Basque Country:

"The townspeople of Durango were very supportive: they came to speak to the Director of the prison and they told him that they would take the children in with them until their families could come and get them, and they took all the children over two years of age into their homes. They cared for them and fed and dressed the children very well. On visiting days, they took them to see their mothers, until little by little the children disappeared from the town as their relatives or friends of the family were able to come and collect them." (p. 121)

Some time later, when the Convent of French Nuns in Durango prison closed, some of the imprisoned women were sent to Amorebieta, others to Saturrarán, Tomasa Cuevas and other, to Santander. The day that they all left the prison, on their way to the railway station, there was a wave of solidarity of such a kind as few have ever seen.

"The departure to the station was extremely moving as it seemed that all the townspeople had agreed to be present; everyone wanted to give us packages, everyone wanted to say goodbye. Of course, they could not come close to us because the guards would not let them, but they were still allowed to give us their packages. We began to sing and we sang as we got on the train and until it left the station, as the women of Durango cried. The song went like this:

"Fare thee well, Durango, Durango of my heart; fare thee well Durango of my heart; when I am free I shall see you again. I do not leave because of the townspeople; they are good people, good people. I leave because I am being taken to another prison." (p. 124)

Although the Basques flew the banner of solidarity very high, elsewhere the women were called whores and the men scoundrels and assassins. What happened in Durango was extraordinary indeed, as other inmates such as Carmen Machado said:

"There is something I wish to make clear, something that has marked me a lot, something that has made me love the Basque People. In Durango, there was a solidarity that I, in Madrid, perhaps because of the astounding repression, I had never before experienced." (p. 135) and also by <u>Pilar Cernuda</u>, from Talavera de la Reina:

> "From Saturrarán I left with the family that had taken me in. It was in the Basque Country that we were received the best. I live there, in Eíbar and since then I have struggled a great deal." (p. 160)

When <u>Ángeles Mora</u>, from Puertollano, was released from Durango, she took a tiny train from Durango to Bilbao. She left the prison wearing a very long coat and realized that fashions had changed. Carrying her bag, she bought a ticket with the money that her companions had collected for her. In the train, everybody looked at her and asked: 'Poor dear, are you coming from the prison?' A man and a woman got up and they went to everyone in carriage asking for some food and money for her. She didn't dare take it but they insisted: 'This is for you, so that you will have something to eat for the first few days'. You cannot imagine how moved she was to see how, since she left the prison, she was sheltered by a chain of true solidarity. She cried but could not eat. They bought her ticket onwards at the station. Another group of people gave her some bananas and wrapped in a bit of paper, some money they had collected, saying: 'Have a good trip'. (p. 165)

<u>Angelina Sánchez Sariñena,</u> from Madrid recalls that although everywhere they were put through a lot, it was in Palma de Mallorca that she found much more solidarity. The people from Palma helped the imprisoned women so much so that they sent them fresh fish every day. Although it was a gift, to supplement our diet, the nuns sold it to us in the canteen. (p. 232)

Tomasa Cuevas describes her arrival at the Bilbao provincial prison, in the pouring rain, carrying their bags and surrounded by Guardias Civiles. They shall never forget, she says, the emotional memory of those groups of people who, right in the town centre and under a violet downpour, pushed at the guards, yelling at them because they were making us walk, soaking wet, carrying the numerous scruffy bags that were that they owned. (p. 291)

Lastly, <u>Antonia García,</u> declared how "In Saturrarán, almost all the food we got was brought in by the Basques, who were wonderful with us; they brought us work, they would sell what we made and spend what they got for it on food for us." (p. 331)

THE GREAT IDEOLOGICAL REPRESSION
IN THE HANDS OF THE CHURCH

> *"Whose are those men who, after kissing their children goodbye, would go off to work as model employees, to torture and murder political prisoners? How did the hired assassins feel and what did they think? The authors of this extraordinary piece of research state that these were normal individuals, delinquents whom immunity allowed them to break all bounds."*

Baltasar Garzón and Vicente Romero, *El alma de los verdugos*.

One of the features of genocide described by Raphael Lemkin in 1944 (*Axis Rule*) refers to the ideological repression of the subjugated that is: the imposition of the oppressed's (national, ideological) identity on the repressed. He often referred to: "Groups who lose their identity and are forced to take on the identity of their oppressors." National Catholicism did exactly that in Franco's victorious Spain. It put into action a radical ideological repression (ideological genocide) to destroy all of the defeated's Republican or working class ideas: trade unionism, republicanism, secularism, free-thinking, progressiveness of all kinds, as well as their faith in the wide range of democratic freedoms that had erupted during that great generation of 1930.

Some have attempted to mellow the impact of this action, calling it re-education, but it was much more than simply a matter of 're-educating'; it was much more radical and all-inclusive. Franco turned to the Catholic Church as his instrument for that monumental repressive operation, especially the prison chaplains but also the clergy in general, both inside and outside the prisons. One must not forget that the clergy put its great ability to mobilize the masses, at Franco's service, occasionally assuming the typically fascist role of a great political party of the masses: huge processions, re-Christianizing the people, befitting the New Spain, a "missionary country".

1.   Prison chaplains

The fulcrum of the great ideological repression began in the jails and the rabid chaplains who saw themselves as 'purveyors of the Divine'. Although prison chaplains were abolished by Victoria Kent in August 1931, Franco reinstituted them by Order 5 October 1938. Priests and nuns became Franco's prison wardens, lords and ladies of the penitentiary world as Gonzalo Amoedo and Roberto Gil stated that the Church was given total and absolute power in Francoist prisons. Chaplains acquired the absolute privilege of reigning as lords and masters, free to proceed with their intent to regenerate, re-educate, control and subjugate the prisoners' resolve.[3] Priests and nuns ruled as much as the Guardia Civil did" [4]

The Church was the cornerstone of National Catholicism's great penitentiary building. It created a penal discourse based on its rules for purging, expiating and degrading "dissolutionary" i.e., democratic, ideas. This was a new and much worse Inquisition. The Church and the victors considered that they had the absolute moral authority to impose their ideas until they had "forced a conversion". They may have not been totally successful in this, but submission and silence still exist, even today.

One of the major instruments that the prison chaplains used was the Regime's great invention of the <u>Redemption of Sentences Through Work Regime</u> of 7 October 1938, Jesuit priest, Pérez del Pulgar's brainchild. More than a means for releasing prisoners from jail, which it practically did not, it became a means for manipulating, brainwashing and destroying the inmates' morale. This deceitful system for commuting sentences was overseen by the Council of Our Lady of Mercy, created by Regime April 1939, whose chairman was the Director General of Prisons, Máximo Cuervo, a fanatic Catholic, assisted by a clerk, an inspector and a priest, appointed by the Cardinal Primate. The ideological pressure directed at the inmates was so great that the release of a prisoner depended on how well he had assimilated the doctrine of the Catholic Church. In other words, a prisoner's release from depended not on how much he had worked to redeem his sentence, but on how well he had learnt his Catechism, as set forth in the 23 November 1940 Decree from the Ministry of Justice.

Amoedo-Gil gives a precise description of the way this worked:
> 9 a.m. Morning mass, with a sermon;
> noon – 1 p.m. and 3 p.m. – 4 p.m. chores;
> 6 p.m. catechism;
> 7 p.m. rosary novena.

One could say that the medieval Cistercian monks were required to engage in fewer religious activities than Franco's prisoners. The National Catholic's sometimes called civilians from outside and seminarians in to assist with this work. Diego San José, a journalist from Madrid who was interned in the San Simón prison described their being "directed by some impulsive and 'pious' young men from Redondela, one or more of whom would later enter the priesthood, without a doubt as a means of washing his mouth out with Holy Water in order to get rid of the bad taste of the paseos in which he had been involved ..." [5]

Of course, from the beginning the Church took it upon itself to carry out the ideological repression in the Francoist prisons, in order to cleanse the 'Godless' and 'Anti-Spain' of their dissolutionary ideas and to implement the cerebral transplantation of the new Fascist ideology. According to Rev. Menéndez-Reigada's *Catecismo Patriotico Español* [iii], the enemies of Spain were: liberalism, democracy and Judaism.[6] "It is the Church's ultimate responsibility to totally eliminate Communism, as well as all ideological and behavioural deviations," stated Jesús Riaño Goiri, a member of the National Catholic Association of Propagandists and a Judge on the Special Court for the Repression of Freemasonry and Communism.

There can be no doubt that the Church's repressive work was one of the fundamental pillars of Francoism. It is not a question of whether the Church was simply collaborating with Francoism, but that it actually was part of Francoism. To this purpose, the chaplains were given *carte blanche* to act at will in the prisons, not only regarding spiritual and religious matters, but even more importantly, concerning all things ideological and political. In other words, the behaviour of the Church and the prison chaplains was the principle vehicle for the Francoist Regime's propaganda.

Chaplains were forbidden to talk with the inmates about their trials or their sentences and especially forbidden to do anything in favour of an appeal or similar. Faithful to Francoist instructions and to the repressive program, the chaplains limited themselves to stress the importance of resignation, submission and waiting for Divine grace. This absence of any kind of intercession when faced with so much injustice from the courts, was another obvious feature of the Church's complicity with the great Francoist repression.

2. Religion as a form of blackmail

Attendance at lessons in the catechism or partaking in the sacraments were incentives continuously dangled in front of the inmates if they desired the most elemental favours such as being allowed to receive correspondence and packages from their families, as well as a means of commuting their sentences: "There will be absolutely no redemption of sentence for anyone who does not know the principles of our Religion." Even being buried in the cemetery could depend on whether the inmate had made confession and kissed the crucifix at the last moment.

Religion as a form of blackmail permeated every aspect of an inmate's life. If a prisoner's children wished to attend school, they had to be baptized. For a marriage to be considered legal, the couple had to have been married in the Church. A woman who was married in a registry office was not considered

---

[iii] *The Patriotic Spanish Catechism.*

a member of the prisoner's family and was therefore prohibited from visiting her husband in prison. Never before had the Church gone so far, not even at the height of the Inquisition.

Before a prisoner could be released on parole, he had to first pass an examination on the catechism (Decree of 23 November 1940). This was a major problem because illiterate individuals, or persons with little schooling, were incapable of understanding the twists and turns of a doctrine that was totally foreign to them. In addition to this there was the supreme humiliation: men and women who had been militant anticlerical during their entire lives, were forced to submit to the victor's ideology if they wished to survive.

May 1942, nationwide prison chaplains met in Madrid, at Chamartin de la Rosa, to set the guidelines for their activities, that can be summarized as follows: a) they must always act in agreement with the prison director; b) attendance at catechism classes is compulsory for all inmates, at least at the elementary level, if they wish to benefit from 'special assignment'; c) chaplains must find the most qualified inmates and have them organize classes or study groups, and perform Saint Ignatius spiritual exercises; d) any inmate who does not repent his sins before his death shall be denied a Christian burial; (e) before an inmate can get 'special assignment' work, he must have been married in the Church; if he has not, he will be listed as single or having had a civil marriage.

Again, a Church wedding was pure blackmail because it was *conditio sine qua non* to receive mail, visits or packages and this applied to both men and women inmates. For example, Miguel Hernández was forced to have a Church wedding in Alicante prison before his wife and son were allowed to visit him.

3. Demonization of the defeated – the 'evil' Rojos

The Church and the chaplains opinion of Republicans in general and prisoners in particular, was that they were no more than animals or evil demons, infra-human beings, the dregs of society. The horror of the Inquisition was insignificant when compared to the New State's demonization of the defeated who had defended the Republican democratic government. The campaign for demonizing the Rojos was massive. The half of Spain whose hopes had been based on a frustrated modernity, found themselves thrashed daily by an official doctrine, by huge doses of reactionary Tridentine Catholicism.[iv] As Mirta Núñez wrote, the chaos within the Church during those dark days is a terrible, unique and unusual case in 20th century Europe.

[iv] Reference to Roman Catholic doctrine as defined at the Council of Trent in the 16th century.

The inmate's principle contact with the clergy took place during Sunday Mass, in the form of a rousing sermon that all prisoners had to listen to standing at attention in the open-air prison patio, regardless of the weather. Some testified that they spent the entire time with their arms raised in the Nazi salute. Others stress how those sermons insulted them as the priest would rage against atheists and Marxists, lecturing them with fits of passion.

José Merino Campos[7], who was captured in the Cordoba mountains in 1947, recalled his experience in Sevilla jail and the notorious, authoritarian Rev. P. Ibarra, S.J. Standing along before the inmates, he began by ordering them to stand at attention. He then made them stand still while he harangued: "*The punishments you are receiving here are nothing compared to that which awaits you in the hereafter.*" The priest was followed by an equally authoritarian female catechist whom they called 'Señorita Cero' who lectured them as if they were already dead: "*Souls, pay attention. Your chances of success in the afterlife are few, because you have done nothing worthwhile in this one.*" One Sunday, the Bishop who came to Seville prison to give the sermon. "*All of you who are in this patio are criminals. That colour that was on your flag will have to be dyed with your own blood.*"[v]

An example of the demonization of the defeated is seen in the Director of Modelo prison in Barcelona's classical statement: "*You must know that a prisoner is worth no more than the ten millionth part of a crap.*"

The Church's total disdain for the 5th Commandment reached unimaginable heights. Already in 1937, a <u>Collective Letter from the Bishops meeting in Synod</u>, stated their acceptance that there would be a mass execution of communists who "*as they die, according to the sanctions of the Law, the immense majority of our communists will have made their peace with the God of their fathers.*" Killing them did not matter; what mattered was that they should have said confession before they were executed.

Pablo Uriel, in his book of memoires,[8] reports a dialogue between two prison chaplains in Aragon:

> "Father B: You who on occasion had the chance to come close to the Rojos at their last moments, did you see any signs of repentance among them?"

> "Father X: None. They are not men, they are pigs. The majority of them do nothing else than protest their innocence and the others even insult us.

---

[v]   The Spanish Republican flag bears three parallel stripes: red, purple and yellow. The Francoist flag, the current one, only bears two stripes: yellow and red. Oddly, the Republican flag is still legal, but it is only extremely recently that anti-Franco Spaniards have begun daring to display it in any form.

Believe me, I often had to contain myself; if I could do what I wanted, I would shoot them myself with my revolver. I know them well. There are vermin and there is only one way to deal with vermin."

Uriel also tells of an incident involving a nun in the Sanidad Barracks, Zaragoza, in 1936, who exclaimed:

"Dear God! I have just been into the autopsy room: there must be at least two hundred bodies there. It is horrible."

When she realized that everyone was looking at her in astonishment, without speaking, she blushed, dropped her eyes and said some words that Paulo would never forget.:

"Dear God. How many evil people there are in this world!"

As far as all the nuns and priests were concerned, the 'evil people' were the Republicans.

4. False accusations; confess or die

The Church closed ranks with the victors through another terrible mechanism: false accusations. It was a system of allegations in which the entire social base of the Regime wallowed, a widespread and typical net of complicity with the Fascist victors, a complicity of blood, a rotten environment in which the Church participated in full as one of the three pillars of Francoism.

If we think back to the words of the Basque monk, Rev. Gumersindo de Estella,[vi] he says that many of those innocent men whose execution he witnessed had been falsely accused by priests (a shameful task in which priests in Gallicia and Castille-Leon, especially, delighted in). This was the case of the sadly famous 'certificates of good behaviour' that the priests in the prisoners' hometowns were asked to issue. In the great majority of these, the priests added to the defamatory allegations at will, in order to present as negative a report as possible for inclusion in the prisoner's military dossier. The same thing occurred with the cases tried under the Law of Political Responsibility where the negative reports from the clergy did such damage. In Cordoba capital, two clergymen were especially notorious for the number of bad reports they issued: a priest, Rev. Ildefonso Hidalgo and a Capuchin monk, Brother Jacinto de Chucena.

[vi] *Vide* Volume II, text and transcriptions in the respective APPENDIX.

In the North of Spain, Julián Casanova[9] cites the case of the priest in the village of La Segarra, who went into great detail with the defamatory allegations he included in the 'revolutionary curriculum' of eighteen inmates in the village jail. At the same time, the priest asked for more townspeople to be punished on the grounds that they: "*blasphemed, were irascible, anti-religious, encouraged expropriations and the murder of members of the clergy, namely one who in addition to being ugly, gross and a coward, was an active member of the CNT.*"

The Church's imposition of religion by force, much more aggressively even than in the distant past when it did so against the Moors, the Jews and the Indians in the Americas, is frequently referred to in the incredible testimonials of those who survived the Blue Hell. As Dr. Sama Naharro told Moreno Gómez July 8 1983 when he was interviewed regarding his experience as a prisoner in Cordoba:

"When Escobar was the Director, there was a Carmelite chaplain called Don Justo who was not very clean and somewhat clumsy, wore a stained habit and never preached sermons 'because they never did anybody any good', as he would say. He was removed and replaced by a wily Jesuit, Rev. García who was about to have me exiled to the Canary Islands because I did not attend Mass. The Director warned me so I went to Mass, unwillingly, always standing in the front row. Several doctors were also involved in the conspiracy as they wanted to get rid of me.

When they wanted to punish a prisoner, they exiled him or transferred him continuously from one prison to another, for a long time. This is what they did to Dr. Sufo who spent two years shunted from one place to the other, on Varela's orders."

Amoedo-Gil described another case involving a 'wily Jesuit' in San Simón, Pontevedra, prison who was actively involved in the firing squads and would tell the inmates that they had to go to Mass. Taking his revolver out, the assembled prisoners were informed they had to tell him who did not go to Mass. He did not care whether he killed one or a hundred and the more he killed the more honoured he would be.

Another survivor, Melquesídez Rodríguez [10], also wrote a Diary in which he described another denizen of the black museum, Nicasio Martín Nieto, the Alcalá de Henares prison chaplain, whom they nicknamed 'Palo Largo', or Big Stick:

"He frothed at the mouth every time he invoked the need to cut the weeds. Days before a saca, regarding which he had already been informed, he repeated that he had to discover and exterminate the black sheep that were hiding among the white ones. The prison chaplain would also beat those who were sentenced to death when they refused to say confession. He incited the prisoners' hatred."

An uniquely dramatic moment certainly was that when the prisoners were subjected to religious pressure during the ceremonies that preceded their execution. Manuel Espejo[11], a Socialist alderman in Dos Torres imprisoned in Cordoba, tells how in the early evening, a Guardia Civil truck would arrive at the prison and call out the names of those who were to be executed. They were taken them to a room to confess. There was a different priest at each saca, monks or Jesuit priests from Cordoba. The prison chaplain was Rev. García, S.J. and he took charge of confessing the most reluctant. He took them to his room and afterwards, whether they had confessed or not, reported that they had. Because of that, many also refused to go into his room. Approximately half in each saca confessed, many of these convinced by Rev. García to whom they owed favours at hard times or in exchange for some food when they were hungry."

In Pozoblanco, the confessor to those who were about to be executed was the Salesion priest, Antonio Do Muiño, whom the inmates called the 'bird of death' because each time he showed up, it was a sign that an execution was imminent. In Villanueva de Cordoba, the confessor was Marcial Rodríguez to whom those about to die were taken to confession the day before. They say that only two prisoners confessed in this jail: Matías Villarreal and Juan Antonio Bustos (the latter of whom did so only to protect his sons, one of whom is a priest today). Moreno Gómez believes that many more actually confessed as he knows of another, unidentified priest, who was also called for confessions. Adding insult to injury, Tomás Cantador Toril told Moreno Gómez what one of his prison companions said after he had confessed: "*Can you believe what the priest just told me? 'My son, if you have any property and you have no heirs, you might as well leave it all to the Church, because you are still going to pay for all you are guilty of.*"

The prisoners' confessor in Montilla was Luis Fernández Casado, a pompous National Catholic priest. He would appear in photographs wearing his cassock, wide-brimmed hat and cloak, surrounded by Falangists. One day, Francisco Solano Martínez' mother, went to Rev. Luis to complain, sobbing as about the mistreatment to which her son was being subject in a Palma de Mallorca Workers Battalion. The priest replied: "*Forget it. He's atoning for his sins.*"

Again, Tomasa Cuevas' work is an encyclopaedia of knowledge of the clergy's repressive actions, by both priests and nuns, in the Francoist prisons. Several testimonials that appear in her book can be found in APPENDIX III.

Although not all priests were quite as nasty as those reported in the testimonials, there was the occasional exception, such as Don José María, a Basque priest in Santurarán, whose kindness and interest in them all, although there was very little he could do to help, they never forgot. (p. 277)

It was a very different matter when she spoke of Amorebieta, where everything was very much worse. The way that the staff (nuns) treated the women was horrible, blackmailing the starving women to force them to repent their sins by controlling how much they fed them. The prison chaplain was a pretentious, offensive devil who considered them as none other than thieves, murderers and prostitutes." (p. 292)

Despite the continuous threats in the event of non-compliance with their order, prison chaplains did enjoy some success in their attempts to morally 'disinfect' the prisons, even organizing choirs to sing at the solemn Mass at Easter, on special Saint's Day, and so on. As mentioned earlier, the Church's influence continued beyond the prison walls as it had its say whenever a prisoner attempted to be released on parole, before which he first had to pass this catechism examination, as Francisco Herencia reports in APPENDIX I.

Our discussion of the chaplains is not complete without a word about the role of nuns as prison wardens. Under the New State, chaplains were sent to men's prisons and nuns to women's prisons. In the latter case, the nuns were much more powerful than the chaplains. In addition to their role as Ministers of the Divine, nuns were also members of the prison staff; chaplains never were.

October 21, 2005, the Prince of Asturias de la Concordia prize was awarded to the Saint Vincent of Paul Sisters of Charity, the order of nuns who controlled several Francoist prisons such as the Provincial Prison of Les Corts, Barcelona; Alcalá de Henares prison; Palma de Mallorca prison and others, following a proposal from the Conference of Bishops.

Their job was to take care of all the internal governance of the prison, maintain discipline among the inmates, teach classes and oversee the workshops. In practice, they administered the prison with favouritism and a chilling lack of humanity. ...The inmates were only fed watery soup with cabbage ... Some women fainted with hunger when at attention in the prison and the nuns did nothing at all. The nuns were so cold, they were inhuman.[12]

Although Victoria Kent expelled nuns and chaplains them from the prisons in 1931 precisely because of their inhumanity, Franco called them back in 1940. In December 1940, 342 nuns belonging to 15 different orders, were scattered amongst 40 prisons.

In Ventas Prison, Madrid, Máximo Cuervo, the Director General of Prisons appointed a young nun of the Order of St. Teresa, Carmen Castro, as Director of the prison after the victory. During the war, she had been part of the 5th column that eventually went over to the Francoist zone in 1937. She got her training as a prison director in San Sebastián, Saturrarán and Santander prisons. She was appointed Director of Ventas Prison after the victory and she governed it with an iron fist. When María Sánchez Arbós, a secondary school teacher in Madrid and in Huesca was imprisoned in Ventas, much to her surprise she discovered that the Director of the prison, Carmen Castro, had been one of her students. It appeared that the latter was somewhat embarrassed by the fact as she approved some of her ex-teacher's, now one of her prisoners, requests such as creating a section in the jail for inmates who were there with their children and a school for young inmates directed by María Sánchez.

María Sánchez was also allowed to collaborate with the 'prisoners' workshop' whose work with crafts was supervised by Matilde Landa, another inmate. The latter, unable to withstand the constant harassment from the Church finally committed suicide in Palma de Mallorca prison. María Sánchez was finally released at the end of 1939; Carmen Castro remained with the Central Inspectorate of Prisons until her death in 1948.[13]

In brief, the Church, as one of the three pillars of the New State, enjoyed its share of power as it embarked on the its task of achieving the ideological repression of the defeated, that is, transplanting the victors' ideology into the minds of the defeated.. To this end, the Church's tactic was to combine methods from the Inquisition with the modern psychological methods of European Fascism. As Moreno Gómez pointed out earlier, the ideological repression of stripping an oppressed peoples of their identity to replace it with that of the oppressors is one of the features of genocide, as described by Raphael Lemkin.

The Church set the pace of the indoctrination and submission in the prisons, as it also engaged in a dark collaboration with the Regime, providing false denunciations for the courts (mercilessly so in some places) and, bureaucratically, by issuing 'bad conduct reports' which caused so much damage and ruined the lives of the defeated. Furthermore, the National Catholic Church reinforced the Regime's penitentiary discourse, by decreeing that the 'offense' was a sin and the 'sentence,' an affliction, and the punishment, a painful process necessary for atonement. In other words, the physical and mental purge was the prisoner's public repudiation of his heretical doctrine. If that were not enough, the Church contributed to entrenching the spirit of Francoism with its great capacity for mobilizing the Catholic masses who prostrated themselves before the Dictator. Clearly, these latter-day Inquisitors thoroughly enjoyed punishing and forcing the 'Godless' to atone for their beliefs.

6. Commuting a sentence through work: the role of the Church as an overseer and manager of the forced labour program.

At the beginning of 1937, as Franco was beginning to realize that he had no idea of what he was going to do and where he was going to put the many thousands of prisoners that were piling up in the prisons, the Church appeared on the scene as an advisor, in the form of a Jesuit, Reverend José Agustín Pérez del Pulgar. A scientist and student of social problems, he fled Rojo Madrid at the beginning of 1937. From Valladolid, Pérez del Pulgar became Franco's theoretician regarding the great mass of prisoners in the Francoist zone, beginning with Decree 281 of May 28 1937 recognizing the prisoners' 'right to work'. The Church-inspired version arrived with the creation of the National Council for the Redemption of Sentences through Work, by Ministerial Order of October 7 1938, based on Decree 281, as it applied to prisoners found guilty of acts of military rebellion. The Council was formally established December 15 1938 and the program was set to start January 1 1939.

Do not think, by any stretch of the imagination, that all prisoners were eligible for this program. The system was only open to prisoners who had already been condemned and were accepted as exhibiting good behaviour. Women, Masons and common criminals (accepted as eligible in 1944, especially black marketeers), among others, were excluded.

Furthermore, the Jesuit's brain child, the *Redemption* program, had nothing to do with any commutation of sentences; the supposed redemption was nothing other than the ideological manipulation and exploitation of labour. All the talk of 'redeeming souls through instruction and persuasion' was rubbish; this was pure and simple brainwashing. The concept of "intellectual work" was added in November 1940, apparently with the same redeeming effects but actually to enable the Church's representative to grade the inmates on the religious and similar courses they attended under the chaplains and nuns' supervision.

The system was in the hands of the National Council for the Redemption of Sentences through Work, which added: 'and Of our Lady of Mercy' in 1942. The council was chaired by the Director General of Prisons, a member of the clergy and some virtuous lady member of the Catholic Action movement. The local branches of the Council (Mayor, parish priest and the usual virtuous lady from the Catholic Action) were those who, in the towns, exercised the real social control both of prisoners out on parole and their families. It was they who determined how much the families would receive from the miserable salary the prisoners were paid for their 'redeeming work' and they who wrote the indispensable certificates of good conduct for the prisoner's release.

In addition to its role as an instrument of social control, the Council provided important national and international propaganda services for the regime, as they proclaimed *urbi et orbi*, the benefactory actions of the 'magnanimous Caudillo', a means of concealing his true nature as a wolf in a sheep's clothing. Some less astute historians have fallen into the trap, letting themselves believe that 'the extermination was not so much of an issue' as the Caudillo provided beneficent alternatives such as the Redemption system. Aforementioned historian Julius Ruiz who professed that he intends to dig deep into the sewers of Francoism, showed a surprising lack of discernment as he swallowed this argument.

There was no official information regarding the Redemption of Sentences before 1943 when the first data regarding the number of prisoners who entered the Redemption system each year during the first five post-war years: 1939 (12,781); 1940 (18,781); 1941: 18,385; 1942 (23,610) and 1943 (23,884) was published.[14] This Memorandum also provides information regarding the number of children of prisoners being taken care of in charitable institutions: 9,050 in 1942 and 12,042 in 1943. Later Memorandums publish the number of prisoners enrolled in the system in 1944 (26,518) and 1945 (17,162).[vii]

Clearly, these figures pale in comparison with the total number of imprisoned. For example, in 1940, 300,000 individuals were held in Franco's Spain, of which only 18,000 had been accepted to the Redemption system. Through the period under study, although this proportion varied little from 5%, the Regime used these figures for propaganda purposes but inflated them greatly, particularly when referring to the data for prisoners released on parole (the numbers usually included the number of prisoners reprieved or pardoned and even of those who were executed).

The 1945 Memorandum gives the following numbers for prisoners freed on parole: 3,654 (inmates condemned up to 20 years in prison) and 7,791 (inmates condemned from 20 years and 1 day to 30 years in prison).

Regarding the Cordoba prison, according to the 1943 Memorandum, 600 inmates were enrolled in the Redemption system; 400 in Jaén; 800 in

---

[vii] José Manuel Sabín in *Prisión muerte en la España de posguerra*, Madrid 1996 and Josep Maria Solé i Sabaté in *Història de la presó Model de Barcelona*, Lleida, 2000 are two historians, among others, who have written on this subject.

Seville; 200 women in Málaga; and 1,300 men in the Dos Hermanas, Seville, Paramilitary Labour Camp. Regarding their professions, of the 6,347 who were enrolled in 1943, almost 4,000 were manual workers, followed by 1,242 bricklayers and stonemasons.

When you come down to it, the reality of the Redemption program was not the release of prisoners but their ideological repression and even worse, their source of slave labour. This is clear in the terminology of the Decree that created the Council when it speaks of work as 'an act of submission and reparation'. Submission, in the lines of the genocidal philosophy of replacing the defeated's identity and ideology with that of the victors. The ideological, moral and class awareness repression. The renunciation of a person's ideals, following which the defeated's lives are forever stained with shame.

Then there is the use of the word 'reparation' that, rather than referring to an atonement of guilt, hides one of Francoism's ugliest intents: 'making the defeat rebuild that which they destroyed'. In other words, it is the defeated who are guilty of creating the damages for which those who instigated the coup and their allies were responsible.

Furthermore, reparation by way of the slave labour of the prisoners, the most vile means of exploiting that immense mass of cheap labour, to the benefit of the New State and the great opportunistic corporations, just as in Nazi Germany. The Church also took full advantage of this source of slave labour to rebuild some damaged churches and convents.

Rev. Pérez del Pulgar, S.J. never ceased proclaiming that this program cemented the Church's ministry and its mandate to bring about the spiritual and social appeasement of Spain through material reconstruction. The Director General of Prisons, Ángel B. Sanz also publicly rejoiced that this program had put this mass of delinquent unemployed to good use.

The newspaper *Rendención*

The National Council for the Redemption of Sentences Through Work's newsletter was a weekly newspaper *Redención* [Redemption], published by the National Catholic Association of Propagandists (ACNP) that spearheaded National Catholicism in Spain. The first issue was published April 1 1939, the first day of victory, and it was continuously published until 1978. The first Editor was José Maria Sánchez de Muniaín, past secretary to Ángel Herrera Oria.[viii] General Máximo Cuervo, Head of the National Prison Service was also a member of the ACNP.

[viii] Roman Catholic journalist and politician. Bishop Emeritus of Málaga and later Cardinal.

Rendención was the only newspaper allowed inside the prisons. Aa bare-faced propaganda instrument as well as tool for indoctrinating the reader, the newspaper recruited its staff among the inmates enrolled in the Redemption system and who, after having been 'redeemed' would become champions of the Regime. This undignified collaboration was rewarded with certain benefits, such as special communications with the inmate staff's families, etc. Each time that an inmate 'was converted' with the First Communion, a Church wedding or the public abjuration of democratic principles, the event was published in *Redención*. Totalitarian and oppressive regimes have always encouraged this type of personal indignity, thereby forever destroying their victims self-respect.

The purpose of the great physical, ideological and slave labour repression was famously broadcast in a NO-DO[ix] government cinema newsreel of the period, that of a very suntanned man with a closed fist that he slowly opens as he raises his right arm in the Nazi salute, saying:

> "And it is here that Franco's Spain regenerates these men as they regain the dignity they had lost. If they demolished a bridge, they are now rebuilding it. If they destroyed a house, they are now reconstructing it. Their days as prisoners are devoted to learning some skills that will make useful beings of them, whilst they atone for their existence as pariahs. All that human trash shall owe Spain its regeneration. From the proletarian mass we created order and accord, we dispelled malice, and like the cripple whose closed fist slowly opens, these men opened their fists as the brotherhood of the open hand and the raised arm received them with the generosity that the Spanish empire of the past always had for the defeated. That is our justice."[15]

---

ix NO-DO is colloquial for "Noticias y Documentales", a series of cinema newsreels created in 1943 as a major source of news, public information, censorship and propaganda for Franco and the Fascist State. Absorbed 1981 into RTVE, the government-controlled TV and radio.

SUBJUGATION OF CHILDHOOD: KIDNAPPING, SEGREGATION AND BRAINWASHING

> *"The Francoist dictatorship, unlike other dictatorships, lasted forty years and had its origin in a genocide that has not yet been openly recognized. Franco killed or exiled half of the country. Spain, today, is still incapable of seeing itself in the mirror of that concealed, silenced genocide."*

Miguel A. Rodríguez Arias, *Esa Memoria.*

1. Children behind bars

The repression of childhood, the manipulation of the children, the social segregation as well as their theft and disappearance, is another of the most pestilent and monstrous chapters of Francoism. The military coup caused death and suffering to everyone, especially to children. Infant mortality, just from the inhuman living conditions, broke all records. To that we have to add other calamities, such as the bombings. A particularly painful chapter was the evacuation of children out of the country, the "children of the war", especially from the Basque Country and Madrid. No less than 37,487 children were sent out of Spain, of which 20,266 were repatriated over time. The remainder were forever lost to Spain.[16]

There follows a brief panorama of the post-war situation regarding children. The New State basically had two general objectives when it came to children: a) the destruction of families by breaking them up and scattering their members, with a view to erasing inherited ideological and class traditions, especially those of the working class; b) secondly, by segregating the children, to subject them to ideological re-education to prevent their being contaminated by their parents' ideas. Again, this is a feature of genocide according to Lemkin: erase the oppressed defeated's identity and impress the victors' identity on them.

At the same time, the Church took advantage of this great operation to impress National Catholicism on Spain. The operation of imposing National Catholicism also involved considerable widespread abuse such as changing a child's identity, arranging for irregular adoptions and out-and-out kidnapping. The UN Working Group on Enforced or Involuntary Disappearances, following a visit to Madrid in September 2013 when the delegation met with several organizations, associations and relatives of the missing, calculated at 30,960 the number of children who disappeared or were kidnapped,.[17]

If under Francoism, parents and families lost all their rights under the law, so did their children. A first step towards the chaotic management of children during the post-war period was the March 30 1940 Order regarding the removal of all children over 3 years of age in jail with their mothers. This began the mass removal of children who were removed from their mothers' care and taken into care by the State.

Nothing better to understand the tragedy of the situation, that to read the direct statements of mothers who were interned with their children and who suffered this humanitarian catastrophe. Beginning with Tomasa Cuevas' book, one of the women she interviews, Julia García Pariente, from Guadalajara, reports how in August, when it was terribly hot, there wasn't enough water to drink. She had a small child who cried because she couldn't give him any water; worse still, when she asked for some they would give her an empty bottle. (p. 85)

Tomasa Cuevas' description of the problem of the children in Durango prison and the remarkable support their mothers got from the townspeople, as well as several other testimonials from inmates are reported in APPENDIX I. The Basque television documentary, *Forbidden to Remember*, also refers to the deaths of 120 women in Saturrarán and of 57 children, 32 of whom died in a single fortnight.[18]

A Catalan television documentary records many testimonials from inmates such as Maria Villanueva and Juana Doña, regarding the lack of everything, especially milk for the children, many of whom fell ill and died. It drew attention to the problem of how could young children survive when they were packed in cattle carts with their mothers, for seven days in a row, from Alicante to Madrid, a horrendous trip during which many children died. As one witness stated, there is no way to describe what they did to them and to their children, unless it is to underline the Regime's intention to exterminate everyone to ensure that nobody would be around to take their revenge.[19]

Ventas Women's Prison in Madrid, the largest worldwide, held 4,000 women in 1945, which gives one an idea of the number of children behind bars or abandoned. Ventas, under the orders of the notorious 'boss ladies' (La Topete, La Chanclitos, La Veneno, La Susana, La Castro, etc), was part of the same great crusade to turn everyone into a Catholic that was sweeping Spain. The Director ordered that all the children had to be baptized. Their godmothers would be ladies from the Falange. The inmates rebelled, stating that if they had no choice but to allow their children to be taken to the baptismal font, at least let their own mothers be their godmothers. The question of religion stuck in many inmates' throats because half a century of working people's lay culture could not be erased in one fell sweep.

'La Topete' (Maria Topete Fernández, sister of General Topete, Director General of the Guardia Civil) actively implemented Vallejo-Nájera's theories. As she wore a military uniform, she was considered to be a "Guardia Civil in woman's clothing". Maria Topete was influential in the opening of a new prison, San Isidro, for Nursing Mothers, next to Segovia bridge in Madrid. This was no beneficial measure. It was a means by which the inmates could be segregated and manipulated.

According to <u>Trinidad Gallego</u>, interviewed by M. Armengou in the *Los Niños Perdidos* (The Lost Children) documentary, in the San Isidro Mothers' Prison, "La Topete applied Vallejo-Nájara's[x] thesis of the need to separate the prisoners' children from their parents' 'evil influence', from the very beginning. She took over the children and enjoyed making their mothers suffer.

The fascist way of thinking, both within and without the prisons, was that the children had to be separated from their parents' ideas and re-educated. One thing was certain. Their mothers knew that if they did not lose their children physically, they would lose them morally and that they could become future enemies of everything that their parents' life represented."

San Isidro prison was inaugurated September 17 1940, with La Topeta as its Director[xi] Segregation was immediate: mothers in the upstairs gallery; the children, in the patio were not allowed to be with their mothers who might nurse them with communist milk. Their mothers were only allowed one a hour a day to be with them. The segregation was such that even their toys were given to them by the prison director. Their mothers rebelled and began making toys themselves.

2. Disappearance and theft of children

Francoism wanted to emulate the Nazi experiments with those it had detained. Apparently lacking the technical perversity of the Germans, Franco fortunately only managed to outline a grotesque scenario based on the theory of a 'Rojo gene' that he also considered was contagious. His right-hand promoter of such nonsense was the aforementioned Dr. Vallejo-Nájera, on whose advice, Franco created the <u>Army Bureau of Psychological Research</u>

---

[x] Antonio Vallejo-Nájera, a high-ranking Army doctor who, after a trip to Nazi Germany decided to practise psychiatry along the Nazi theories, which he brought back to Spain. He believed in a close relationship between Marxism and mental inferiority and because of the association of antisocial Marxist psycopaths and social unrest, their offspring must be segregated from childhood from their parents in order to protect society from such a terrible plague.

[xi] La Topete died in 2000 at the age of 100.

(August 23 1938), an imitation of a similar organism Himmler created in 1935 in Nazi Germany. The purpose of this Bureau was to research the bio-psychiatric roots of Marxism, in an attempt to find the 'Rojo gene'. Colonel Vallejo-Nájera set to work studying 297 members of the international brigades captured in Burgos and 50 women imprisoned in Málaga. His study purported to demonstrate the 'mental inferiority' of the Marxists.

Vallejo-Nájera concluded that Marxists were not only mentally inferior, but they were also dangerous and, consequently, unqualified to bring up their children. This then led to the proposal of 'segregating these subjects from childhood, so as to free society from such a terrible plague.' Recently, Juan Sánchez Vallejo has shown how Francoism also had recourse to insane asylum inmates to justify its repression of Republicans on the grounds if their presumed madness.[20]

The Vallejo-Nájera theory was applied during the 1940s and 1950s as in Spain, like in Argentina and elsewhere, the theft of children was institutionalized under law. Law of December 4 1941 endorsed the kidnapping of children as it permitted the government to change the children's name and surnames, which made it almost impossible for their families to find them and get them back. As A. Rodríguez Arias stated: "With this theft of children, Franco committed the whole gamut of crimes against humanity, the entire range of crimes that are continuously being presented to the International Criminal Court."[21]

As families were destroyed, scattered or de-structured, and any that managed to survive were subjected to social exclusion and starvation, particularly as many fathers had been executed and their mothers imprisoned, the Regime developed its arguments in favour of its theft of the children, decreeing that:

> "All families who cannot not show that they have the means to educate their children according to the principles of the Glorious National Evolution, must give the State custody of their children."

Understandably, few defeated families could comply with that requirement. As parents were unable to obtain certificates of economic, ideological and religious, compliance with the Regime, etc., the State took their children, just as they did with children who had attained 3 years of age with their mothers in prison. A great many mothers whose children were thus kidnapped from their arms, never saw them again.

The stew that fed the wave of the theft and disappearance of children was, most especially, misery and poverty. The extreme state of misery broke the traditional domestic universe of the woman and this triggered an entire chain of acts against childhood: children taken into care by the Welfare Authorities, placed in foster homes and in hospices, ending with the dark, slippery slope of irregular adoptions.

There was, however, another recourse for children of poor families whose parents were unable to feed them, which was to place them with foster parents. This was a common custom in Andalusia during the 1940s and 1950s but Moreno Gómez has not seen any reference to this anywhere; only those who came from the country towns, such as he, knew of this. The method was to send minor children to live with small and medium-sized landowners where they would help with the field work or in taking care of the cattle, in exchange only for food and lodging, and some clothes.

Rojo children, regardless of how charitably they were treated in a community, were always looked down on by the victors, scorned, shunned and despised, regardless of the official paternalistic rhetoric. One who was interviewed by Günter Schwaigaer in his documentary, describes his experience as a 9 year-old in 1936:[22]

> "I had to put up with some very disagreeable moments, many insults. We could not leave the house, we were always insulted with calls of 'communists and thieves', almost always so. When eleven of us made our First Communion [in Santa Cruz de la Salceda, Burgos] and we were taken to eat, I had to go home because some said: 'communist, what are you doing here? Other times, when I went to get a piece of bread, a lady would call out from the balcony of her house saying 'Rojo, get away you are going to dirty my door' and I would go home in tears."

A women who was also interviewed in the same documentary told of how, a young girl at the time, was called Roja and told to go home to Russia. She did not want anything to do with that town and vowed that as soon as her father was released, she would take him away from there. She still not forget them. There were similar testimonials in the *Prisoners of Silence* documentary: "They kicked us out of many places because we were Rojos. You could not speak of anything; you had to keep quiet. I am still afraid to speak out. When one does not speak of something, that something slowly disappears, slowly disappears."

Another misfortune that fell on children during those dark times, was the problem of the "children of war", those who had been sent outside the country during the war. Francoism created a pirate scheme, the Falange Foreign Service whose sole purpose was to hunt down and kidnap the "children of war" who lived outside Spain. Many were captured in Leningrad and Hitler sent them back to Franco where custody of these children was usually given to the Welfare Authorities.

In 1943, 21 children were sent back to Spain without, as Montse Armengou said, telling their parents. The parents of a child from Santander found out that their son had been returned but when they went to get him, the authorities refused to hand him back. He was sent to the Welfare Authorities where he was forbidden any contact with his family 'because they were unsuitable to educate him'.[23]

On another occasion, 180 children arrived in Madrid. Some parents heard of this but many others never found out because the Regime had ordered that they should not be told. It was all carefully organized to prevent the children from having any contact with Republican families and to encourage their adoption by right-wing families. Kidnapping these children abroad was very profitable.

As mentioned earlier, the UN Working Group on Forced Disappearances calculated that 30,960 children were stolen by Francoism, based on the Report of Penal Court Number 5 (Diligencias Pr. 399/08 V, October 16 2008), the report of the Audiencia Nacional (a type of Supreme Court), on Montse Armengou's book *The Lost Children of Francoism,* and on data from the Brotherhood of St. Paul (1944-1954) which was given custody, by the State, of that number of 'disappeared' children, distributed over 258 centres, who had lost all contact with, the education and loving care of their parents; i.e. 'disappeared' both physically and other emotionally.

All this was part of the program to 'regenerate the children of the Rojos'. Another NO-DO newsreel declared that it was:
> "The sacred mission of recovering thousands of children of Spain and of saving them from misery, to hand them over, healthy and regenerated, to the Fatherland."

One of the children sent to the Welfare Authority, Francisca Aguirre, is quoted in Montse's book as saying:
> "The nuns would assemble us and tell us clearly that we were rubbish, children of criminals... We knew that we were guilty, but we did not understand of what."

Eugenio Álvarez, from Asturias, is quoted as saying:
> "I know all the hymns of the Falange and the Church backwards. We were punished by sending us to bed without dinner, night after night, we were so hungry... They stole everything from me: my childhood, society, my family, my parents' ideals."

It was a truly Machiavellian program destined to erase their identity: their names (name and surname), their identification with their family, their social class, their ideology. It is inconceivable today how Francoism managed to destroy the backbone of the Republican family. One cannot imagine, nor does one want to know, nor is one told about it, not at school, not in the community, nor in the media.

This was a monumental fraud against historical justice. One of the great irreparable damages that the Allies committed against a progressive, innovative, hopeful and noble Spain was to allow the country to remain in Franco and the National Catholic Church's hands for 40 years, allowing them to act at will with all the time in the world to continue their terrible Nazi-inspired programs with impunity. The European democracies are to be blamed for a large part of this catastrophe, whose effects endure to this day and will continue to do so.

The 'official' theft of Rojo children, a massive New State operation, had unimaginable dimensions and was accompanied by all sorts of irregularities and abuse of power, against which the children and their parents were totally impotent. This was a clear crime of lèse humanité.

Tomasa Cuevas recounts the tragedy of her fellow inmate, Anastasia, mother of six. At the end of the war, the youngest was eleven months old. Both parents were arrested and the children were left to shift for themselves in an maddened and terrified Madrid. Everyone was suspect, everyone was considered Rojo unless he could show proof that he, or she, had been a Falangist for years. Both parents were sentenced to death and her husband was shot. Anastasia, saw her sentenced commuted to thirty years in jail and she was sent to Saturrarán prison. She had tried to find her children when she was in Ventas. All that her neighbours knew was that someone, they believed from the Welfare Authorities, had taken them away. She continued to search from Saturrarán. Nothing. Her children were not to be found in any hospice or children's home. José Maria, a kind Basque priest, the Saturrarán chaplain, did his utmost to find them. It took him some time and trouble. The children, who had been given a different surname, had been interned in a provincial hospice, apparently in Ciudad Real." (p. 286) This was the road taken by thousands of children who 'disappeared' under Franco.

Tomasa tells of her companion Clara, from Andalusia who was arrested with her husband at the end of the war, both charged with being communists. He was executed and she was condemned to death but her sentence was commuted to thirty years in prison. She was imprisoned with her younger daughter who was only a few months old. She was allowed to say goodbye to her husband as he was taken to the firing squad. Many years later, her mother-in-law and her mother were able to take her daughters to Segovia to visit her in prison. The eldest was working as a servant in Madrid; the younger, very little ones, were able to visit her. She did not know them nor did they know her. The girls looked at her with amazement. For many years they had been told that she was an evil woman, which is why she was in prison. The poor creatures looked and listen to the woman who was looking so fondly at them. She managed to keep from crying until the gate of the jail closed behind them. (p. 289)

When they took Elena Tortajada, from Ciudad Real, out to be executed, she handed her infant son to her fellow inmates, in front of the guards and the soldiers, saying: "I give you my son and ask that you educate him and teach him to respect my beliefs and to never forget why his mother died." (p. 165)

It was very difficult for these destroyed families to retain their beliefs amongst themselves. It was because of them that the Regime beat them. Yet the State and the Church who saw themselves as the traditional defenders of the family were responsible for destroying more families than in all Spanish History. Today, sanctimonious clergy speak out in defence of the family, but they do not deceive those who know their history and what they did against thousands of hundreds of families in Spain. *"There are at least 30,000 persons in Spain today who still do not know who their parents were. They were given to Catholic families and their true identity wiped from the records."*

That is what the Historic Memory is all about – to fully understand the present and correct the errors of the past. The problem is that in Spain, the State did its best to erase 40 years of the Historic Memory of its people. Outside Spain, some 80 years after the beginning of the civil war, almost nobody knows the history of the genocide. A tragic history that is gradually being unveiled, despite lingering fears among the descendants of the supporters of the legal government, with every electoral victory of the right-wing parties in the country.

3.   The Social Welfare Authority

In pre-war Spain, charity was always brought to public attention more frequently than justice, especially at times of economic depression, unemployment, hunger or calamity, when the ruling class in Andalusia opened their purses to set up soup kitchens for the hungry, although a more philanthropic assistance would have been helping people find work or get better wages.

In 1936, faced with the great wartime humanitarian catastrophe created by the military coup and the war, the better-off classes' inclination towards charitable actions was elevated to the nth degree by the great propaganda umbrella of National Catholicism kindness, a social welfare apparatus promoted as the "Falange's work of love to provide 'moral and material' assistance to hundreds of poor, abandoned or orphaned children."

In the beginning, this was primarily a volunteer organization run by Falangist men and women, namely Mercedes Sanz Bachiller (widow of Onésimo Redondo) and Javier Martínez de Bedoya, from Valladolid, together with several clergymen of course, to make sure that bread was accompanied by a good dose of religious instruction. Pedro Cantero Cuadrado, one of the best-known of its chaplains, made of this work his lifelong career.

Order of December 29 1936 establishing the Assistance to children and the elderly program, under the Ministry of Governance, published 3 January 1937 in the Official Government Bulletin, was accompanied by public appeals for charity to help fund the program.[xii]

The first Social Welfare Congress was held in Valladolid (September 13-18 1937); the second, in the same town, one year later (October 16-23 1938) and the third, now under the bugle calls of victory, at the end of December 1939. The latter was inaugurated by a euphoric Mercedes Sanz Bachiller, the first to coin the designation Social Welfare and closed by Serrano Súñer who led a delegation from the Falange and caused a great upheaval by removing Social Welfare from the aegis of the Ministry of Governance and assigning it to the Falange, thus removing any relative independence the welfare program to provide assistance to orphaned children had so far enjoyed. Mercedes Sanz was forced to resign and she was replaced by Pilar Primo de Rivera.

New Social Welfare regulations were formalized by Decree May 17 1940. The institution now was established as an official organization, a member of the FET and the JONS, dependant on and under the aegis of the State. The official nature of the Social Welfare Program was thus recognized for the first time, which enabled it to have assets of its own, the product of donations. Its budget was set by the State.[24] The new body, clearly modelled on the Nazi *Winterhilfe*, was yet another example of Franco's attraction to European fascism.

Decree of November 23 1940, in addition to reaffirming that the orphans or children of prisoners were subject to the guardianship of the State, snubbed the numerous existing welfare organizations, emphasizing its duty to entrust the education of orphans to persons 'of impeccable moral character who would ensure their educations from a religious, ethical and national viewpoint'.

[xii]   The volunteer Winter Welfare organization obtained increasing autonomy following the publication of a series of decrees such as General Order of February 3 1937 and of March 10 of the same year.

As time went by, as the victors began to tire of so many appeals for charity and giving so many alms to Rojo children, the program began to find itself in serious financial difficulties. Consequently, <u>Order of 23 May 1942</u> declared that all Spaniards had to wear a Social Welfare badge and that the so-called 'Blue sticker' had to be displayed in all public places (cinemas, bars, restaurants, etc.).

October 7 1937, the Regime created the Social Service for the New State's virtuous women. This was a kind of 6-month military service intended to provide staff assistance to the Welfare Authority, either on a daily basis or as resident wardens in homes for women in religious establishments or the so-called Recovery Colonies-Homes. The 'Welfare' ladies and the members of the Women's 'Militia' rarely got on with each other.

The key to all this Francoist charity work was not just its material assistance, but most especially, religious instruction. The Social Welfare's evangelization work was praised, particularly the mass christening campaigns, first communions and church marriages of parents, as well as its multiple actions as part of the troika of civil, military and clerical authorities. In 1939-1940, the Madrid branch of the Social Welfare Authority celebrated: 9,872 christenings, 6,642 first communions, 1,116 church weddings, in addition to obtaining several religious vocations (9 in Oviedo; 22 in all of Spain in these two years alone). There were 24,513 christenings in Spain in 1940.[25]

The daily Social Welfare routine included saying the rosary, praying before and after meals, days of spiritual retreat and sermons from clergy expert in attracting the masses. A declaration on the occasion of the 1944 general meeting of Social Welfare Advisors, clearly showed how over and above welfare itself, the majority of their tasks were focused on Francoist and religious manipulation, re-education and ideological repression:

> "Children who eat in the refectories shall attend religious instruction at the parish church and at school.
> Adults who are receiving assistance shall be given religious instruction and written propaganda.
> Social Welfare activities must be energized by the spirit of the Christian and Spanish family.
> Thanks are given to the Catholic organizations for their collaboration.
> Cordial gratitude and pledges of unbreakable support of Franco."

No matter how charitable the founders of the *Winter Welfare* wanted the organization to be, the Social Welfare Authority was corrupted from the inside by the manipulation of Francoist religious-patriotic fanatics. In a recent

(2002) heated declaration, Mercedez Sanz Bachiller insisted that she was not trying to turn the children in Francoists. She just wanted to make them become anti-Communists. Ricard Vinyes, speaking in Montse Armengou's documentary, affirmed that the Social Welfare Program was no more than a set of concentration camps for children, not with a view to exterminating them but to totally make them over. It is interesting to note, when you look at old photographs, that the Welfare children are all wearing the Falange uniform: dark blue shirts, light-coloured trousers and badges.

The welfare organization was divided into several different sections that became increasingly more complex with time. The first sections were **Children's Soup Kitchens**, for abandoned orphans from Valladolid, whose parents had been assassinated. They were cared for by volunteers, with prayers and patriotic songs. Next were **Brotherhood Kitchens**. These began in 1937 as assistance for the 'freed populations' - adults and children over 12 years of age. By the end of 1938, they had already fed 71,430 adults to whom they served 4.4 million meals. There were **Refugee Soup Kitchens** for right-wing individuals who had returned to the Francoist zone, especially via Portugal and France. Destitute women in general were cared for in **Homes for Pregnant Women and sick mothers**, in the **Recovery Colonies**.

Not all of the above existed everywhere. More widespread were the Soup Kitchens and the Brotherhood Kitchens, and the Refectories because of the general misery and great number of orphans. A great many parents had been executed, others died in battle and others had disappeared. The **Infants Feeding Centres** were for poor and orphaned children up to the age of 2 and they were nothing special – provision of some milk and medical care. Do not forget that any child suffering from a contagious disease, and there were a great many, were prohibited from going to these centres. **Creches** took care of and housed poor and orphaned children from the age of one month to three years, and even these had an educational touch. **Day Care Centres** took in children of the same age but only in capital cities and large towns as they were for children with working mothers and fathers. **Children's Homes** boarded children from the ages of three to seven who were segregated according to their sex. **Residential Schools** boarded children from seven to twelve years of age. In 1942, there was one such school in Valladolid whose rules of admission were the following: 50% places for orphans of the revolution and the war; 25% for children who are disabled because they are orphaned or poor; and 25% for beggar children. **Summer Camps for Children**. Originally created for weak or convalescing children, they also had to attend intensive indoctrination events in the form of politico-social and religious talks.

The Welfare Authority was in total chaos during the first days of victory, as it tried to meet the needs of numerous 'liberated towns' in the Centre-South of Spain and Madrid. During the first days of April 1939, it distributed more than 750,000 meals. With victory, charitable fascists began at last to act in Madrid in an attempt to compensate for their failure in November 1936, when they appeared with trucks full of melons that rotted as the trucks waited unloaded on the side of the road.

No sooner was victory announced in the North of Cordoba, at the end of March 1939, the Social Welfare organized a caravan to take help to the towns and villages in Los Pedroches district. The caravan arrived in Alcaracejos 28 March but they found the town deserted and partially destroyed. They drove around several other towns with their truck of food, until they reached Almadén. 1940 reports, presumably referring to the end of 1939, speak of 50 Social Welfare Food Centres for Children, providing assistance to 50,000 children. This number was obviously insufficient as of this number, 28,000 were children fed in 16 centres in Madrid.[26]

In 1941, the 5th Anniversary of Social Welfare was celebrated throughout Spain with great pomp and circumstance and multiple newspaper articles praising the 'magnanimous Caudillo's' great welfare work. A great fuss was made of the 61 welfare centres in Spain (Soup Kitchens for Children and Children's Homes) that had assisted 48,186 children, including 11,869 orphans in residential care. Again, it is presumed that these figures refer to 1939.

Figures reported for 1941 were 2,254 Children's Soup Kitchens, feeding 288,548 children and 1,355 Brotherhood Kitchens feeding 333,396 persons.[27] There is additional information. In Cordoba, Public Soup Kitchens were created in 1937, supplying daily meals. In 1940, long lines of starving Cordovans waited for food at the Kitchens on Calle Santa Marta. There was a Creche on the Paseo de la Victoria. In 1942, the Cordovan press published numerous photographs of huge lines of hundreds of children on many streets in central Cordova, waiting for their meal. All are wearing uniforms: girls with white skirts and boys, also in white, with a Sam Browne type belt across their chests, in the Falangist manner.[28]

1941 was a terrible year all over Spain. This was the year of the great slaughter in the Francoist prisons. Countless executions by firing squads in the capitals and an upsurge in the application of the Law of Fugitives. Inmates were being decimated by the increasing lack of food. Earlier, in this book, we spoke of the Pro-Inmate association that had been formed in Cordoba to which the regime reacted violently by arresting some hundred individuals. Hunger in 1941 went well beyond the Social Welfare expectations and in January, City Hall was forced to create a '**Municipal Winter Soup Kitchen**' in the Mother of God and Saint Raphael Asylum. A month later, the Municipal Soup Kitchen was providing more than 2,000 meals to beggars.[29] So much for the 'Great, Free Spain'.

Social Welfare Assistance – Cordoba end of 1941		
Organization	*Type*	*Number Assisted*
Province		
72 Soup kitchens	Children	9,000
54 Brotherhood kitchens	Adults	4,500
Palma del Rio Creche	Poor/orphaned children	429
Capital		
2 Soup kitchens	Children	1,500
2 Brotherhood kitchens	Adults	1,500
San Rafael creche	Children	841
San Gonzalo residential school	Children	85
San Acisclo & Santa Vitoria home	Children	73
Calle Manríquez Orphanage	Children all ages	Countless
Soup kitchen	Beggars	2,000

In October 1942, there was a decrease in the Welfare services that at the time were providing help to between 12 and 15,000 persons in Cordoba capital and province.[30] In the province, there were 63 Children's Soup Kitchens with 7,334 children; 22 Brotherhood Kitchens for 1,990 adults. In the capital, the two Soup Kitchens served 1,260 and the 4 Children's Soup Kitchens, 431 children, plus an additional 500 in the Food Centre. In December, 2 Children's Homes cared for 183 resident and 602 day-care children.

In Cordoba, the Welfare Authority headquarters were on Emilio Luque square. The provincial Delegate was Demetrio Carvajal Arrieta. The Woman's Section was on Calle Sevilla and the provincial Delegate was Mercedes Ordóñez Oria (the national delegate, Pilar Primo de Rivera, visited Cordoba March 1942).[31]

Undoubtedly, this was social chaos with a hyperbolic dimension, totally beyond belief today, even though today we speak of another uncontrolled catastrophe during the years that followed. In reality, country people always lived from one catastrophe to another.

The Social Welfare Authority's had a budget of half a million pesetas in 1941, which was not much. That sum included the 80,000 pesetas it received from the sale of the required Blue Stickers countrywide. The

Pozoblanco Municipality contributed with 225 pesetas a month in 1940. Not all municipalities contributed in this manner. Already in February 1941, the Villanueva de Córdoba municipality had expressed its alarm at the great number of people benefitting from welfare (children, elderly, widows, relatives of inmates, etc.). Nothing else was to be expected because on those dates, half of the townspeople, both men and women, were imprisoned in Francoist jails. Villanueva de Cordoba did not officially support the Social Welfare's 'work of charity' until 1947 when it paid a monthly subscription of 100 pesetas for Blue Stickers but only after it was pressured by the provincial Welfare delegate.

In Villanueva de Cordoba, the Welfare Soup Kitchen was located on Calle Real (today the *Hogar del Pensionista*[xiii]). It is there that one saw long lines of hungry people, many of whom came from the Los Bretes Group of Schools where many people who had lost everything with the end of the war, were housed. A legion of children roamed the streets begging and a number of these were taken in by local families. In January 1941, the Villanueva Municipality increased the number of food rations served daily at the Soup Kitchen by 100.

The Municipality also took advantage of public holidays and religious festivals during the year, to organize charitable works in favour of the hungry. September 29 1939, the Feast of Saint Michael, the patron saint of the town, it served an 'extraordinary repast for the imprisoned and poor people of the town'. The Falange would also participate in these charitable actions for the children of the tortured, executed, imprisoned and excluded in general, during the 1940s. The Juvenile Section organized a *Reyes*[xiv] campaign for used clothing for poor children in 1941. At the end of that year, the *Acción Católica*, *Obreras Parroquiales* and *Conferencias de San Vicente de Paúlo* (religious sister/ brotherhoods to which the flower and cream of the upper class belonged) organized a Christmas party for the poor.[32]

As mentioned earlier, the Social Welfare Soup Kitchen in Villanueva de Cordoba was on Calle Real, whereas the children in residential care were taken in by the nuns at the Cristo Rey Convent. There they were fed, housed, educated and received religious instruction. There were around 80 girls in residential care. They were primarily taught how to sew and how to pray. In November 2012, Moreno Gómez spoke with Virtudes, from Fuentes de Andalusia, Seville, who told him her story. In 1936, they assassinated her father, her mother (who was eight-months pregnant) and her grandmother.

---

xiii   Home for Pensioners.
xiv   Twelfth Night, the Spanish Christmas festivity in January in honour of the Three Wise Men, or Kings.

Virtudes, 14 months old at the time, was taken in by some aunts but the nuns showed up and took her to their convent by force, where they kept her until she was 13 years old. "They taught me how to sew, how to pray and to beg for the convent, but they did not teach me my sums." Today, Virtudes is a woman of unlimited energy. "Before, one could not speak, but today I speak out loud and nobody pays attention."[33]

As to the boys, at the beginning of the 1940s, about 50 children from destitute Rojo families (parents executed, imprisoned, guerrillas, etc.) were cared for under a day-care regime at the Cristo Rey Convent. The boys would arrive in the morning when they were taught how to say the rosary, then some ABCs and numbers, and finally given military training. Curiously, it was the nuns who taught them to march to the following rhyme: "*Jay, jop, jaro / los fusiles de los rojos son de palo*". After parading around the patio, they were given lunch and then sent home.[34]

In Montemayor, the children under care of the Welfare Authorities and the elderly from the Brotherhood Soup Kitchen, were treated with a special meal December 8 1941, in celebration of the Duchess of Frias' saint's day. The tale of this event is a perfect example of what was common practice on such occasions:

> "Once desert was over, both the guests and the servers raised their right arms high and sang *Cara al Sol,* ending with cries of Viva! Duke of Frias!" Their spokesperson added: "We thank their Excellencies the Duke and Duchess of Frias, for this example of Christian charity and we hope that it will be extended in favour of the humble and the needy, and for the good of the New Spain to which we all aspire."[35]

The work of the Social Welfare Authority (renamed Ministry of Social Affairs under the democracy) in Cordoba was overseen by the National Delegation under Mercedes Sanz Bachiller until the end of 1939, with headquarters at Calle Abascal number 39. Some of the heads of the Cordoba provincial delegations were: Amparo Bahamonde, appointed September 15 1937; Luis Nicasio Garrido Lama, February 1 1938; Manuel León Adorno, February 1 1940; Salvador Marco Martí, May1 1941; Demetrio Carvajal Arrieta, August 1 1941. Thus, we conclude this overview of a work of charity that is so rarely spoken of today, following what could be considered the Regime's watchword: Execute the parents, then be charitable with their children.

4. National Council of St. Paul for Prisoners and Convicts

In addition to the Social Welfare Authority, additional assistance was provided by the National Council of Saint Paul for Prisoners and Convicts, created by the Ministry of Justice by Decree July 26 1943 to administer the State's guardianship of the children of prisoners enrolled in the redemption program.[36]

This new organization was nothing else than a branch of the Council for the Redemption of Sentences through Work that, in October 1941, was already overseeing the care of 3,000 children of prison inmates, for whom it paid for their education and other needs. This was a dramatic increase in assistance as earlier that year, in February, the Council only reported 202 such children under its care. At the same time, reports in the local press referred to more than 6,000 children of inmates who were still not getting any help. Much of this could be explained by the confusion in the manner by which their parents were being shifted from prison to prison.

In theory, the Council of St. Paul's uplifting mandate was to take in prisoners' children and care for their upkeep and instruction. In practice, however, 'instruction' was a euphemism for brainwashing, ideological repression, preventing them from being contaminated with their family's Rojo ideology, ensuring that they are cleansed of all of the oppressed's beliefs and impressing the oppressors' ideas on them. All this for the Rojo children whom they sanctimoniously described as "That divine mass regarding which we have to rectify their parents' mistakes".[37]

An important feature of the Council of Saint Paul's actions was its avowed purpose to take advantage of the separation of parents and children – parents behind bars and children out on the street and in religious institutions – to control the families of all the disaffected. This, in pursuit of the so-called 'magnanimous Caudillo' great task of 'disinfecting' Spain and abolishing all dissolutionary, i.e., democratic, ideas. As Ricard Vinyes stated, this was solely another name for Franco's massive re-education project, whereby the control of the children had already been programmed by Order March 30 1940 regulating how long children were allowed to remain with their mothers behind bars.

The Francoist penitentiary system did not only target the prisoners with physical and ideological repression, it kidnapped their children in order to 'disinfect' and re-educate them, to erase all memories that the children might have of their parents and the ideals they defended.

Ángela Cenarro Lagunas described the manner by which the prison universe institutionalized these practices. [38] Children's visits to their parents in prison could be stopped if they wardens felt that there was a risk that the children might be 'scandalized by their parent's advice'. During the holiday months, the Council only allowed parents to see their children after it had received a favourable report on the 'living and moral situation' of the family. Worst of all, with its brutal National Catholic campaign against children, its loathing of their parents and the brainwashing of their offspring, the Regime actually was successful in getting many children to disown and hate their families.

There is a famous October 5 1945 letter to *The Times* from Tomás de Boada, President of the National Council of Saint Paul for Prisoners and Convicts, containing some facts, some lies and especially, some scandalous "declarations". A fragment of this letter is reproduced below:

> "During my current visit to England, I have noticed that there is a campaign of lies regarding how Justice is administered in Spain… Fewer than 23,000 inmates are currently housed in our penitentiaries. The prison population immediately after the end of the civil war was some 250,000 criminals convicted of common crimes punishable under the laws of all civilized nations. I have personally examined many sentences, without having found a single one that was based on a political motive. The Council cares for a large family of about 1,500,000 persons, among inmates, convicts and families."[xv]

Boada's only correct statement was that Francoist penitentiary repression affected 1,500,000 persons, prisoners and their immediate families. The number he gives for prisoners under Franco soon after the end of the war is a lie as the total exceeded 300,000. Another blatant lie was that those sentenced under Franco were tried only for common, not political, crimes This was pure propaganda, a typical example of Franco's usual mendacious policy when addressing an international audience as he played lip service to International agreements. Foreign governments, either ingenuously or hypocritically, believed him. At the end of 1947, only 2% of all prison inmates in Spain were officially classified as common criminals. In other words, 98% of the remainder of those imprisoned in Francoist prisons had been tried and sentenced by court martial for purely political reasons.

[xv] The full text of this letter can be consulted on the Internet but in Spanish only. The original letter could not be found after a search of *The Times* archives. The above text is translated from Spanish.

FINAL COMMENTS REGARDING A PERIOD OF REPRESSION NEVER BEFORE SEEN IN SPAIN

The 1947-1949 Triennium of Terror

Located in the final stages of this book in three volumes, having reached the limits of permissible space, it is still important to give the reader a minimum indication of the massive repression with which Franco terrorized the Spanish countryside during the period that Moreno Gómez has called the Triennium of Terror (1947-1949), a period regarding which there were serious precedents in 1946 and a bloody ep ilogue in 1950.

Since 1987 Moreno Gómez has consistently drawn attention to this new Francoist despotic turning of the screw in its repression of the civilian population (fathers, mothers, sisters, wives, and other relatives of those who had fled to the mountains, including many with presumed links with them, which in many cases simply did not exist). Today, however, many historians of the period have not yet reached this last great chapter of the Francoist repression, the one that sowed the greatest amount of terror in the rural world, with some assistance from the city police forces.

In guerrilla vocabulary, this is often described as 'repression in the plains', as opposed to 'repression in the mountains'. In the case of the repression in the plains, more than looking for fugitives or those opposed to the Regime, the real purpose was to sow such terror in the countryside that no guerrillas would be able to survive in the maquis. It was a scorched earth policy whereby the liberal application of the Law of Fugitives or simple summary executions, were responsible for the death of 1,500 persons throughout Spain during those three years.

Pay attention, all you half-baked negationists, literati of the Regime, members of the 'third Spain', and liars and prevaricators of all kinds. Also take note you, who like Julius Ruiz, without knowledge of the cause, fatuously nourish, the theory that the Francoist repression decreased significantly after 1941, totally disregarding the fact that there still were many more deaths to come after that dark date in the history of Francoism.

Moreno Gómez regrets that the scope of this book is not sufficient for him to go into great detail regarding the tragedy of the Triennium of Terror, especially in the Cordoba countryside, but in other Spanish provinces as well . He does, however, refer the reader to two of his previous books that deal with this subject and all the horror of Francoism that comes into play, unrestrained, over all the Spanish countryside:

Cordoba en la posguerra (La represión y la guerrilla, 1939-1950) [Post-war Cordoba. Repression and Guerrilla, 1939-1950]. Cordoba, 1987, in which he introduces his preliminary study of this dark period in Spanish history,

and his primary work on this subject:

La resistencia armada contra Franco. Tragedia del maquis y la guerrilla [Armed Resistance Against Franco. The Tragedy of the Maquis and the Guerrilla.] Crítica, Barcelona, 2001, in which he presents an exhaustive study of that which was the serious criminality of the Triennium of Terror.

In addition to several articles, Moreno Gómez co-authored another book, also in Spanish: *Morir, matar, sobrevivir. La violencia en la dictadura de Franco.* [Die, Kill, Survive. Violence under Franco's Dictatorship]. Crítica, Barcelona, 2002, which provides data regarding the Triennium of Terror in the rest of Spain, as he talks of those who fled, who became guerrillas and members of the resistance. (None of these books is currently available in English.)

Regarding documentaries regarding the 1948 terror, Moreno Gómez mentions two recent ones in particular, that he considers especially awesome. The first of these, *Muerte en El Valle* (Death in El Valle) by Cristina M. Hardt, CM Pictures for Channel Four Television, 2005, www.muerteenelvalle.com, is about a crime in a small town in Léon province, in 1948, when the Guardia Civil applied the Law of Fugitives to two farmers, one of whom, Francisco Redondo.

Many years later, his granddaughter, Cristina M. Hardt who was living in New York, decided to tell the world what Franco's Regime had done to him. She went to El Valle and asked questions, searched and researched the facts, no matter how scared the townspeople and her relatives still were of being seen speaking to her.

In his little old farmhouse in the country, Francisco and his wife sheltered guerrillas. One day, an informer turned them into the Guardia Civil who raided the farm and burnt the house down. The guerrillas escaped but Francisco and his wife were arrested and taken to Bembibre prison where they were horribly tortured. Six days later, they took Francisco Redondo and his wife Florentina into a field where they shot them both. Back in El Valle, Cristina had the guts to discover which Guardia Civil had shot them, she went to his house and recorded her interview with him. Only an American is capable of such bravery. In Spain, nobody would dare to do so a thing.

The second awesome documentary that Moreno Gómez mentions is practically unknown in Spain: *La isla de Chelo* [Chelo's Island], Play Film IBCinema, 2008, by Odette Martínez, daughter of the ex-guerrilla 'Quico'. This is the story of another tragedy in El Barco de Valdeorras, Galicia.

The film recounts the sufferings of the Rodriguez Montes family because two of their sons had gone over to the guerrillas. The Guardia Civil went to their farmhouse, ordered the parents to come out and shut their daughter Consuelo in the sheep pen. After a while, they called her to come out and say goodbye to her parents. Her mother held her hand tight, begging them to leave her alone, but they put Consuelo back with the sheep. They ordered her parents to go down a footpath, where the Guardias brought them down with a burst of gunfire that the young girl heard from the corral. Hours later, neighbours came and took her to the place where her parents had been killed and where they buried them. Some time later, the Rodriguez brothers came down from the hills and took their sister back with them. She spent three years in the hills where she was known as 'Chelo'.

The relentless Francoist repression of those it considered its opponents, both before and after this bloody period, lasted until 1950. Fifteen years killing people so that "Thirty years from now, none of this scum will be alive" as the Seville executioner, Captain Diaz Criado liked to say. In 1950, the Law of Fugitives was still being applied in some places in Spain, as in Nerja, Málaga.

Beginning July 18 1936, Spain suffered a never-ending ordeal that was so much more than simply the slaughter of so many people. It was the concentration camps, mass arrests, killing through starvation in the prisons (just as in the Nazi camps), slave labour, forced labour battalions, deporting prisoners from their home towns after their release, the lack of food and widespread hunger, social exclusion, blacklists of defeated prevented from working, purges, rationing, black-markets, courts martial, mass torture, firing squads, summary executions or Law of Fugitives until 1950. Especially as regards the defeated or disaffected, it was shaving women's heads, the castor oil treatment, stripping women naked in public and other gross humiliations, the disappearance and kidnapping of children, imposition of religion by force, brainwashing children, official theft and seizure of the defeateds' property, the purposeful destruction of families, and so much more.

All of this Moreno Gómez described in great detail in this work as he provides solid proof, based on his in depth research and interviews with survivors and eye-witnesses of Fascism's crimes against humanity, many of which are in agreement with Lemkin's descriptions of acts of genocide.

Crimes that the reactionary sectors in Spain (the Military, the Falange and Church, in the barracks, the casinos and church vestries) committed as they attempted to emulate the terrible form of Fascism practised by the Rome-Berlin Axis. The July 18 1936 military coup led to a terrible civil war whose end in 1939 brought neither peace nor reconciliation, nor forgiveness, nor amnesty, none of that by which all Spaniards, both victors and defeated, could come together.

On the contrary, far from encouraging a reconciliation of parties, the victors embarked on a cruelty in which they wallowed without restraint, with an indescribable fury and an unmeasurable desire for revenge that is unique in the history of Spain, as they forced the defeated to bite the dust for almost four decades. The result was a colossal humanitarian catastrophe as Francoists and National Catholicism rode roughshod over every form of human rights past and present, added to which half a million eminent intellectual Spaniards, an irreplaceable brain drain that was forever lost to the country.

For all the wealth of detail, this book only pretends to disclose the tip of the iceberg of that which really occurred. He who wants to know, knows; he who does not, let him continue to hide his head in the sand or to contribute to the great lie, another popular national sport.

Moreno Gómez concludes, for the reader's reflection of this tale of a terrible conflict, by quoting the Greek Herodotus', father of History, introduction to his work *Histories:*

"Herodotus of   Halicarnassus hereby publishes the results of his inquiries, hoping to do two things: to preserve the memory of the past by putting on record the astonishing achievements both of the Greek and the non-Greek peoples; and more particularly, to show how the two races came into conflict".

Endnotes for Chapter II

1   Tomasa Cuevas Gutiérrez. *Testimonios de mujeres en las cárceles franquistas.* (Eye-witness Accounts of Women in Franco's Prisons). Instituto de Estudios Altoaragoneses, Huesca, 2004 (1ˢᵗ Edition, Casa de Campo, Madrid, 1982).

2   Basque TV documentary. *Prohibido recordar* (No Remembering). Tentazioa Rec, Moztu, Pais Vasco, 2010.Do

3   Gonzalo Amoedo López y Roberto Gil Moure, *Episodios de terror durante a Guerra Civil na provincia de Pontevedra. A illa de San Simón,* Xerais, Vigo, 2007, p. 85.

4   Sr. Prado Girón, nephew of the famous guerrilla from Léon, Manolo Girón. Testimonial in the Catalan television documentary *Los niños perdidos del franquismo* (Francoisms lost children). Montse Armengou & Ricard Belis. 2002.

5   Diego San José. *De cárcel en cárcel* (From jail to jail). Do Castro, La Coruña, 1988.

6   Julián Casanova in *La Iglesia de Franco* (Franco's church). Critica-Bolsillo, Barcelona, 2005, p. 299.

7   José Merino Campos. Interviewed by Moreno Gómez in Córdoba, 22 February 1981.

8   Pablo Uriel, *Mi guerra civil* (My Civil War). Introduction by Ian Gibson. Self-published, Valencia, 1988.

9   Julián Casanova, *La iglesia de Franco* (Franco's Church). Annotated edition, Crítica, Barcelona, 2005.

10   Melquesídez Rodríguez Chaos, *24 años en la cárcel,* Forma, Madrid, 1977, pp. 162 and 97.

11   Manuel Espejo. Interviewed by Moreno Gómez in Madrid January 1984.

12   María Salvo i Iborra. *Interviú* magazine, 17 October 2005. Also testimonials from previously referenced work by Ricard Vinyes, Tomasa Cuevas, Fernando Hernández Holgado and an email from the Andalucia CGT 29 October 2005.

13   Carlos Fonseca. *Trece Rosas Rojas* (Thirteen Roja Roses). Temas de Hoy, Mardid, 2005.

14   *Memoria que eleva al Caudillo de España y a su Gobierno el Patronato Central para la Redención de Penas por el Trabajo, de 1943.* (Memorandum from the Caudillo of Spain and his Government regarding the National Council for the Redemption of Sentences Through Work., 1943). Madrid.1944.

15   Text transcribed from the *Presos del Silencio* (Prisoners of Silence) documentary by Mariano Agudo and Eduardo Montero. Intermedia Producciones, Seville, 2005.

16   Francisco Moreno Gómez. "La represión en la posguerra" (Postwar repression) in *Víctimas de la guerra civil* (Victims of the civil war). Temas de Hoy, Madrid, 1999, p. 286.

17   Preliminary report of the UN Working Group on Enforced or Involuntary Disappearances after a visit to Madrid, Spain, 30 September 2013.

18   *Prohibido recordar* (Forbidden to Remember). Basque television documentary by Josu Martinez and Txsaber Larreategi, de la ETB, Tentazioa Rec, Basque

Country, 2010.

19 *Los niños perdidos del franquismo* (The lost children of Francoism). Catalan television documentary by Montse Armengou and Ricard Belis. Televisió de Catalunya, 2002.

20 Juan Vallejo. *La locura y su memoria histórica.* (Madness and its Historic Memory). Ediciones Atlantis, Madrid, 2013.

21 A. Rodriguez Arias. Interviewed in the documentary *Esa Memoria* (That Memory) by Dominique Gautier and Jean Ortiz, Creav Atlantique, France, April 2011.

22 Interviewed in Günter Schwaigaer's documentary, *Santa Cruz, por ejemplo* (Holy Cross, for example), Austria, 2005.

23 Montse Armengou and Ricard Belis, The Lost Children of Francoism, op. cit.

24 Mónica Orduño Prada, *El Auxilio Social (1936-1940). La etapa fundacional* (The Social Welfare Program – The foundation). Escuela Libre Editorial, Madrid, 1996.

25 Ángela Cenarro Lagunas, <<Historia y memoria del Auxilio Social de la Falange>> (History and memory of the Falange's Social Welfare Program). *Pliegos de Yuste,* issues 11-12, 2010.

26 *Azul* newspaper, Córdoba, 18 October 1940.

27 *Córdoba* newspaper, 30 October 1941. With the following headlines: 'Social Welfare obeys. Intense social, moral and religious reconstruction. 6,000 christened. 150,000 first communions. 2,000 marriages legalized.'

28 *Córdoba* newspaper, 3 November 1942.

29 Azul newspaper, Córdoba, 24 January 1941. "Campaign against begging in Córdoba. City Hall creates a Municipal Winter Soup Kitchen with a sum of 50,000 pesetas. The Falange will collaborate with all its means."

30 *Córdoba* newspaper of 23 April 1942 published a very complete list of all those assisted in the Soup Kitchens.

31 *Azul* newspaper, Córdoba, 17 March 1942.

32 Minutes of the Meetings of the Villanueva de Córdoba Municipality dated 28-8-39; 31-12-40; 28-1-41; 25-2-41; 16-12-41; and 18-3-1947.

33 Interview with Moreno Gómez on the occasion of a Historic Memory Conference, Seville, 24 November 2012.

34 Ernesto Caballero Castillo, testimonial from one of those boys.

35 *Azul* newspaper, Córdoba, 13 December 1941.

36 There is an ancient publication on this matter with several authors: *Crónica del Patronato Nacional de San Pablo* (Chronicles of the National Council of Saint Paul). Ministry of Justice, Madrid, 1951, 379 pp.

37 Mirta Núñez, op. cit.

38 Ángela Cenarro Lagunas. "La institucionalización del universo penitenciario franquista" (The institutionalization of the Francoist prison universe), in *Una inmensa prisión* (An Immense Prison), Crítica, Barcelona, 2003.

APPENDIX I

Testimonials regarding other aspects of the multi-repression and the Spanish holocaust Conditional freedom, slave labour

<u>Matias Romero Badia</u>. VILLANUEVA DE CÓRDOBA

- "At about 11 p.m. on the night of 9 May of the Year of Victory, a short 2nd Lieutenant [probably the notorious Teniente Pepinillo] accompanied by several drunken Falangists appeared in the room on the first floor of the building where the prisoners were held [Juan Herrero's house on Calle Conquista], and who, revolvers in hand, had come to 'say warm good-nights to the inmates': "Let's see. Where is the bastard who said that if he had a hoe he could make a hole in the roof of this house and get away? You have five minutes to tell me who he is and if you don't, I have a truck outside the door to cart you all to the cemetery."

About half an hour later they returned, revolvers in hand and he repeated the question. As the inmates again refused to comment, he pulled out a list with the following names: Bartolomé "El Floro" Pozuelo, a sheep shearer, and Francisco "Floro el Manco" Pozuelo, his son, and took them away. About an hour later, they returned, barely able to walk. The Lieutenant, pistol in hand again, repeated the same question and getting the same reply, read out another name: Alfonso"El Papel" Ibáñez Tamaral whom they took to headquarters where a group of tormentors, including Pedro "El Barbero", were waiting.

And so on, back and forth, the same question and the same response. The Lieutenant kept on repeating "If anybody present still lives at the end of the night, he shall never forget the night of 9 May of the Year of Victory"…

CÓRDOBA. *Regarding his transfer to the Provincial Prison from the Alcázar, Winter 1942.*

- "We were transferred to the Provincial Prison in two groups. The first group marched along the banks of the River Guadalquivir to their new destination; in the second, we were formed into sets of two and three, some of us shackled to each other, others tied to the other with wires. Each prisoner had to carry his backpack over his shoulder. Once we were lined up indian file, usually in groups of some two hundred, each one was tied to another with a long rope, head to tail, to prevent any attempted escape. Closely guarded, we began walking along the riverside until we arrived at the New Prison, which was still under construction."

Antonio "El Cano" Álvarez. POSADAS. *Report to the local Historic Memory Association.*

- "We were sleeping one night in the anthill that was the local jail, when there was a banging at the door. 'Who is it? a guard asked. 'Come on out… We're going to have some fun!' someone replied. They took my father and another person from this town out to Plaza Mártires., where a ring of many Señoritos and their sons were amusing themselves with castor oil, some were pouring gasoline, another was wielding a lash, another…. and so on. They beat my father so badly, we had to use pincers to remove his shirt."

Miguel Hernández. ORIHUELA. *Diary and letters written in the Orihuela jail.*

- "I feel much worse here than I did in Madrid. There, nobody, neither those who received nothing, suffered such hunger as we do here, and we did not see the suffering and the diseases that are everywhere in this building. My fellow townspeople are especially interested in showing the evil that lies in their hearts and I have been seeing this first-hand ever since I fell into their hands.

    The Señoritos will never forgive me for having put the little intelligence and learning that I have at the service of the people. These are the most brutish individuals you can imagine. But they will not f… with me or anybody else. Every moment they are making me waste now, each beating, they will have to work for.

    I do not want to leave whilst they still are scoundrels and blackguards in this world. Tell me how you get along in this labyrinth of hunger and misery in which we have been placed…"

Testimonials from inmates in Córdoba Provincial Prison

José Sáez Jiménez. Letter to Moreno Gómez from Caracas, Venezuela, March 24 1986. *Regarding his father in Córdoba Provincial Prison 1941.*

- "Every morning, they took a new victim from the cells, swollen like a balloon, to add to the list of those who died from some supposed disease that the imprisoned doctors were forced to certify. Faced with such a situation, my father denounced it to the authorities, regardless of the threats he received and that almost cost him his life."

Carlos Menéndez. DOS TORRES. *Regarding his treatment in Córdoba Provincial Prison.*

- "We ate rotten beans, mouldy turnips, squash and more, without olive oil. I was present when we left our cells as they inspected the several individuals who died each day. The death certificates, complete with diagnosis, had already been signed. The only thing missing were each dead man's personal details."

Manuel Espojo Blanco. DOS TORRES. *Driver for prison Director Escobar.*

- "One of the dormitories was occupied by those who were dying of hunger. It was a dismal scene because they were no more than skeletons who could not even stand up. They were grouped in the two dormitories above the offices in the centre of the prison. When they died, they put several bodies in the same casket and there still was room left for more. On the other hand, the inmates suffering from typhus were kept in the infirmary. The sleeping mats had to be burnt to get rid of the bed bugs and the lice."

Adriano Romero. VILLANUEVA DE CÓRDOBA and Member of Parliament for PONTEVEDRA. *Describes the dormitories in the old Córdoba prison, under the Alcázar.*

- "The dormitories in which we were packed, like a herd of sheep, had so little sleeping space that it was often less than 20 centimetres wide per person. They were located in an underground area of the old Alcázar that had at one time served as stables, under three corners of the patio, some 20 metres long and some seven or eight metres wide, to serve a prison population of more than 1,000 inmates... there just wasn't enough room for everybody in the patio.

  In the 350 inmate dormitories, there was a single open air toilet that we could not use during the day. An epidemic of typhus broke out amidst this appalling misery, with no sanitary conditions, with a food ration that did not supply even one fourth of the calories that a human needed to live. If you add those who died from hunger to those who died from typhus, they liquidated a third of the prison population. Some six hundred persons who had been turned into living skeletons survived... This Dantesque scenario of dead and men turned into skeletons from hunger and typhus, was repeated in all the most important prisons in Spain. All those who had nobody to help them was condemned to starve to death."

Francisco Gómez Herencia. NUEVA CARTEYA. *Regarding hunger and parasites.*

- "It is almost impossible to describe those days of horror, of anguish, of unrelenting hunger. During the day we would drag our miserable bodies from one patio to another, not even able to sit on the ground because the parasites that covered it, the logical result of the total lack of sanitation, would crawl over our bodies... We were treated worse than animals and I still have several scars to remind me of that unforgettable stage of my life. If we were treating in a humiliating and savage manner, our despair grew even more at mealtimes: the only food we were given was a watery soup made from boiled cauliflower stalks in which, to give it an appearance of containing something nourishing, they threw cubes of fat that they used to grease the cartwheels.

  For twelve months, our lives slowly slipped away. The few of us who survived did so thanks to the proximity of our families who, with a superhuman effort, sent us some food when they could. We would have all died if it had not been from a young officer who, horrified with the sadism with which we were treated, informed Madrid. An inspector was sent and when he asked to see where the food was stored, all they could show him was a shack containing some rotten turnips."

Miguel Regalón. VILLANUEVA DE CÓRDOBA. *Regarding medical treatment.*

- "Every afternoon, when we were sent to our cells, several inmates who had died from hunger remained on the patio floor. We had to brush the lice off those who could not move from their mats because they were dying. They were covered with infected, foul-smelling sores. Dr. Sama, who lives in Córdoba and was also imprisoned, can attest to this, as he wrapped cotton around his ankles to keep the lice from infecting him.

  In Summer, with temperatures above 40ºC in the patio, we were given no water and whenever some relative brought a water bottle, the guards would break it. One inmate from Adamuz caught a little bird that had fallen from roof and ate it raw. The guards beat him and that was the last we saw of him. The lack of vitamins (avitaminosis) began to manifest itself with a swelling of the face, the legs and the skin on our testicles. One day I was lucky in that my family brought me a canteen of olive oil and some oranges. I went into the patio, to share a spoonful of oil and a bit of orange peel with those who could no longer stand. One inmate, nicknamed 'El Panolo', died with some olive oil and bit of orange in his mouth."

132

Released on Probation, the so-called Conditional Freedom

Miguel Regalón. In a letter to Moreno Gómez from VALENCIA April 1986. *Regarding the 'delights' of living as a parolee.*

- "I was released on parole and was constantly under supervision, followed by informers from all social classes, and the police would send me Communist propaganda in the mail to see if I would fall into their trap by distributing it. I was provoked, to see how I would react, but as I had a wife and daughter, grinned and bore it and humiliated myself. This is why I often say that I have more than nine lives."

Ernesto Caballero Castillo. VILLANUEVA DE CÓRDOBA.

- "Something else were the daily signing ins at the Guardia Civil barracks that many men and women were required to attend, usually at the end of the day. At times there was a huge crowd of people in front of the gates to barracks, waiting for some guards to come out with their lists and check off their names so that they could go home... until the next day. If they felt like it, the guards would stop this or that person, interrogate them harshly and give them a beating or two, for no reason other that they were working men.

  In addition to the constant fear that one might be kept back and interrogated, the required appearances made it impossible for one to work in the countryside as it forced the parolees to remain in town all day, because of which many families went hungry.

  My mother was forced to attend these signing ins for a long time. Also with my brother and me... every afternoon. I was about 9 years old at the time and my brother about 11. Both of us had been working in the fields, taking care of the cattle, but we were forced to leave those jobs and stay in town doing nothing."

- "Every afternoon, the Falangists would go to the bus stop to see who was coming back into town and, when they felt like it, they arrested them again, together with any of their family who were waiting for them. At a minimum, they kept them closed up in the country jails for a few weeks, when they did not shave their heads or beat them.

  The people who waited at the bus stop were terrified of the uniformed and armed Falangists... One day, my mother arrived on the bus..."

Forced labour and the Workers' Battalions

Pedro Gómez González. VILLARALTO. Letter to Moreno Gómez from Córdoba, December 16 1986. *Description of the conditions in Workers Battalion 28, Company 4, La Bacolla, near Santiago de Compostela, where he was put to work in building an airfield.*

■ "The most rotten tricks were the rule here. The boss was a Commander in the Engineers, the greatest bastard I ever met. Each Battalion worked eight hours, one in the morning and the other in the afternoon. The morning Battalion had to rise at 5 a.m. We were given a mug of coffee and we were marched five by five, holding each other by the hand, escorted on either side by a soldier who carried a rifle and a whip. It was a 3 km march to the job. The other Battalion began worked from 1 p.m. to 9 p.m. When dinner was served, boiled cabbage, it was already 11 p.m.

It was exhausting work. We had to dig and fill 8 or 10 metre-and-a-half wagons with earth and we had to take them along a path to level a hilly area. We were put into groups, each under the command of one of the most bloodthirsty sergeants or corporals, who lashed us and made us work without stopping. We were given very little clothing and paid nothing, despite the fact that the work had been given to a private contractor.

When one of us escaped, the rest of us were punished by having to attend instruction sessions after work. Two friends of mine from the same town managed to escape but we later heard that the Guardia Civil had caught them in León railway station. They were sure killed because we never heard of them again. Another friend of mine from Villaralto, Alfonso Luna, was beaten with a sharp pointed stick they jammed into his arm. When they finally took him to Santiago Hospital it was too late; he died the following day from gangrene.

There was a great deal of hunger. The poor chap who received nothing from his family, was condemned to death. Many starved to death. When we arrived, we were only fed some broth and cattle greens. We looked like starving beggars, eaten up with misery. We were housed in an ancient tannery. At night, shivering with cold, we watched the stars through the holes in the roof.

The commander laughed at us when he saw us; he called us the "sons of the Pasionaria". Many companions could not work because they were too weak to walk and they fainted. When we returned to the camp from work, those who were able to stand went to look for food in the garbage cans for anything edible – fish guts and other rubbish. You had to see it to believe it."

Excerpts of testimonials from the award-winning 2009 Spanish television documentary on the Dos Hermanas, Seville, labour camp: *Prisoners of Silence.*

- "It was very, very difficult for the inmates' families. My mother had reached the end of her tether because of so much suffering. Four of her sons died. There was no end to her pain and she had run out of tears.

- In addition to the hunger, it was the humiliation.

- Families could visit on Sundays and Holy Days, but it cost an enormous amount and we had to travel long distances. We came from Jaén and after we got to Dos Hermanos, we had to walk 8 kms to get to the prison camp. Once at the camp we could see my father from a distance, behind a wire fence. We had to shout to speak to him. Instead of making him happy to see us, it made him very sad. My mother cried non-stop and so did the children.

- One day, four or five drivers escaped – one from Córdoba, another from Gibraleón, the others from Morón. They made the mistake of not going far away and a few days later they were caught and taken to La Corchuela, which began with 3,500 prisoners and they added another 3,500 from El Arenoso. The fugitives were shot in front of everybody and we were made to march past the bodies. 'Eyes right! Eyes right!'. It was a day of silence."

APPENDIX II

EXTERMINATED IN THE PRISONS IN CÓRDOBA CAPITAL DUE TO HUNGER AND HARDSHIPS

PP = Provincial Prison, Plaza del Alcázar 5
NP = New Prison, on the road to Pedroches

8-May-1939, PP
Francisco González Heredia, 61, bricklayer, acute nephritis, Almería.
23-May-1939, PP
Antonio Gómez Leal, 29, farmer, suffocation, Hinojosa del Duque.
Alfonso Martín Rojas, 25, suffocation, Villa del Río.
13-June-1939, PP
Juan Moreno Tejada, blacksmith, suffocation, Badajoz.
Germán Ramírez Madrid, 25, farmer, suffocation, Espiel.
Francisco Juárez Zapata, 21, suffocation, Granada.
Rafael Luque Serrano, 32, farm worker, suffocation, Carcabuey.
23-August-1939, PP
Jacoba Centeno Tena, 59, housewife, performation of the stomach, Badajoz.
17-September-1939, PP
Juan Boquizo Delgado, 79, manual labourer, collapse, Lopera.
9-October-1939, PP
Rafael González Roldán, 22, manual labourer, tuberculosis, Nueva Carteya.
21-October-1939, PP
Luis Pérez Escués, 74, manual labourer, gastroenteritis, Lopera.
1-November-1939, PP
Joaquín Palma Delgado, 62, salesman, asystole, La Victoria.
5-November-1939, PP
Antonio Ramírez Mesa, 54, road worker, myocarditis, Cabra.
1-December-1939, PP
Pedro Muñoz Burgos, 59, manual labourer, myocarditis, Lucena.
28-December-1939, PP
Félix Pulgarín Agenjo, 44, manual labourer, acute nephritis, Fuenteobejuna
3-January-1940, PP
Francisco Guerrero Cáceres, 43, tar worker, acute nephritis, Puente Genil.
11-January-1940, PP
Francisco Sáez de la Torre, 50, soldier, tuberculosis, Madrid.

10-February-1940, PP
> Rafael Cruz Fernández, 40, manual labourer, heart attack, Monturque.

11-February-1940, PP
> Cristóbal Jiménez Sevillano, 44, manual labourer, bronchitis, Aguilar.
> Francisco Rodriguez Palos, 52, manual labourer, chronic nephritis, Puente Genil.

15-February-1940, NH
> Francisco López Hierro, 52, manual labourer, bronchitis, Peñaflor.

20-February-1940, PP
> Pablo Barja Peláez, 47, tool sharpener, chronic nephritis, Porcuna.
> Juan Fructuoso Quesada, 74, manual labourer, laringeal epithelioma, Posadas.

7-March-1940, PP
> José Blázquez Milara, 53, miner chronic bronchitis», Belmez.
> Miguel Garcia Madrid, 61, blacksmith, cerebral haemorrhage, Montoro.

10-March-1940, PP
> Antonio Vázquez Pérez, 57, manual labourer, chronic nephritis, Cerro Muriano.

13-March-1940, PP
> Luis Garcia Orihuela, 58, manual labourer, valvular heart disease, Villaralto.

14-March-1940, NH
> José Moreno Hernández, 47, manual labourer, bronchial asthma, Posadas.

21-April-1940, NH
> Francisco Talballido Blanco, 53, manual labourer, pneumonia., Navas Concepción.

3-June-1940, PP
> Tomás Martinez Barber, 20, entrepreneur, heart attack, Villaviciosa.

16-June-1940, PP
> Manuel Montserrat Leonard, 25, manual labourer, heart attack, La Carlota.

4-July-1940, NH
> Francisco Cebrián Amil, 32, manual labourer, tuberculosis, Adamuz.

18-July-1940, PP
> Antonio Luna Hidalgo, 28, manual labourer, tuberculosis, Morón de la Frontera
> José Siles Jiménez, 29, bricklayer, epilepsy, Almodóvar del Rio.

2-August-1940, PP
> Isabel Cañete Molina, 40, housewife, diabetes, Baena.
> Miguel Álvarez Tena, 37, miner, suffocation, Pueblonuevo.

13-October-1940, PP
> Domingo Valenzuela Salamanca, 27, market gardener, bronqu., Albendin.

3-November-1940, NH
> Miguel Garcia Gómez, 28, manual labourer, tuberculosis, Villaviciosa.

15-November-1940, NH
Antonio Pozo Gañán, 68, manual labourer, myocarditis, Adamuz.
7-December-1940
NH Eusebio Corrales Trujillo, 54, miner, heart attack, Belmez.
PP Antonio Ruiz Garcia, 58, manual labourer, uremic coma, Priego.
15-December-1940, PP
Manuel Hurtado Torres, 57, manual labourer, enterocolitis, Cabra.
24-December-1940, NH
Alfredo Ramos Vázquez, 58, farmer, nephritis, Fuenteobejuna.
29-December-1940, NH
Manuel Cárdenas Delagrima, 42, farm worker, rheumatic endocarditis. ,Granada.
30-December-1940, NH
Ramón Girado González, 48, farm worker, mitral insufficiency, Villanueva del Rey.
3-January-1941, NH
Juan Miguel Lao Gordillo, 58, manual labourer, arteriosclerosis, Valenzuela.
6-January-1941
NH Julián Prieto Carmona, 30, manual labourer, apoplexy, Pueblonuevo.
PP Vicente Martin López, 22, manual labourer, anemia, Alicante.
8-January-1941, NH
Juan J. González Hidalgo, 42, miner, enterocolitis, Pueblonuevo.
12-January-1941, PP
Juan Peña Delgado, 50, manual labourer, nephritis, Villanueva del Rey.
Juan Sierra Rabanera, 49, manual labourer, nephritis, Granada.
14-January-1941, NH
Aquilino Estévez Risquez, 65, farm worker, myocarditis, El Viso.
Francisco Alberca Alberca, 66, barber, gastric ulcer, Posadas.
23-January-1941, NH
Manuel Torresilla Ferré, 43, butcher, endocarditis, Constantina.
27-January-1941, PP
Alfonso Moreno Bajo, 63, miner, angina, Vva. del Duque.
29-January-1941
PP Antonio Benitez Frutos, 63, manual labourer, heart attack, Zalamea Serena.
NH Julián Lama Maiz, 51, manual labourer, anemia, Cañete de las Torres.
31-January-1941, PP
Antonio López Bravo, 60, cattle breeder, heart attack, Trasierra.
2-February-1941, NH
José Cano Rodriguez, 53, manual labourer, cirrhosis of the liver, Baena.
4-February-1941, PP
Agustin Roiza Morales, 50, manual labourer, heart attack, Calzada Calatrava.
6-February-1941, NH
Luis Hemica Gómez, 51, manual labourer, anemia, Azuaga.

Dimas Marta Flores, 60, carpenter, enterocolitis, Hinojosa.
Ramón Garcia Martinez, 37, manual labourer, nephritis, Bujalance.
Ernesto Diaz Naranjo, 57, manual labourer, bronchopneumonia, Villanueva del Rey.

8-February-1941, NH
Alfonso Valverde Shepherd, 62, manual labourer, intestinal epithelioma, Adamuz.

9-February-1941, NH
Juan B. Sánchez Pizarro, 50, manual labourer, mitral insufficiency, Vvillanueva. del Rey.

15-February-1941, PP
Argimiro Sánchez Garcia, 24, heart attack, Villanueva Córdoba.
Antonio López Sánchez, 65, heart attack, Villanueva de Córdoba.
Ramón Molina Gutiérrez, 65, policeman, heart attack, Córdoba.

16-February-1941
PP Juan Miguel Jnez. Santiago, 61, painter, heart attack., Benamargosa.
José Castro Murillo, 51, manual labourer, heart attack, Granada.
NP Pablo Sánchez Moreno, 78, farm worker, «rheumatism», Castro del Rio.

17-February-1941, PP
Luis Dobao Martinez, 42, manual labourer, emaciation, Palma del Rio.

18-February-1941, PP
Vicente Riañoz Martin, 33, manual labourer, emaciation, Peñarroya.

20-February-1941, NH
Francisco Horcas Castro, 57, bricklayer, anemia, Valenzuela.

22-February-1941, NH
Francisco Pareja Valdivia, 54, manual labourer, myocarditis, Priego.

23-February-1941, PP
Enrique Martin Junca, 57, Municipal Secretary., emaciation, Córdoba.
Jesús Chacón Rodriguez, 40, manual labourer, emaciation, Alcázar de San Juan.

24-February-1941, NH
Melquiades Ruiz Porras, 50, miner, pneumonia., Peñarroya.
Estanislao Tirado Roldán, 45, enfermero, heart attack, Madrid.

25-February-1941, NH
Juan A.Rodriguez Roig, 49, miner, pericarditis, Peñarroya.
Bartolomé Regalón Sabariego, 56, manual labourer, anemia, Córdoba.

26-February-1941, NH
Pedro Guerrero Ruiz, 52, manual labourer, myocarditis, Murcia.
Antonio Sánchez Villaseca, 51, manual labourer, myocarditis, Hinojosa.

27-February-1941
NH Diego Redondo Rodriguez, 32, manual labourer, pneumonia., Pozoblanco.
PP Hilario Celaya Pozo, 46, manual labourer, emaciation, Zalamea Serena.

28-February-1941
PP José Olmo Martinez, 57, manual labourer, emaciation, Espiel.
Florentino Figueroa Expósito, 47, manual labourer, emaciation, Puente Genil.
NH Ant. Pérez Caballero, 65, manual labourer, cerebral haemmorhage, Doña Mencia.
Alejandro Alamillos Muñoz, 42, manual labourer, anemia, Villanueva de C.

1-March-1941, NH
Juan Perea Garcia, 56, miner, arteriosclerosis, Hinojosa.

2-March-1941
NH Juan Rabadán Lucena, 42, manual labourer, endocarditis, Espejo.
PP Rafael Guerrero Malaver, 27, manual labourer, emaciation, Málaga.

3-March-1941, NH
Pedro Caballero Cardito, 44, coal merchant, anemia, Palma del Rio.
Antonio Barrios Lozano, 32, shoemaker, gastric ulcer, Peñarroya.

4-March-1941
NH Blas Acosta Méndez, 57, manual labourer, pneumonia., Montoro.
Martin Garcia Jurado, 29, tradesman, acute anemia, Belmez.
Justo Monge Ramos, 52, manual labourer, endocarditis, Hinojosa.
Pablo Alcalde Plazuelo, 49, miner, myocarditis, Espiel.
PP Alfonso Mansilla Calvo, 59, manual labourer, emaciation, Baena.
Manuel Expósito Márquez, 50, manual labourer, hepatic epithelioma, Córdoba.

5-March-1941, PP
Manuel Reyes Guerra, 68, manual labourer, emaciation, Palma del Rio.

6-March-1941
PP Félix Migallón Román, 38, manual labourer, emaciation, Añora.
Rafael Onieva Huete, 61, mailman, emaciation, Córdoba.
NH Vicente Mesa Polo, 62, manual labourer, mitral insufficiency, Doña Mencía.
Antonio Lorenzo Torremocha, 52, shoemaker, nephritis, Constantina.
Manuel Moreno Ramírez, 46, shoemaker, congest. cerebral, El Viso.

7-March-1941, NH
José Tartajo Ochando, 44, manual labourer, nephritis, Villaviciosa.
José Baena Lozano, 66, manual labourer, myocarditis, Baena.

8-March-1941
NH Pedro Moreno Jurado, 53, bricklayer, nephritis, Pozoblanco.
Demetrio Parra Farm workers, 54, manual labourer, anemia, Hinojosa.
Bautista Ventura Jurado, 66, manual labourer, heart attack, Villanueva del Rey.
Juan Montilla Gallardo, 43, manual labourer, arteriosclerosis, Valenzuela.
Antonio Cosano Mansilla, 20, manual labourer, pneumonia., Puente Genil.
Rufo Madrid Sánchez, 35, shoemaker, heart attack, Valdepeñas.
PP Felipe López Serrano, 27, manual labourer, heart attack, Villafranca.

10-March-1941
>PP Rafael Caracuel López, 18, manual labourer, emaciation, Montilla.
>NH Antonio Pérez Muñoz, 57, manual labourer, myocarditis, Pueblonuevo.
>José Blázquez Pérez, 74, miller, heart attack, Fuenteobejuna.
>Juan Horcas Castro, 66, manual labourer, arteriosclerosis, Valenzuela.

11-March-1941
>NH José Elices Pérez, 42, railway worker, anemia aguda, Rota.
>Acisclo Jurado Villarejo, 56, manual labourer, anemia, Pozoblanco.
>Pablo Morillo Castro, 49, farmer, endocarditis, Fuenteobejuna.
>PP José García Sánchez, 39, manual labourer, emaciation, Espiel.
>Críspulo Daza Peña, 67, manual labourer, emaciation, Santa Eufemia.

12-March-1941, NH
>Manuel Delgado Buenrostro, 31, manual labourer, acute anemia, Puente Genil
>Francisco Colorado Fernández, 25, baker, anemia, Marchena.
>PP Jacinto Vega Luque, 40, manual labourer, emaciation, Castro del Río.

13-March-1941
>NH Francisco Sánchez Mediavilla, 58, manual labourer, anemia, Almodóvar.
>José Barroso Gómez, 51, mechanic, anemia, Azuaga.
>PP Juan López Vallejo, 20, manual labourer, emaciation, Bujalance.
>Guillermo Muñoz Neira, 30, miner, emaciation, Huelva.
>Rafael Córdoba Ariza, 53, manual labourer, emaciation, Córdoba.

14-March-1941, PP
>Francisco Escobar García, 34, manual labourer, emaciation, Córdoba.
>José García Peralta, 18, carpenter, emaciation, Córdoba.
>Mateo Majuelos Torres, 39, manual labourer, emaciation, Villanueva de Córdoba

15-March-1941
>NH Antonio Vega Amaya, 28, stone mason, emaciation, Morón de la Frontera
>Francisco González Serrano, 47, manual labourer, pneumonia, Montoro.
>Francisco Bonilla Cubiles, 60, manual labourer, anemia, Cádiz.
>PP Luis Ruiz Mora, 20, manual labourer, emaciation, Córdoba.

16-March-1941
>NH Juan Ortega Fuentes, 54, manual labourer, anemia, La Carlota.
>PP Antonio Ortega Baena, 27, manual labourer, emaciation, Rute.

17-March-1941
>PP Leopoldo Pernil Huertas, 21, shoemaker, emaciation, Valverde del Campo.
>NH Ángel de la Fuente Ramirez, 41, railway worker, acetonemia, Málaga.
>Ramón Garcia Guerrero, 53, mule driver, pneumonia., Montoro.

18-March-1941
>NH Antonio Ruiz Lozano, 39, manual labourer, acute anemia», Villaviciosa.
>Antonio Calabria Molero, 56, manual labourer, epitelioma, Posadas.

PP Juan Lavado López, 39, manual labourer, emaciation, Castro del Rio.
Estanislao Trujillo Garcia, 30, cattle breeder, emaciation, Las Quemadas.
Antonio Ruiz Navajón, 50, manual labourer, emaciation, Santa Eufemia.

19-March-1941, PP
Antonio Martinez González, 26, manual labourer, emaciation, Cazorla (Jaén).
Francisco Pérez Sillero, 34, manual labourer, emaciation, Loja (Málaga).

20-March-1941, PP
Antonio Sánchez Núñez, 28, carpenter, emaciation, Córdoba.

21-March-1941
PP Antonio Gamazo Diaz, 49, farm worker, emaciation, Arcos de la Frontera
NH José Vargas Gutiérrez, 49, miner, emaciation, Belmez.
Fernando Martinez Magaña, 51, manual labourer, anemia, Almeria.

22-March-1941
PP Miguel Romero Cabezas, 46, manual labourer, emaciation ,Villanueva de Córdoba
NH Narciso Ruiz Ceballos, 57, manual labourer, anemia, Villanueva de Córdoba

23-March-1941, NH
José Gómez Márquez, 71, baker, anemia, Dos Torres.

25-March-1941
NH Manuel Calvo Manzano, 36, manual labourer, anemia, Cabeza Buey.
Pedro Gallardo Pérez, 63, manual labourer, anemia, Badajoz.
PP Juan Fernández Diaz, 46, manual labourer, emaciation, Villarreal.
José Murillo Risquez, 49, manual labourer, emaciation, Villanueva de Rey.

26-March-1941, NH
Valeriano Rodriguez Garcia, 64, manual labourer, anemia, Belmez.
Basilio Horrillo Sereno, 56, miner, anemia, La Granjuela.

27-March-1041, PP
Julián Ruiz Gómez, 45, entrepreneur, asystole, Madrid.

28-March-1941, NH
Gonzalo Delgado Sánchez, 49, ferrov., bronchitis, Toledo.

29-March-1941, NH
Juan Serrano Ruiz, 46, manual labourer, anemia, Montoro.

30-March-1941, NH
Juan López Romero, 47, manual labourer, emaciation, Villanueva de Córdoba.
Santiago Ambrosio Arroyo, 54, miner, acute anemia, Belmez.
Juan Ibáñez González, 34, soldier, emaciation, Valencia.
Antonio José Peña Agenjo, 55, miner, emaciation, Villanueva del Rey.

31-March-1941
NH Ernesto Medina Aceituno, 25, manual labourer, acute anemia, Alcalá la Real.
Antonio Ruiz Muñoz, 19, metalúrgico, anemia, Córdoba.

PP Francisco Sanz Moreno, 38, manual labourer, coma, Villa del Rio.

1-April-1941

PP Francisco Céspedes Vázquez, 55, mailman, tuberculosis, Almeria.

NH Francisco Salinas Toledano, 53, manual labourer, emaciation, Bujalance.

Pedro Sánchez González, 57, manual labourer, emaciation, Villanueva del Rey.

2-April-1941

NH Miguel April Molina, 28, manual labourer, estaphylophemia, Espiel.

Eustaquio Lozano Pedraja, 29, bricklayer, emaciation, Peñarroya.

Ángel Bejarano Blanco, 49, miner, anemia, Peñarroya.

Zacarías Pérez Trujillo, 37, manual labourer, emaciation, Iznájar.

PP Miguel Jiménez Farm workers, 40, plasterer, emaciation, Puente Genil.

3-April-1941

PP César Buenahora Pascual, 49, road worker, heart attack, Madrid.

Roque Herrera Bejarano, 45, coal merchant, tuberculosis, Villanueva de Córdoba

NH Juan Gómez Jiménez, 45, manual labourer, anemia, Adamuz.

Juan García Guerrero, 56, manual labourer, anemia, Montoro.

Manuel Estévez Barragán, 55, bricklayer, anemia, Fuenteobejuna.

4-April-1941

NH Manuel TaMay Dávila, 48, manual labourer, anemia, Zalamea de la Serena.

July Caballero Madueño, 30, salesman, nephritis, Villaralto.

José Aguilar Espada, 57, manual labourer, emaciation, Palenciana.

PP Antonio Ortiz Pérez, 25, employee, emaciation, Sevilla.

5-April-1941

NH Rafael Pons Luque, 58, market gardener, emaciation, Posadas.

Francisco González Cobos, 59, manual labourer, emaciation, Granada.

Felipe Caballero Polonio, 47, foundry hand, emaciation, Belmez.

PP Antonio Soto Arte, 25, bricklayer, tuberculosis, Priego.

6-April-1941, NH

José Moya Díaz, 54, manual labourer, anemia, Pedroche.

Juan A. Rodríguez Ruiz, 50, manual labourer, anemia, Belalcázar.

Joaquín Espinosa Gómez, 40, manual labourer, anemia, Cabra.

7-April-1941

NH Antonio de la Torre Nevado, 30, manual labourer, tuberculosis, Villaviciosa.

José Rodríguez Calvo, 28, manual labourer, pneumonia., Belalcázar.

Rafael González Berengena, 41, manual labourer, anemia, Villanueva del Rey.

Juan Ruiz Criado, 40, shoemaker, acute anemia, Montoro.

Luis Serrano Yepes, 46, plasterer, emaciation, Espejo.

PP Roque Arenas Garrido, 28, manual labourer, enterocolitis, Arjonilla.

8-April-1941, NH

Luis Bagre Maestre, 52, manual labourer, anemia, Fuente Palmera.
José Ticiba Montoro, 61, mechanic, anemia, Priego.
Rafael Sánchez Galán, 52, miner, anemia, Villanueva del Duque.

9-April-1941, NH

Antonio Buenosvinos Rebaño, 42, manual labourer, emaciation, Cañete.
Antonio de la Fuente Arribas, 52, manual labourer, anemia, Villaviciosa.

10-April-1941, NH

José Olmo Rísquez, 46, market gardener, anemia, Córdoba.
Toribio Valderrábanos Agredano, 64, manual labourer, emaciation, Fnteobejuna.
Salvador Molina Mora, 48, manual labourer, emaciation, Luque.
Pedro Giménez Berenguer, 24, manual labourer, anemia, Posadas.

11-April-1941

NH Juan Franco Navarro, 50, manual labourer, mitral insufficiency, Palma del Río.
Juan López Guisado, 62, manual labourer, anemia, Fuente Palmera.
Andrés Márquez Moncayo, 66, manual labourer, anemia, Fuenteobejuna.
Juan Fernández Romero, 46, shepherd, anemia, Torrecampos
Antonio Arroyo León, 64, manual labourer, anemia, Baena.
Miguel Prieto López, 39, manual labourer, nephritis, Granada.
Celestino Calvo Calvo, 48, anemia, Villaviciosa.
PP Antonio Cuadrado Cuadrado, 55, carter, emaciation, Adamuz.

12-April-1941, NH

Antonio Expósito Caracuel, 53, manual labourer, heart attack, Montilla.
Benito Márquez Muñoz, 38, manual labourer, anemia, Cardeña.
Juan A. Margarín Millán, 30, farm worker, anemi, Peñarroya.

13-April-1941, NH

José Padilla Rojano, 60, manual labourer, emaciation, Baena.
Francisco Calzadilla Barbado, 64, manual labourer, anemia, Montilla.
Antonio Gordillo Luque, 28, manual labourer, anemia, Valenzuela.
Juan Fernández Barrigón, 32, manual labourer, anemia, Hornachuelos.
José Marín Palacios, 24, mechanic, anemia, Jaén.

14-April-1941, NH

Martín Vallejo Aljarilla, 48, manual labourer, emaciation, Valenzuela.
Antonio Flores Serrano, 51, manual labourer, anemia, Belalcázar.
Antonio Viso Peña, 56, manual labourer, emaciation, Villanueva del Rey.

15-April-1941, NH

Alfonso Calles Peinazo, 62, manual labourer, anemia, Montoro.

16-April-1941, NH

Rafael Romero Benavente, 20 months, enterocolitis
Prudencio Bravo Martín, 48, hat maker, heart failure, Badajoz.
Luciano Capilla López, 37, shoemaker, congest. cerebral, Hinojosa.

18-April-1941

NH Maximiliano Bravo García, 46, mailman, úlcera gástrica, Belmez.

PP José García García, 26, barber, emaciation, Pueblonuevo.

Pedro Ceballos González, 58, basket weaver, emaciation, Fuente Tójar.

19-April-1941

NH Eugenio Galán Cepas, 44, manual labourer, heart failure, Villaharta.

PP Eduardo Guerrero Aguilar, 65, bricklayer, Córdoba.

21-April-1941, NH

Manuel Castro Orellana, 32, manual labourer, tuberculosis, Sevilla.

22-April-1941, NH

Francisco Murillo Sánchez, 62, blacksmith, enterocolitis, Hinojosa.

23-April-1941

NH Amador Jiménez Roldán, 43, manual labourer, enterocolitis, Pedro Abad.

José Luna Rivas, 41, manual labourer, heart failure, Puente Genil.

Joaquín Monzonis Alemán, 25, manual labourer, anemia, Alicante.

PP Antonio Vázquez Barrera, 18, manual labourer, emaciation, Peñarroya.

Manuel Rodríguez Hidalgo, 52, manual labourer, pellagra, Dos Torres.

24-April-1941, NH

Alfonso Alcalde Palacios, 27, blacksmith, tuberculosis, Belmez.

25-April-1941, NH

Juan Caseos Gallardo, 46, manual labourer, anemia, Belalcázar.

Miguel Amor Arroyo, 28, baker, heart attack, Cabra.

26-April-1941

NH Estaban Manuel Rubio Vinagre, 35, manual labourer, pneumonia, Fuenteobejuna.

Antonio Obrero Hernández, 37, bricklayer, cerebral haemmorhage., Posadas.

PP Rafael Sedo del Águila, 17, cook, heart attack, Almeria.

27-April-1941, NH

José Feligrana Silva, 61, dealer, myocarditis, Llerena.

Liderio Revuelto Pedregosa, 22, manual labourer, tuberculosis, Villaviciosa.

Antonio Solis Romero, 45, manual labourer, anemia, El Carpio.

Tomás Cachinero Oliveros, 52, manual labourer, enterocolitis, Montoro.

Antonio López Blanco, 40, miner, anemia, Alcaracejos.

28-April-1941, NH

Antonio Baza Granados, 47, farmer, anemia, Los Blázquez.

Manuel Moreno Bedmar, 56, manual labourer, anemia, Villa del Rio.

29-April-1941, NH

Antonio Luque Alcántara, 40, manual labourer, enterocolitis, Castro del Rio.

Antonio Garcia López, 53, carter, anemia, Valenzuela.

30-April-1941, NH

Julián Páez Nieto, 38, manual labourer, septicemia, Almedinilla.

Pedro Moreno Pulgarin, 58, manual labourer, anemia, Córdoba.
Manuel Cuevas Serrano, 53, septicemia, Córdoba.
1-May-1941, NH
Antonio Monterroso Guadalupe, 31, manual labourer, anemia, Navas de la C.
Juan Mora Delgado, 22, anemia, Cádiz.
2-May-1941, NH
Antonio Torralbo Caballero, 47, manual labourer, anemia, Villanueva de Córdoba
3-May-1941, NH
Gabriel González López, 60, manual labourer, pneumonia, Pedroche.
4-May-1941, NH
José Tena Paredes, 65, manual labourer, anemia, Badajoz.
5-May-1941, NH
Rafael Leiva Manrique, 40, electrician, tuberculosis, Puente Genil.
6-May-1941
NH Juan Bailén Ortega, 45, metal worker, anemia, Torrecamplos
Antonio Torres González, 45, manual labourer, anemia, Almeria.
PP Pedro Cabrera Gálvez, 30, manual labourer, pellagra, Montoro.
Francisco Cabrera Garcia, 24, manual labourer, tuberculosis, Villanueva de Córdoba
7-May-1941, NH
Antonio Pedregosa Blanco, 33, manual labourer, anemia, Villaviciosa.
Ildefonso Hidalgo Escribano, 57, entrepreneur, arterioescl., Montoro.
8-May-1941, NH
Andrés Salido González, 43, waiter, tuberculosis, Jaén.
Antonio López Garcia, 59, railway worker, «pneumonia., Cabeza del Buey.
10-May-1941, PP
Alfonso Pérez Lorencio, 26, tradesman, tuberculosis, Madrid.
Leopoldo Galán Cepas, 48, manual labourer, emaciation, Villaharta.
11-May-1941, NH
Jesús Fernández Moreno, 24, anemia, Dos Torres.
Juan Lara Muñoz, 52, manual labourer, pneumoniaonia, Villa del Rio.
13-May-1941, NH
Pablo Aranda Prado, 27, manual labourer, enterocolitis, Hinojosa del Duque.
Francisco Garrido Molina, 56, manual labourer, enterocolitis, Pedroche.
Manuel Prieto Navas, 42, tree feller, tuberculosis, Puente Genil.
21-May-1941
NH Francisco Muñoz Pozo, 60, manual labourer, enterocolitis, Cardeña.
PP Críspulo Pontes López, 24, manual labourer, enterocolitis, Belalcázar.
Juan Santofimia Cantador, 51, manual labourer, embolism, Villanueva de Córdoba

22-May-1941, NH
> Mariano Ginesta Santos, 31, mechanic, pneumonia., Valencia.

23-May-1941, PP
> Antonio Moral Rider, 34, manual labourer, heart attack, Posadas.

25-May-1941, NH
> NH Plácido Campaña Gutiérrez, 21, manual labourer, enterocolitis, Castro del Río
> Cristóbal Vílchez Rodríguez, 53, manual labourer, pneumoniaonía, Jaén.
> PP Antonio Pérez López, 19, manual labourer, emaciation, Guadalajara.

26-May-1941, NH
> Juan Rojas Holanda, 61, manual labourer, bronchopneumonia, Pedro Abad.
> Alfonso Rojas García, 43, bricklayer, enterocolitis, Pedro Abad.
> Manuel Fernández Paz, 34, manual labourer, enterocolitis, Villanueva del Rey.

27-May-1941, NH
> Juan Cuadrado Salnia, 54, manual labourer, anemia, Adamuz.

28-May-1941, NH
> José Cruz Ortiz, 36, manual labourer, enterocolitis, Baena.

29-May-1941, NH
> Martín Serrano Torrico, 57, manual labourer, pneumonia., Pozoblanco.
> Pascual Garrido Calé, 55, manual labourer, malaria, Granada.

30-May-1941, NH
> Ángel Marina Gamero, 26, sawyer, enterocolitis, Madrid.
> Antonio Montero Alguacil, 28, manual labourer, enterocolitis, Fuenteobejuna.

31-May-1941, NH
> Andrés García Garrido, 25, manual labourer, enterocolitis, Castro del Río.

1-June-1941
> NH José A. Aranda Monterroso, 57, baker, enterocolitis, La Granjuela.
> Francisco Romero Díaz, 53, miner, enterocolitis, Pozoblanco.
> PP José Vila López, salesman, emaciation, Málaga.

2-June-1941
> NH Cristóbal Rodríguez López, 30, manual labourer, nephritis, Málaga.
> Juan Gil Torres, 27, manual labourer, enterocolitis, Huelva.
> PP Juan Cabezas Molina, 52, manual labourer, uremia, Sevilla.

5-June-1941, NH
> Manuel Armada Lozano, 67, baker, pneumonia., Posadas.

6-June-1941, NH
> Blas Esquina Orellana, 58, manual labourer, enterocolitis, La Granjuela.

9-June-1941, NH
> Juan Pérez Castelo, 64, manual labourer, myocarditis, Hinojosa del Duque.
> Joaquín Frutos Vaquero, 29, manual labourer, enterocolitis, Pedroche.

10-June-1941
> NH Manuel Arroyo García, 26, manual labourer, reumatismo, Jaén.

José Manuel Nogales Herrera, 20, manual labourer, enterocolitis, Peñarroya.
PP Alfredo Gómez Lucena, 48, manual labourer, emaciation, Córdoba.

11-June-1941, NH

Pedro Reyes Ramos, 49, manual labourer, malaria, Montoro.

13-June-1941, NH

Manuel Castillo Borrego, 55, manual labourer, pneumonia., Villa del Río.

16-June-1941, NH

Anastasio Cabanillas Ponce, 33, miner, enterocolitis, Brazatortas.
Amador Lora García, 53, mason, anemia, Alanís.

17-June-1941

NH José Muñoz Rodríguez, 36, manual labourer, tuberculosis, Valsequillo.
PP Jorge Blanco Conde, 31, bricklayer, agranulositosis, Sta. Eufemia.

18-June-1941, NH

Manuel Brocal Martínez, 55, manual labourer, nephritis, Montoro.
Ángel Gallardo Perales, 26, office clerk, gastric ulcer, C. Real.

19-June-1941, NH

Luis Núñez Núñez, 28, farm worker, enterocolitis, Cádiz.
Ignacio Ríos Cornejo, 29, manual labourer, malaria, Valsequillo.
Juan A. Peláez Santiago, 57, farmer, nephritis, Montoro.

21-June-1941, PP

Antonio Fimia Espino, 34, bricklayer, enterocolitis, Córdoba.

22-June-1941, PP

Manuel Bolaños Veria, 61, dealer, asystole, Córdoba.

23-June-1941

PP Alfonso Cejudo Redondo, 22, manual labourer, enterocolitis, Villanueva de Córdoba
NH Nicolás Mateo Rodríguez, 33, manual labourer, anemia, Badajoz.
José García Cachinero, 60, road worker, bronchitis, Villanueva de Córdoba

24-June-1941, PP

Gabriel Vázquez García, 24, coal merchant, enterocolitis, Alcaudete.

25-June-1941, PP

Juan Molina Gómez, 58, manual labourer, septicemia, Málaga.
José Valverde Ruiz, 77, manual labourer, pneumonía, Pedroche.
Manuel Sánchez Alamillo, 54, manual labourer, enterocolitis, Alcaracejos.
Daniel Rodríguez Guisado, 58, manual labourer, enterocolitis, Fuente Palmera.

27-June-1941, NH

Pedro Moreno Martínez, 55, manual labourer, enterocolitis, Bujalance.
Luis Romero Jiménez, 23, barber, tuberculosis, Cádiz.
Melitón Tejada Cabanillas, 39, butcher, enterocolitis, Peñarroya.

28-June-1941, PP

Juan Manuel Sánchez Moreno, 21, manual labourer, tuberculosis, Hinojosa.
Antonio Roda Delgado, 37, manual labourer, anemia, Úbeda.

Juan A. Romero Horrillo, 26, manual labourer, enterocolitis, La Cardenchosa.

29-June-1941

PP José Ramírez Martín, 23, bricklayer, enterocolitis, Málaga.

José Luna Dios, 37, manual labourer, tuberculosis, Baena.

NH Juan Barba Jiménez, 56, manual labourer, anemia, Doña Mencía.

Vicente Fernández Cabrera, 60, manual labourer, «emaciation», Villanueva del Rey.

30-June-1941, NH

Luis Fernández Méndez, 29, manual labourer, anemia, Palma del Río.

1-July-1941

NH Alfonso Ruiz Tabas, 36, manual labourer, enterocolitis, Hinojosa.

PP Antonio Acosta Romero, 40, manual labourer, enterocolitis, Sevilla.

Pedro Cuadrado Cerezo, 37, bricklayer, enterocolitis, Adamuz.

2-July-1941, NH

Juan Quero Bazán, 61, manual labourer, enterocolitis, Montoro.

3-July-1941

NH José Trujillo Badillo, 27, manual labourer, enterocolitis, Ciudad Real.

PP Francisco Herrera Espinosa, 41, manual labourer, asystole, Cádiz.

4-July-1941, PP

Serapio Ortuño Delgado, 40, enterocolitis, Zamoranos.

5-July-1941, PP

José Bautista Losada, 60, cook, enterocolitis, Jerez de la Frontera

José Ruiz Priego, 51, manual labourer, enterocolitis, Carcabuey.

Antonio Romero Moreno, 20, manual labourer, tuberculosis, Villanueva de Cordoba

7-July-1941, PP

Agustín Góngora Serrano, 19, mechanic, pelagra, Lucena.

Rafael Cádiz Miranda, 57, manual labourer, gastroenteritis, Ciudad Real.

Miguel Zarnoza Pérez, 50, market gardener, enterocolitis, Torrecampo.

8-July-1941

PP José SotoMayr Palma, 43, baker, tuberculosis, Aguilar.

NH Antonio Jurado García, 31, bricklayer, anemia, Belmez.

Feliciano Rubio López, 31, road worker, tuberculosis, Hinojosa.

9-July-1941, NH

Juan Boquizo Martínez, 43, manual labourer, gastroenteritis, Villanueva del Duque.

10-July-1941, PP

Manuel Jurado Alamillos, 28, manual labourer, gastroenteritis, Villanueva del Duque.

11-July-1941, NH

José López Checa, 37, miner, mitral insufficiency, Linares.

13-July-1941, NH

Antonio García Torrico, 40, manual labourer, enterocolitis, El Guijo.

14-July-1941, PP
Florencio Moreno Barcala, 35, metalworker, uremia, Madrid.
José Rodríguez Fernández, 59, charcoal worker, emaciation, Córdoba.

18-July-1941, NH
Antonio Murillo Méndez, 54, manual labourer, enterocolitis, Badajoz.

21-July-1941, NH
Santiago Rubio González, 23, manual labourer, tuberculosis, Espiel.

25-July-1941, NH
Antonio Nogales Trenado, 50, manual labourer, enterocolitis, Badajoz.

29-July-1941
NH Mateo Tejero Jiménez, 50, manual labourer, enterocolitis, Fernán Núñez.
Cristóbal Pacheco Lopera, 29, manual labourer, pneumonia., Iznájar.
PP Juan Criado Orihuela, 40,designer, tuberculosis, Cabra.

31-July-1941, NH
Fidel García Cáceres, 60, manual labourer, enterocolitis, Villaviciosa.

2-August-1941, NH
Federico Rodriguez Mata, 31, manual labourer, tuberculosis, Jaén.

3-August-1941
NH Antonio Bocero Rodriguez, 32, manual labourer, enterocolitis, Fuente Carreteros.
PP Dolores Jiménez Fernández, 40, housewife, pellagra, La Victoria.

4-August-1941, NH
Antonio Salinas Pozuelo, 49, manual labourer, mitral insufficiency, Pedro Abad.
Francisco Mayrga Hurtado, 60, manual labourer, enterocolitis, Lucena.

6-August-1941
NH Francisco Gómez Ramos, 51, farm worker, enteritis, Belmez.
PP Miguel Cortés Alhaja, 22, marble worker, peritonitis, Mérida.
Manuel Gordillo Jurado, 17, manual labourer, heart attack, La Cardenchosa.

7-August-1941, NH
Juan Madrid Ramos, 50, shoemaker, enteritis, Bujalance.
José Peláez Garcia, 44, manual labourer, myocarditis, Pueblonuevo.

8-August-1941, NH
Miguel Ortiz Luna, 26, tradesman, enteritis, Villafranca.

9-August-1941
NH Francisco Gómez Márquez, 28, manual labourer, tuberculosis, Montilla.
PP Matias Fresno de la Orden, 43, mechanic, uremia, Almadén.

12-August-1941, PP
Manuel Ropero Calleja, 65, miner, enterocolitis, Fuenteobejuna.

14-August-1941
NH Manuel Cortés Cerezo, 54, barber, mitral insufficiency, Adamuz.

PP Juan J. Jiménez Caballero, 49, salesman, pneumonia., Cabra.

15-August-1941, NH
Manuel González Rodriguez, 44, manual labourer, tuberculosis, Hornachuelos.

16-August-1941, NH
Antonio Romero León, 49, manual labourer, emaciation, Baena.
Pedro Robles Rosauro, 43, manual labourer, mitral insufficiency, Bujalance.

19-August-1941, PP
Pedro Garcia Carretero, 22, manual labourer, tuberculosis, Cardeña.
Modesto Prats Aguilar, 49, barber, heart attack, Villanueva del Duque.

20-August-1941, PP
Manuel Márquez Peinado, 29, manual labourer, tuberculosis, Dos Torres.
Francisco Lucena Márquez, 52, employee, heart attack, Montilla.
Francisco Priego Parrado, 35, manual labourer, skull fracture, (possible suicide).

21-August-1941, NH
Manuel Gómez Torrico, 51, manual labourer, pneumonia., Villaralto.

25-August-1941, NH
Agustin Arévalo Marta, 38, manual labourer, neumonia, Pedroche.

26-August-1941, NH
Conrado López Aláez, 31, manual labourer, enterocolitis, Dos Torres.

28-August-1941, NH
Atanasio Garcia Ramos, 50, manual labourer, enterocolitis, Espiel.
Juan Rodriguez Luque, 60, manual labourer, Septicemia, Fernán Núñez.
Ventura Peinado Madueño, 52, manual labourer, pneumonia., Dos Torres.

6-September-1941, NH
Severo Gómez Gozalbo, 40, farmer, enterocolitis, Pozoblanco.
Aniceto López Romera, 24, manual labourer, tuberculosis, Villaviciosa.
Valentin Aragonés Hidalgo, 47, miner, septicemia, Castuera.

9-September-1941, PP
Demetrio Herruzo Rayo, 51, manual labourer, tuberculosis, Hinojosa.

10-September-1941, NH
Amador Lozano Heras, 49, manual labourer, bronchopneumonia, Baza.

11-September-1941, NH
Francisco Pérez Cerezo, 30, manual labourer, tuberculosis, Cáceres.

17-September-1941, NH
Antonio Moya Torrico, 27, manual labourer, tuberculosis, Hinojosa.
Vicente Triviño Agenjo, 54, farm worker, arterioescl., Los Blázquez.

22-September-1941, NH
Ángel López Redondo, 34, entrepreneur, tuberculosis, Santa Eufemia.

24-September-1941, NH
Modesto Cidoncha Cidoncha, 64, manual labourer, pneumonia., Freobejuna.

26-September-1941, PP
    Enrique Garcia Álvarez, 28, sailor, nephritis, Alcalá del Rio.
2-October-1941, NH
    Antonio Calvo Garcia, 44, manual labourer, heart failure, Belmez.
3-October-1941, NH
    Manuel Cotán Mejias, 42, manual labourer, enterocolitis, Sevilla.
    José Villalba Benavides, 43, manual labourer, enteritis, Posadas.
4-October-1941, NH
    Joaquin Mateo Ramos, 26, manual labourer, tuberculosis, Jerez de la Frontera
    Alfonso Ojeda Fernández, 60, manual labourer, erysipelas, Posadas.
5-October-1941, NH
    José Torralbo Carbonero, 29, weaver, nephritis, Villanueva de Córdoba
    Francisco Ballestero Martinez, 44, manual labourer, tuberculosis, Almodóvar.
6-October-1941, NH
    Andrés Luque Regalón, 27, manual labourer, tuberculosis, Adamuz.
7-October-1941, NH
    Francisco Castillejo Molero, 35, office clerk, tubercul., Peñarroya.
8-October-1941, NH
    Santiago Mantas Pontes, 60, manual labourer, pneumoniaonia, El Carpio.
    Pablo Aranda Algar, 36, manual labourer, tuberculosis, El Carpio.
    Gregorio Cabrera Mansilla, 34, cattle breeder, influenza, Vva. del Duque.
9-October-1941, NH
    Rafael Alberca Segura, 34, manual labourer, septicemia, Adamuz.
16-octub re-1941, NH
    Juan M. Nacarino Molina, 63, school teacher, uremia, Palma del Rio.
    Antonio Ferrero López, 56, manual labourer, rheumatism, Dos Torres.
17-October-1941, NH
    Benito Pedregosa Uclés, 46, shoemaker, nephritis, Valenzuela.
    Aurelio Martin Infantes, 26, manual labourer, tuberculosis, La Granjuela.
18-October-1941, NH
    Benito Cejudo Moreno, 44, manual worker, enterocolitis, Villanueva de Cordoba
    Manuel Herruzo Mora, 34, carpenter, tuberculosis, Cardeña.
20-October-1941, NH
    Juan Martin Perea, 55, bricklayer, colitis, Belalcázar.
22-October-1941, NH
    Ángel Morales Peña, 38, manual labourer, meningitis, Hinojosa del Duque.
23-October-1941, NH
    Ángel Barbancho Cano, 55, manual labourer, septicemia, Fuente la Lancha.
    Francisco Ferrero Lavrador, 46, manual labourer, bronchitis, Torrecampo.
    Pedro Martin Infantes, 37, miner, enterocolitis, La Granjuela.

24-October-1941, NH

Francisco Mejias Cerezo, 58, manual labourer, bronchopneumonia, Adamuz.
Antonio Nevado Expósito, 63, manual labourer, mitral insufficiency, Villaviciosa. Fernando Ruiz Galán, 39, manual labourer, tuberculosis, Almodóvar del Río.

25-October-1941, NH

Antonio Álvarez Cobos, 45, manual labourer, enterocolitis, Villaviciosa.

26-October-1941, NH

Elias Jiménez Blanco, 49, manual labourer, pneumonia., Santa Eufemia.

27-October-1941, NH

Rafael Martinez Castilla, 29, manual labourer, influenza, Adamuz.
Dionisio Diaz Serrano, 41, manual labourer, reumatismo», Dos Torres.

28-October-1941, NH

Miguel Padilla Torrecilla, 41, manual labourer, arthritis, Almeria.
Antonio Escamilla Garcia, 59, manual labourer, arteriosclerosis» Vva de Córdoba

29-October-1941, NH

Federico Moral Otero, 29, manual labourer, tuberculosis, La Carlota.

30-October-1941, NH

Manuel Romero Rodriguez, 40, miner, influenza, Belmez.

1-November-1941, NH

Antonio Casán Molleja, 34, manual labourer, tuberculosis, Pedro Abad.

2-November-1941

NH José Moreno González, 61, manual labourer, enterocolitis, Alcalá la Real.
Emiliano Vioque Tribaldo, 65, farm worker, enterocolitis, Dos Torres.
PP Juan Pérez Martinez, 60, manual labourer, emaciation, Villanueva de Córdoba

3-November-1941, NH

José Muñoz Muñoz, 34, manual labourer, enteritis, Cardeña.
Antonio Rodriguez Rodriguez, 48, manual labourer, nephritis, Granada.

4-November-1941, NH

Mario Pérez Fernández, 47, shoemaker, pneumonia., Espiel.
Elias Ruiz González, 40, farmer, asystole, Hinojosa del Duque.

5-November-1941, NH

Antonio Ballesteros Cañete, 42, manual labourer, tuberculosis, Luque.
José Español Blasco, 40, farm worker, pneumonia., Villanueva. del Duque.

6-November-1941, NH

José TaMay Pérez, 39, bricklayer, enterocolitis, Utrera.

10-November-1941, PP

Ángel Novemberas Ortiz, 48, manual labourer, epitelioma laringeo, Villaviciosa.

11-November-1941, NH
Diego Ortega Pérez, 87, manual labourer, rheumatism, Adamuz.
14-November-1941, NH
Manuel Sánchez Garcia, 43, manual labourer, enterocolitis, Castuera.
15-November-1941, NH
Pablo Santamarta Expósito, 50, coal merchant, enterocolitis, Priego.
17-November-1941, NH
Santiago Benitez del Rey, 43, manual labourer, pneumonia., Espiel.
18-November-1941, NH
Manuel Melendo Carrillo, 45, manual labourer, arteriosclerosis, Villa del Rio.
José Agüera Ortiz, 48, manual labourer, enterocolitis, Almodóvar del Rio.
19-November-1941, NH
Martin Muñoz Frutos, 41, manual labourer, uremia, Cabeza del Buey.
20-November-1941, NH
Juan Romero Gómez, 47, shepherd, tuberculosis, Villaralto.
22-November-1941, NH
José Sánchez Gómez, 47, manual labourer, enterocolitis, Villaviciosa.
Urbano Martinez Martinez, 37, manual labourer, tuberculosis, Cuenca.
24-November-1941, PP
Bibiana Romero Gómez, 70, unemployed, enterocolitis, Villanueva de Córdoba
27-November-1941, PP
Joaquin Mendoza Carpio, 46, manual labourer, heart attack, Castro del Rio.
28-November-1941, NH
Pedro Gómez Moreno, 28, manual labourer, bronchopneumonia, Montoro.
Antonio Fernández Gómez, 56, manual labourer, influenza, Villaralto.
29-November-1941, NH
David Garcia Toril, 46, manual labourer, enterocolitis, El Viso.
Francisco Murillo González, 49, manual labourer, rheumatism, Villanueva del Rey.
30-November-1941, PP
Mª Josefa Hidalgo Rodriguez, 35, housewife, enterocolitis, Montoro.
1-December-1941, NH
José Plaza Cuevas, 42, manual labourer, influenza, Fuente Palmera.
Agustin Murillo Sánchez, 60, blacksmith, enterocolitis, Hinojosa.
2-December-1941, NH
José Escamilla Garcia, 66, bricklayer, enterocolitis, Villanueva de Cór.
Felipe Molina Herruzo, 46, manual labourer, bronchopneumonia, El Guijo.
3-December-1941, NH
Julián Madueño Muñoz, 37, manual labourer, avitaminosis, El Viso.
Pedro Hidalgo Caballero, 66, manual labourer, enterocolitis, Montoro.

5-December-1941, NH
Francisco Santiago Gordillo, 42, manual labourer, enterocolitis, La Granja de T.

6-December-1941, NH
Diego Valiño Trejo, 53, farm worker, septicemia, Badajoz.
PP Juliana Almena Moreno, 54, s. l., myocarditis, Belalcázar.

8-December-1941, NH
Ángel Diaz Morales, 41, miner, enterocolitis, Fuente la Lancha.
Juan Olarte Gutiérrez, 43, railway worker, enterocolitis, Cerro Muriano.

11-December-1941
NH Joaquin Ruiz Moreno, 28, tin worker, influenza, Guadalcanal.
PP Juan Sánchez Vela, 55, manual labourer, enterocolitis, Jaén.

12-December-1941, NH
Ramón Cano Moya, 38, manual labourer, septicemia, Baena.

15-December-1941, NH
Juan Moyano Platero, 56, manual labourer, septicemia, Villanueva del Río.

16-December-1941, NH
Francisco Romero Horrillo, 60, shepherd, endocarditis, Ojuelos Altos.

17-December-1941, NH
Francisco Benítez Molero, 47, manual labourer, enterocolitis, Bujalance.

18-December-1941, NH
Juan Romera Moya, 46, manual labourer, pneumonia., Morente (Bujalance).
Antonio Cuevas Estrada, 56, manual labourer, tuberculosis, Posadas.

19-December-1941, NH
José López Abad, 28, manual labourer, Septicemia, Carmona.

20-December-1941
NH Juan José García López, 45, manual labourer, typhus, Valenzuela.
PP Baroncio Zarza Nieto, 40, manual labourer, cerebral haemorrhage, Ávila.

21-December-1941, NH
Bartolomé Morales Fernández, 62, manual labourer, enterorragia, Hinojosa.

22-December-1941, NH
Luciano Tapia Morales, 60, manual labourer, nephritis, Baena.
Antonio Briones Molina, 47, manual labourer, typhus, Fuente Tójar.
Manuel López González, 25, manual labourer, valvular lesion, Torrecampo

23-December-1941
NH José Serrano Fernández, 45, manual labourer, arteriosclerosis., Dos Torres.
Pedro Moya Sánchez, 28, manual labourer, typhus, Pedroche.
Manuel Pérez Romero, 50, manual labourer, cerebral embolus, Sevilla.
PP Antonio López Bejarano, 21, manual labourer, tuberculosis, Añora.

25-December-1941, NH
Francisco Medina Pérez, 38, manual labourer, typhus, Montoro.

26-December-1941, NH

Rafael Écija Casas, 35, manual labourer, septicemia, Cabra.

Ángel García Gallego, 52, entrepreneur, enterocolitis, Cabeza del Buey.

Francisco Romero Velasco, 37, manual labourer, septicemia, Cañete de las T.

27-December-1941

NH Francisco Perales Lozano, 41, manual labourer, pneumonia., Marmolejo.

PP Victoriano Torrico Sánchez, 23, manual labourer, tuberculosis, Alcaracejos.

28-December-1941, NH

Víctor Ruiz González, 38, manual labourer, uremia, Hinojosa del Duque.

Juan Sánchez Álvarez, 22, manual labourer, tuberculosis, Hinojosa.

Casimiro Padillo Izquierdo, 61, manual labourer, rheumatism, Castillo Locubín.

Manuel Cerdán Roca, 25, manual labourer, enteritis tuberculosa, Teruel.

29-December-1941, NH

Juan Jurado Jiménez, 23, office worker, tuberculosis, Bujalance.

Pablo Segovia Morales, 32, manual labourer, typhus, Belmez.

30-December-1941, NH

Rafael Toledano Pino, 51, manual labourer, enterocolitis, Adamuz.

2-January-1942, PP

Antonio Doblas Muñoz, 59, manual labourer, tuberculosis, Moriles.

5-January-1942, NH

Cirilo Romero Rísquez, 38, manual labourer, rheumatism, Torre

Salvador Luque Valverde, 36, manual labourer, enteritis tuberculosa, Adamuz

Pedro Hernández Vicente, 54, manual labourer, enterocolitis, Almería.

6-January-1942

NH Ignacio Millán Fernández, 22, manual labourer, typhus, Peñarroya.

Adalberto Serrano Rodas, 52, school teacher., encefalitis, Cuenca.

PP Alejandro Márquez Rguez., 47, miner, emaciation, Fuenteobejuna.

7-January-1942, NH

Manuel Figueroa Villa, 54, school teacher, hipertensión, Pte. Genil.

8-January-1942, NH

Ramón Roso Gomater, 24, manual labourer, tuberculosis, Cádiz.

9-January-1942

NH Antonio Ortega Ponce, 27, manual labourer, tuberculosis, Huelva.

PP Isidoro Valle Jiménez, 60, manual labourer, tuberculosis, Lucena.

10-January-1942, NH

Zacarías Muñoz Fernández, 60, entrepreneur, typhus, Conquista.

Antonio Vigara García, 55, manual labourer, cerebral haemorrhage, Belalcázar.

12-January-1942, NH

Andrés Paredes Tapia, 56, manual labourer, tuberculosis, Valsequillo.

Antonio Martínez Nieto, 59, manual labourer, enterocolitis, Adamuz.
Esteban Cejudo Montes, 57, barber, arteriosclerosis, Doña Mencía.
13-January-1942, NH
Jacinto Cano Asencio, 57, manual labourer, arteriosclerosis., Montoro.
Antonio Rojas Martínez, 43, bricklayer, anemia, Cañete de las Torres
Manuel Carmona Leiva, 35, chauffeur, typhus, Montoro.
José Barber Tena, 34, manual labourer, arteriosclerosis, Villaviciosa.
Lorenzo Guillén Buenosvinos, 47, manual labourer, enterocolitis, Bujalance.
Cándido Toril López, 58, blacksmith, pneumonia., Fuenteobejuna.
14-January-1942, NH
Calixto Santos Cabezas, 47, salesman typhus, Villanueva de Córdoba
15-January-1941, NH
Cristóbal Serrano Castro, 37, manual labourer, nephritis, Luque.
Sebastián Blanco Blacksmith, 55, manual labourer, typhus, Torrecampo
16-January-1942, NH
Antonio Mariscal Jurado, 36, manual labourer, tuberculosis, Villaviciosa.
19-January-1942, NH
Alejandro Delgado Moyano, 26, manual labourer, myocarditis, Torrecampo
20-January-1942, NH
Juan Fernández Navarrete, 31, manual labourer, typhus, Villaviciosa.
21-January-1942, NH
José Aranda Ávila, 57, manual labourer, typhus, Fuente la Lancha.
Miguel Cejudo Fernández, 57, farmer, heart attack Sta. Eufemia.
Isidro Díaz Guerrero, 44, manual labourer, enterocolitis, Obejo.
Manuel Murillo Martínez, 54, miner, arteriosclerosis, El Hoyo.
Francisco Barbero Tena, 38, manual labourer, typhus, Villaviciosa.
23-January-1942, NH
Juan López Flores, 37, manual labourer, endocarditis, Fuente Palmera.
26-January-1942, NH
José González Nevado, 32, manual labourer, tuberculosis, Villaviciosa.
Francisco Gallego Toledano, 35, baker, typhus, Montoro.
28-January-1942, NH
Manuel Caballero Alcalde, 53, manual labourer, arteriosclerosis, El Viso.
31-January-1942, NH
Juan J. Gómez Calero, 51, bricklayer, tuberculosis, La Granja de T.
4-February-1942, NH
José Peña Valverde, 51, manual labourer, mitral insufficiency, Adamuz.
6-February-1942, NH
Francisco Vázquez Gallego, 23, miller, typhus, Badajoz.
10-February-1942, NH
Antonio López Pescuezo, 57, baker, pneumonia., Villanueva del Río.
15-February-1942, NH
Luis Núñez Alonso, 56, market gardener, nephritis, Castuera.

21-February-1942, NH
> Manuel Rivera López, 30, miner, tuberculosis, Pueblonuevo.
>
> Antonio Serrano Castro, 55, muleteer, pneumonia., Fernán Núñez.

24-February-1942, PP
> Lucia Garcia Valverde, 55, housewife, enterocolitis, Adamuz.

26-February-1942, NH
> Juan A. Hidalgo Medina, 37, manual labourer, pneumonia, Belalcázar.

3-March-1942, PP
> Salvador López Rabadán, 45, manual labourer, acute nephritis, Luque.

4-March-1942, PP
> Agustin Jurado Fernández, 20, manual labourer, tuberculosis, Hinojosa.

5-March-1942, PP
> Diego Soler Jerez, 19, manual labourer, tubercular meningitis», Huelva.

8-March-1942, PP
> Antonio Carmona Relaño, 51, manual labourer, pneumonia, Adamuz.
>
> Ignacio Martinez Rguez., 51, boiler maker, angina, Bujalance.

17-March-1942, PP
> Domingo Aguayo Caballero, 18, bricklayer, tuberculosis, Baena.

21-March-1942, PP
> Juan Carracedo Culebra, 33, manual labourer, tuberculosis, Obejo.
>
> Carmen González Zarza, 48, housewife., laryngeal epithelioma, Estepa.

26-March-1942, PP
> José Alfaro Puerto, 56, miner, stroke, El Viso.

31-March-1942, PP
> Francisco Dominguez Sierra, 35, foundry worker, mitral insufficiency, Peñarroya.

9-April-1942, PP cárcel de mujeres,
> Malio Giraldo Molero, 7 months, enterocolitis, Badajoz.

11-April-1942, PP
> Juan Hernández Peña, 30, stoker, bronchopneumonia, Espiel.
>
> Sinforiano Paredes Dominguez, 33, rialway worker, mitral insufficiency, Peñarroya.

13-April-1942, PP
> Antonio Chacón Benitez, 35, muleteer, tuberculosis, Villaviciosa.

14-April-1942, PP
> Tomás Gómez Marin, 40, manual labourer, tuberculosis, Castro del Rio.

17-April-1942, PP
> Antonio Pantoja Pérez, 56, manual labourer, stroke, Córdoba.

20-April-1942, PP
> Cristóbal Medina Muñoz, 42, manual labourer, endocarditis, Rute.

27-April-1942, PP
> Antonio Caballero González, 47, miner, uremia, Alcaracejos.

30-April-1942, PP
> José Lázaro de Diego, 59, manual labourer, cirhosis of the liver, Bujalance.

7-May-1942, PP
> Galo Adamuz Montilla, 45, school teacher pneumonia., Córdoba.

8-May-1942, PP
> José Sepúlveda Arjona, 38, miner, tubercolisis, La Carolina.

13-May-1942, PP
> Jacinto Sánchez Campillo, 34, manual labourer, cerebral haemmorhage., Iznájar.

14-May-1942, PP
> Rafael Expósito Leal, 48, manual labourer, pneumonia. ,Adamuz.

21-May-1942, PP
> Antonio Jaut Castilla, 19, manual labourer, tuberculosis, Pozoblanco.

27-May-1942, PP
> Adriano Valencia Quero, 47, manual labourer, myocarditis, Alcaudete.
> Manuel Puerto Nieto, 51, manual worker., heart attack, Villanueva de la Serena.

28-May-1942, PP
> Pedro Morillo Pinto, 29, shoemaker, pneumonia., Badajoz.

14-June-1942, PP
> Francisco Santofimia Carrillo, 33, manual labourer, tuberculosis, Córdoba.

20-June-1942, PP
> Aquilino Sánchez Navarro, 53, foundry worker, mitral insufficiency, Peñarroya.

2-July-1942, PP
> José Trujillo Muñoz, 55, painter, heart attack, Málaga.

26-August-1942, PP
> Eulalio Medrán Gañán, 26, manual labourer, tuberculosis, Dos Torres.

29-August-1942, PP
> Eufemio Cabello Merlo, 30, manual labourer, tuberculosis, Villaviciosa.

8-September-1942, PP
> Miguel Oviedo Rodríguez, 18, manual labourer, tuberculosis, Añora.

7-October-1942, PP
> Julián Vergara Ventura, 56, manual labourer, enterocolitis, Fuenteobejuna.

9-October-1942, PP
> Antonio Patiño Suárez, 28, baker., enterocolitis, Pto. Santa María.

8-November-1942, PP
> Manuel Ruiz Romero, 40, manual labourer, enterocolitis, Pozoblanco.

21-November-1942, PP
> María Sanz Cisneros, 63, housewife, gastric epithelioma, El Viso.

16-December-1942, PP
> Francisco Carrillo Nevado, 44, manual labourer, tuberculosis, Pedroche.

20-December-1942, PP
>Eusebio Castro Robles, 58, manual labourer, enterocolitis, Granada.

15-January-1943, PP
>Rafael Pedraza Farm workers, 26, manual labourer, pyloric ulcer, Vva. de Córdoba.
>Manuel Jiménez Jurado, 4, pneumonia., Bujalance, (women's prison)

2-February-1943, PP
>Manuel Mendoza Garcia, 24, manual labourer, enterocolitis, Granada.

15-February-1943, PP
>Antonio Medina Romero, 40, manual labourer, pneumonia., Pedroche.

17-February-1943, PP
>Pablo Garcia Rubio, 52, manual labourer, heart failure, Villaralto.

25-March-1943, PP
>Cándido Olot Munich, 52, farmer, septicemia, Lérida.

1-April-1943, PP (possible suicidie),
>Bernardino López Morales, 30, road worker, fractured skull, Villanueva del Duque.

8-April-1943, PP
>José Belmonte Blanco, 48, manual labourer, pulmonary gangrene, El Viso.

16-April-1943, PP
>Gabriel Rodriguez Ordóñez, 25, manual labourer, heart attack, Luque.
>Antonio Cañero Llamas, 66, tradesman, gastric ulcer, Fernán Núñez.

19-April-1943, PP
>José Fernández Castillejo, 52, miner, asystole, Peñarroya.

28-June-1943, PP
>Baldomero Corredera Ávila, 40, manual labourer, uremia, La Carlota.

12-July-1943, PP
>Juan Pablo Caballero Romero, 31, farm worker, tuberculosis, Hinojosa.

20-July-1943, PP
>Antonio Morenas Polaina, 38, butcher, tuberculosis, Jaén.

7-August-1943, PP
>Miguel Bolaños Cabrera, 69, manual labourer, asystole, Montoro.

11-August-1943, PP
>Roque Serrano Fernández, 43, manual labourer, hemoptisis, Dos Torres.

29-August-1943, PP
>Victoriano Ollero Moreno, 55, manual labourer, tuberculosis, El Viso.

16-September-1943, PP
>Manuel Carmona Garcia, 21, manual labourer, myocarditis, Montoro.

17-October-1943, PP (women's prison),
>José Toro Luque, 7 meses, meningitis, Priego.

24-November-1943, PP
>José Ortiz Arjona, 75, gastric ulcer, Palenciana.

13-January-1944, PP
> Agustin Morilla Tejada, 62, farmer., cerebral embolus» Venta del Charco.

1-February-1944, PP
> Bartolomé Muñoz Garcia, 38, manual labourer, Maltese fever, Sevilla.

11-June-1944, PP
> Joaquin Sánchez Sánchez, 41, miner, tuberculosis, Peñarroya.

1-July-1944, PP
> Miguel Diaz López, 22, manual labourer, tuberculosis, El Viso.

17-October-1944, PP (possible suicide),
> Joaquin Garcia Lázaro, 32, bricklayer, ruptured liver and torn lungs, Adamuz.

11-April-1945, PP (possible suicide),
> Rafael Garcia Gutiérrez, 51, baker, skull fracture, Villanueva de Córdoba.

5-June-1945, PP
> Juan Luque Rubio, 50, manual labourer, syncope, Montilla.

28-June-1945, PP
> Juan Molina Jiménez, 21, manual labourer, heart attack, Fernán Núñez.

23-September-1945, PP
> Ignacio García y García del Barrio, 55, tradesman., bronchopneumonia, Montilla.

20-January-1946, PP
> Francisco Manosalvas Medina, 60, tradesman, septicemia, Pedroche.

7-June-1946, PP (possible suicide),
> Francisco Romero Paredes, 24, boiler worker, fracture of the spine., Belmez.

3-July-1946, PP
> Florencio López Cortés, 50, cattle breeder, heart attack, Torrecampo.

3-August-1946, PP
> Juan Díaz Martínez, 23, goatherd, tuberculosis, Montoro.

7-August-1946, PP
> Antonio Avilés Díaz, 26, farm worker, meningitis, Pedroche.

20-August-1946, PP
> Antonio Fabre Sánchez, 48, telegraphist, heart attack, Rota.

31-August-1946, PP
> Juan Sánchez Cabrera, 29, manual labourer, heart attack, Almería.

2-September-1946, PP (women's prison),
> María Gómez Aguilar, 3 days, Córdoba.

9-October-1946, PP
> Juan Morales Rodríguez, 64, coalman, asystole, Badajoz.

21-October-1946, PP
> José Fernández Gómez, 54, manual labourer, heart attack, Villaralto.

8-November-1946, PP
> Mª Antonia Baena Granado, 82, housewife, brain haemorrhage, Rute.

4-December-1946, PP
    José Palma Martínez, 27, basket weaver, tuberculosis, Jaén.

5-January-1947, PP (suicide, according to his son José "Comandante Ríos".)
    José Murillo Alegre, 49, cattle breeder, hanging, El Viso.

27-January-1947, PP
    Isabelino Granados Moya, 51, manual labourer, pneumonia., Villanueva.
    del Duque.

TOTAL: 756

APPENDIX III

Testimonials of the clerical repression and of the situation of the children behind bars.

Manuel Espejo. DOS TORRES. *Regarding the pressure to confess ritual in Córdoba prison. Interview with Moreno Gómez in Madrid January 1984.*

- "At night, a Guardia Civil truck would arrive at the prison, they called the names of those who were to be executed and took them to a room to confess. There was a different priest at each saca, monks or Jesuits from Córdoba. The prison chaplain was Fr. García, S.J. and he took charge of confessing the most reluctant. He took them to his room and afterwards, whether they had confessed or not, said they had. Because of that, many also refused to go into his room. Approximately half in each saca confessed, many of these convinced by Fr. García to whom they owed favours at hard times or when they were hungry."

Flor Cernuda. QUINTANAR DE LA ORDEN. *Testimonial recorded by Tomasa Cuevas, regarding Ocaña prison.*

- "In Ocaña, we were taken to Mass. During Mass, another priest and minister of God, would give us a sermon on how evil the Rojos were but they, as they were so good, were willing to forgive... to forgive our souls but they would have to kill our bodies because it was our bodies who had sinned."

Agustina Sánchez. Regarding Ventas prison in Madrid. Testimonial recorded by Tomasa Cuevas. *Regarding the day they executed her mother-in-law, Josefa Perpiñán July 24 1939.*

- "She came out looking like a ghost and she was taken to the chapel. There were another six women with her. They executed all seven. They had been taken to the church the night before, from where they took them to the chapel; the priest told them to entrust their souls to God because they were going to die. The next morning, at 6 a.m., at the last moment, they were given a crucifix to kiss. My mother-in-law grabbed the crucifix and threw it at the priest's head. She did not kill him because he ducked.... As they took the woman away, I was made to leave the church so that I could not go into the gallery and see in what condition they left. I was told that the women's lips were dark purple, almost black.. I was so upset that the only reason they were killing my mother-in-law was because they could not capture her son."

Regarding her experience in Amorebieta prison from which she was released:

- "I was called for my examination and the priest told me that I had religion by a thread and that I would leave here when he wanted to let me go. 'Do you see this finger?' he asked. 'With it I have often pulled the trigger against Rojos. I have killed a lot. My only regret is that I have not killed them all.'"

Francisco Gómez Herencia. NUEVA CARTEYA, CÓRDOBA. *Regarding his being examined regarding the catechism before he could be released from jail.*

- "One day, after I had spent four years in prison, the Director told me that if I could pass the catechism examination and answer the priest's questions satisfactorily, I could be released. The Director himself, Don Faustino, gave me a catechism to study. A few days later he called me: 'Herencia, how are you getting along with what I gave you?' 'The same, Don Faustino', I replied. 'I just cannot get this into my head.' The Director, seeing that it was pretty much the same after a few days, call an old village priest to come in and examine me and the Director himself helped me answer the questions. This is how I was able to go free."

The situation of the children behind bars.

Tomasa Cuevas. DURANGO prison. *Description of the problem of children in prisons and the support given by the townspeople of Durango to their mothers.*

- We were more than two thousand women in that prison There were a great many children ranging from a few months of age – some were born in jail – up to three and even four years of age. The Government then issued an Order by which children older than three years could not accompany their mothers in prison. Where did these children go? To a children's home. There were some problems: in some cases, it was friends or relatives who asked to be allowed to take the children. Unfortunately, we were in the North of the country and we were all from Centre and even some, Andalusia. The Government had set a deadline by which the older children had to leave the jail and their mothers were getting desperate. What would happen to their children? The townspeople of Durango were brilliant. They went to the Director and told him that they would take these children until their families could come and get them.

The little ones who stayed with their families had a hard time of it; they only had the same food as the inmates to eat, no more milk or anything else. Two died not long after. When the townspeople heard of this and that others were not faring very well, they sent in jugs of milk to be shared by the mothers." (pp. 11-122)

Nieves Waldemar. Imprisoned in the Convent of the French Nuns in Guadalajara, told Tomasa the following:

- "There were just fourteen square metres with a toilet just for us; where at night, a mass of children and women slept; what one child had, the others would catch: pimples, scabies, all those illnesses that are infectious just because of the overcrowding... They executed two sisters-in-law in Auñón, Guadalajara, and when they left to be shot, with their fists raised, one of them said: 'Companions, do not salute, because you will be punished, but think of my children, I am leaving my children!' This is what the married one said. Her husband, a member of the elite police force, had been executed. This woman left her children to be taken care of by whoever wanted to because all of her relatives had been executed." (pp. 92-93)

Carmen Machado. From Madrid, reporting on some very serious figures for DURANGO prison:

- "The tragedy of these mothers was horrible: the children were not given any special food; they had to eat the same as their mothers. Many women were not able to receive any food packages because their homes had been destroyed and all their relatives had disappeared. There was an epidemic of encephalitis lethargica: the same children whom we had seen playing happily the day before, began to fall asleep and most of these never woke up. I particularly remember a little boy from the province of Toledo, an amusing little chap, one of the children who died from the encephalitis. I imagine that I see him, during the vigil of his body, wrapped in a blanket until they came to get him the next day. (p. 133)

Carmen Riera. Is extremely blunt as when gives an interview to the *Prohibido recordar* (Forbidden to remember) documentary, *She describes her horrible experience in Santurrarán prison:*

- "Regarding the children, more than thirty died in ten days, including my daughter. When she died, the moved me to a room where they took her little casket. The nuns picked some flowers for her and began lamenting 'Oh how exciting, another little angel who loves God!' I could not stand it anymore and kicked them out of the room. I spent the whole night sitting on the floor, next to my daughter's casket.

APPENDIX IV

POST-WAR FIRING SQUAD EXECUTIONS IN CORDOBA CAPITAL
2 June 1939 – 21 February 1945

Individual, small group and mass executions compiled and annotated for the Democratic Memorial of Spain investigation of the Francoist genocide in Cordoba.

[Francoists refused to recognize the rank the prisoners-of-war held with the Republican army when they were captured and they only recorded the names of the executed and their lowest pre-war rank [*as given in italics in brackets*]. The highest rank each held when they were captured is nevertheless indicated here following their name.]

1939

2 June (1)
> Juan B. Ruano Muñoz, 43, bricklayer, Porcuna

11 July (1)
> Alfonso Hernández Carrillo, 32, carpinter, Beas de Segura

26 August (1)
> Rafael Guerrero Juárez, 51, electrician, Espiel

1 September at 6:15 a.m. (4)
> Antonio Juárez Guerrero, 26, mechanic, Alora (Málaga)
> Francisco Bermúdez Canales, 54, farm worker, Baena
> José Bermúdez Expósito, 36, farm worker, Baena
> Isidoro Povedano Muñoz, 37, farm worker, Priego

28 October at 2 a.m. (2)
> José Navajas Espejo, 38, manual labourer, Posadas
> José Mesa Frías, 31, farm worker, Alcalá la Real

<u>6 November</u> (1)

    Benjamín Gil Bona, 20, manual labourer, Aljuna (Valencia)

<u>8 November at 6 a.m.</u> **(11)**

    José Matas Jiménez, 39, farmer, Puente Genil
    José Luna Granados, 26, farm worker, Puente Genil
    Miguel Rey Balaguer, 25, manual labourer, Puente Genil
    Diego Cornejo Morales, 36, farm worker, Puente Genil
    Feliciano García Haba, 23, farm worker, Peraleda de Zaucejo
    Antonio Zurita Montero, 26, farm worker, Cañete
    Ricardo Rubio Calero, 27, Pozoblanco[i]
    Manuel Moya Vivo, 28, bricklayer, Villacarrillo (Jaén)
    Juan Durán Lorenzo, 34, farm worker, Azuaga
    José Cuevas Simonis, 44, farm worker, Posadas
    José Pérez Pozo, 49, farm worker, Gilena

<u>9 November</u> (3)

San Rafael cemetery

    Rafael Martínez Arenales, 55, businessman, Villaviciosa
    Justo Deza Montero, 39, farm worker, Puente Genil[ii]
    Antonio Molina Romero, 28, farm worker, Puente Genil

<u>6 December at 6:30 a.m.</u> (6)

La Salud cemetery

    Antonio Sánchez Cabello, 19, bricklayer, Puente Genil
    Juan B. Sánchez Aguilar, 50, farm worker, Puente Genil

San Rafael cemetery

    Manuel Martín Balsera, 26, farm worker, Badajoz
    Felipe Espinosa Casablanca, 31, manual labourer, Badajoz
    José Jiménez Vargas, 24, barber, Lora del Río
    Salvador Sánchez Fernández, 29, basket weaver

<u>15 December</u> (2)

    Domingo Muñoz Mérida, 32, farmer, Almodóvar del Río
    Juan Muñoz Torres, 29, farm worker, Posadas

1940

<u>7-January at 7:15 a.m.</u> (1)

---

[i] Prisoner of war captured 1938 in Vinaroz (Castellón), Political commisar in the army and son of *El Calor*, the famous Socialist.

[ii] Famous Cordovan Socialist. Chairman of the Puente Genil War Committee, alderman as of 1931. During the war, lived in Pozoblanco where he presided over a farmer's cooperative. Went valiantly to his death exhorting his cellmates to make sure that so much bloodshed should not go unpunished.

El Alcázar Provincial Prison
    Francisco Cruz González, 40, manual labourer, Dos Torres

17 January at 7 a.m. (2)
Casillas artillery range
    Narciso Sánchez Aparicio, 50, Lieutenant Colonel [*Artillery Major*]
    from Santa Clara (Cuba)[iii]
    Esteban Rodríguez Domingo, 45, Major [*Artillery Lieutenant*], Valencia[iv]

20 January at 6:30 a.m. (3)
    Luís Giménez Romero, 29, farm worker, Espejo
    Bartolomé Higuera Caballero, 31, farm worker, Villafranca
    Andrés Caballero García, 27, farm worker, Villafranca

27 January at 7 a.m. (2)
Casillas artillery range
    José Bueno Quejo, 43, Commander [*Infantry Captain*], Vitoria[v]
    Luís Soler Espiauba-Cánovas, Major [*Infantry Lieutenant*], Cartagena[vi]

29 January (1)
    Juan Aranda Martos, 41, carpinter, Cordoba

28 February at 6 a.m. (3)
    Eugenio Giménez Blanco, 30, manual labourer, Posadas
    Juan Sánchez Muñoz, 37, manual labourer, Posadas
    Juan Codines Galvez, 27, farmer, La Rambla

[iii] Infantry major in Segovia ordered to organize a battalion of volunteers 17 July 1936. Promoted Lt. Colonel, served as General Staff Officer. 1938, Chief of Staff first, of the XVIIth Army Corps and later, the XXIII Army Corps. Source: 5 October 1987 letter to the author from Carlos Engel.

[iv] At the end of the war was serving with the Light Artillery Regiment 6, in Murcia. Ordered to suppress the rebellion in Albacete. Promoted to Captain in 1936 and to Mayor in 1938. Source: Carlos Engel.

[v] When war broke out, was in command of the garrison in Santoña and refused to support the coup. He commanded a unit in defense of the Port of Escudo, which later became the 2nd Division of the Santander Army Corps. Promoted to Major in 1937. When Santander fell to the Nationalists, he went to France and from there, to the Centre of the country where he was appointed Chief of Staff of the 22nd Division of the Andalusia Army Corps. Was tried by court martial in Cordoba 5 September 1939. Posthumously fined 5,000 pesetas under the Law of Political Responsibilities. Source: Carlos Engel, op. cit. and Jesús Gutiérrez Flores, undated letter to the author from Santander.

[vi] Had retired to Almería in 1936. With the war, re-enlisted. Promoted to Captain, then to Major in 1938. Fought in the Granada sector with the 54 MB of the 23rd Division of the XXII Andalusia Army Corps.

<u>18 March at 6 a.m.</u> **(19)**

 Francisco Mejías Sánchez, 28, farm worker, Hornachuelos
 José García Rodríguez, 46, miner, Hornachuelos
 Emilio Ramos Cantador, 60, farm worker, Hornachuelos
 José Linares Pérez, 34, farm worker, Hornachuelos
 Antonio Núñez Pulido, 36, farm worker, Hornachuelos
 Hilario Expósito Flores, 32, farm worker, Obejo
 Higinio Morales Moraza, 35, businessman, Obejo
 Tomás Flores Puerto, 39, manual labourer, Obejo
 Francisco González Gavilán, 38, bricklayer, Almodóvar del Río
 Manuel Berjillo Rodríguez, 29, farm worker, Almodóvar del Río
 Francisco Gómez Galindo, 30, farm worker, Benamejí
 Manuel López Moya, 30, farm worker, Morente
 Gabriel Serrano González, 28, farm worker, Villa del Río
 Cristóbal Sáinz Marín, 35, farm worker, Villa del Río
 Rafael Casado Castro, 27, bricklayer, Villafranca
 Gonzalo Obrero Duque, 30, farmer, Villafranca
 Rafael Muñoz Navarrete, 25, farm worker, La Rambla
 Francisco Haro Manzano, 33, farm worker, Bujalance
 Isidoro Martínez Trucharte, 56, farm worker, Baena

<u>5 April at 6 a.m.</u> (6)
Casillas artillery range

 Lorenzo Almaraz de Pedro, 52, Captain [*Infantry Lieutenant*], Badajoz[vii]
 Damián Contreras Moreno, 39, Major [*Infantry Lieutenant*], Torredonjimeno[viii]
 Felipe Gallardo Linares, 53, Major [*Infantry Lieutenant*], Linares[ix]
 Eugenio Muñoz Hoyuela, 34, Major [*Infantry Lieutenant*], Palencia[x]
 Antonio Fernández Sánchez, 44, Captain [*Artillery Lieutenant*], Murcia[xi]

[vii] Had retired to Badajoz in 1936. When this city fell, fled to Portugal where he embarked on the ship *Nyassa* that took many refugees to Tarragona. Re-enlisted and rose to the rank of Captain. Fought in Catalonia, then with the Military Headquarts of Almería, then with the XXIII Army Corps and lastly, in June 1938, the Levante Army Corps.

[viii] Enlisted as Lieutenant with the Jaén Volunteer Battalion No. 4 and promoted Captain November 1936. Commanded the 148 MB of the 37th Division of the VII Army Corps of Extremadura. Promoted Major June 1938.

[ix] Retired 2nd Lieutenant, re-enlisted, promoted Lieutenant October 1936, then Captain and Major (June 1938). Always fought with the Army of Andalusia.

[x] Was a Guarda de Asalto posted in Linares in 1936. Rose to Captain December 1936. 1938 transferred to the Army of the Centre and in July promoted Major.

[xi] Serving in Cartagena when war broke out. Promoted Lieutenant October 1936 then Captain March 1938. Remained the entire war with the 3rd Costal Artillery Regiment of Cartagena. It is not known how he came to be executed in Cordoba.

Enrique Medina Vega, 50, Major [*Captain*], Chafarinas[xii]

8 April at 6 a.m. (24)
Rafael Pérez Alcaide, 25, office worker, Cordoba
Bernabé Menor Molleja, 28, Villa del Rio
Bernardino Escabia Molleja, 27, Villa del Rio
Miguel Mantas Cantero, 27, Villa del Rio
Lorenzo Moyano Morales, 25, Villa del Rio
Francisco Moreno Rojas, 27, Villa del Rio
Ildefonso Platero Rojano, 66, Villa del Rio
Ignacio Pino Gutiérrez, 25, Aguilar
José Redondo Mata, 33, Navas de la Concepción (Sevilla),
Francisco Carbadillo Sánchez, 27, Navas de la Concepción (Sevilla)
Antonio López Rodriguez, 44, Hornachuelos
Pedro Mangas López, 25, Hornachuelos
Manuel Garcia Palomares, 43, Hornachuelos
Rafael Guerra Morales, 31, Guadalcázar
Antonio Nieto Romero, 37, Puente Genil
Juan M Giménez Rodriguez, 45, Castro del Rio
Francisco Sánchez Garcia, 38, Villanueva de Cordoba
Alfonso Ayuso Tinahones, 33, Adamuz
Cristóbal Padilla Garcia, 31, Adamuz
Francisco Caballero Garcia, 28, Villafranca
José Arrabal Muñoz, 35, Arenas del Rey (Granada)
Vicente Rubio Molero, 33, Hinojosa del Duque
Amalio Molina Macias, 30, Villamayor de Calatrava (Ciudad Real)
Juan A Muñoz Barba, 42, Cabra

20 April at 6 a.m. (5)
El Alcázar Provincial Prison
Ángel Gómez Ortega, 32, market gardener, Posadas
Rafael Torronteras Zafra, 36, ironmonger, Posadas
Alfonso Sánchez González, 22, marble worker, Posadas
Félix Cuenca Cruz, 39, farm worker, Villa del Rio
Juan Barrera Reyes, 48, farm worker, Adamuz

4 June at 6 a.m. (16)
Juan Barrazosa Castro, 24, chauffeur, Palma del Rio
Juan Fuentes Sánchez, 38, manual labourer, Palma del Rio
Antonio Garcia Garcia, 36, market gardener, Palma del Rio
Antonio Benitez González, 32, manual labourer, Palma del Rio

[xii] Had retired to Almeria as Captain. Re-enlisted October 1936 and promoted Major. Commander of Almeria Machine Gunners. Ended the war with the Almeria Recruiting Office. Source: Carlos Engel.

José Castillo Sánchez, 38, ironmonger, Hornachuelos
Juan Diaz Martinez, 52, manual labourer, Posadas
Luis González Navajas, 63, farmer, Posadas
Antonio Sánchez Olmo, 25, farmer, Espiel
Antonio Franco Muñoz, 25, manual labourer, Espiel
Daniel Arévalo León, 34, farm worker, Villaviciosa
Francisco Álvarez Izquierdo, 33, farm worker, Villafranca
Virgilio Ferri Vidal, 41, hat maker, Valencia
José Alcaide Manso, 49, farm worker, La Rambla
Francisco Caballero Bueno, 33, salesman, Rute
Ramón Romero Fernández, 48, tradesman, Montoro
Ildefonso Ruiz Santiago, 38, farm worker, Valenzuela

6 June at 6 a.m. (17)
Enrique Morales Guzmán, 31, manual labourer, Fuente Palmera
Bartolomé Martinez Abúndez, 33, manual labourer, Posadas
José Grande López, 56, manual labourer, Villa del Rio
Francisco Serrano Serrano, 62, chauffeur, Villa del Rio
Diego Solaz Cruz, 37, bricklayer, Montoro
Julián López Muñoz, 43, manual labourer, Montoro
Miguel Martinez Martinez, 30, farmer, Almodóvar del Rio
José Alcalde Machuca, 35, lawyer, Espiel
Antonio Olmo Sánchez, 50, manual labourer, Espiel
Juan Torres Rivera, 38, businessman, Villafranca
Miguel Torres Tripiana, 27, manual labourer, Villafranca
Antonio Lainez Carrasco, 28, railway worker, Puente Genil
Antonio Vega Casas, 45, manual labourer, Palma del Rio
Rafael Fernández Diaz, 40, manual labourer, Hornachuelos
Ildefonso Santiago Lara, 55, farm worker, Valenzuela
Juan Ruiz Rubiales, 42, bricklayer, Ubrique, resident Cordoba
Juan Morata López, 35, manual labourer, Ciudad Real, resident
Cordoba

8 June at 5 a.m. (13)
Juan Fuentes Ruiz, 41, manual labourer, Montoro
Bartolomé Mazuelas Sánchez, 34, farm worker, Montoro
Francisco Rodriguez Torres, 38, farm worker, Montoro
Antonio Navarro Aguilar, 29, manual labourer, Palma del Rio
Ruperto Muñoz Martinez, 24, manual labourer, Palma del Rio
José Pérez Reyes, 34, farm manual labourer, Palma del Rio
Rafael Polonio Delgado, 32, farm worker, Palma del Rio
Manuel Diaz Sánchez, 41, manual labourer, Palma del Rio
Juan Felipe Martinez Murillo, 34, manual labourer, Hornachuelos
Francisco Palacios Bernal, 56, farm worker, Almodóvar
Bartolomé Torralba Pastilla, 35, mechanic, Villa del Rio

Cristóbal Navajas Manchado, 34, farm worker, Villa del Rio
Pedro Berenguer Diaz, 55, manual labourer, Posadas

22 June at 5 a.m. (18)
Juan González Guirado, 37, bricklalyer, Palma del Rio
Miguel Pavón Fernández, 37, manual labourer, Posadas
Manuel Girona Rodriguez, 48, farmer, Posadas
Antonio Fructuosa Garcia, 36, manual labourer, Posadas
José Garcia Garcia, 35, manual labourer, Hornachuelos
Manuel López Rodriguez, 37, manual labourer, Hornachuelos
Francisco Cardo Camacho, 27, manual labourer, Hornachuelos
Rafael Ruiz Moya, 38, farmer, Adamuz
Antonio Gómez Torres, businessman, Villafranca
Manuel Garcia Castro, 43, transportation, Villa del Rio
Francisco Palma Prieto, 34, farm worker, Aguilar
Francisco Dios Muñoz, 29, bricklalyer, Villafranca (Bujalance)[xiii]
José Ranchal Tartajo, 38, manual labourer, Espiel
Antonio Zamora Espinar, 32, farm worker, Iznájar
Daniel de la Torre Nevado, 52, farm worker, Villaviciosa
Manuel Noguera Guisado, 36, manual labourer, Silillos (Fuente Palmera)
Antonio Redondo Heras, 47, manual labourer, Fuenteobejuna
Antonio Medina Pedregosa, 23, farm worker, Cordoba

10 July at 4 a.m. (1)
Antonio Ruiz Martinez, 45, manual labourer, Palma del Rio

20 July at 5 a.m. (6)
Antonio Sánchez Calet, 44, manual labourer, Montoro
Batolomé Porras Ruano, 43, farmer, Montoro
José Lara Olmo, 57, manual labourer, Montoro
Juan A. Villaverde Vega, 32, manual labourer, Montoro
Francisco Garcia Guilarte, 34, farmer, Montoro
José Quero Izquierdo, 26, farmer, Lopera

30 July at 5 a.m. (2)
Manuel Sánchez Pérez, 28, manual labourer, Montoro
Francisco Jurado Guiérrez, 36, butcher, Villanueva de Cordoba

12 September at 6 a.m. (11)
Tomás de la Torre Barbero, 42, farm worker, Villaviciosa

[xiii] Famous Captain Paco of the Villafranca Battalion. His heroism was sung by the poet Pedro Garfias in his book *Héroes del Sur* and by Joe Monks, an Irish member of the International Brigade, in his book *Con los rojos en Andalucía*, Renacimiento, Seville, 2012.

Antonio Aranda Pulido, 29, farmer, Villaviciosa
José López Arribas, 24, farm worker, Villaviciosa
Juan Muñoz Arribas, 36, farmer, Villaviciosa
José Cabello Calvo, 25, farmer, Villaviciosa
Alberto Merino Pérez, 23, farm worker, Castro del Rio
Antonio Francos Ruiz, 39, manual labourer, Palma del Rio
José Deña Velasco, 31, farmer, Constantina (Sevilla)
Francisco Cuesta Gutiérrez, 66, farmer, Almodóvar del Rio
Manuel Tapiero Cáceres, 47, manual labourer, Fuente Palmera
Santiago Mantas Cuenca, 34, bricklayer, Villa del Rio

20 September at 6 a.m. (7)
Rafael Cuevas Alcaide, 27, potter, Villaviciosa
Tomás Lopera González, 36, manual labourer, Villaviciosa
Diego González Misa, 28, farm worker, Villafranca
Manuel Lucena Padilla, 36, farm worker, Espejo
Antonio Garcia Urraco, 29, farm worker, Hornachuelos
Manuel Colomina Benitez, 30, baker, Montoro
Antonio Almenara Muñoz, 35, farmer, Palma del Rio

30 September at 6 a.m. (6)
José Dios Criado, 61, farm worker, Castro del Rio
Miguel Porcel Redondo, 49, tradesman, Castro del Rio
Francisco López Morales, 45, farm worker, Villa del Rio
Juan Solas Hernández, 41, manual labourer, Hornachuelos
Emilio Santiago Lara, 45, runner, Valenzuela
Francisco Cerezo Requena, 42, farmer, Cordoba

11 November at 6:30 a.m. (1)
Manuel Diaz López, 26, barber, Baños de la Encina (Jaén)

12 November at 6:30 a.m. (2)
Antonio Mármol Alonso, 34, manual labourer, Adamuz
Juan Rojas Arenas, 34, manual labourer, Pedro Abad

27 November at 6:30 a.m. (1)
Ernesto López Vidal, 60, hospital administrator, Agudos, Lugo

18 December at 7 a.m. (4)
San Rafael cemetery
Francisco Alcaide Cruz, 27, Santa Eufemia
Vicente Lillo Morente, 32, Palma del Rio
Manuel Andújar Rosa, 48, Palma del Rio
Manuel Qesada López, 43, Montoro

20 December at 7 a.m. (3)

Juan José Velasco Mateos, 39, farm worker, Santiago de Calatrava (Jaén)
Manuel Portero Romero, 51, manual labourer, Santiago de Calatrava (Jaén)
Sebastián Romero Urbano, 30, manual labourer, Santiago de Calatrava (Jaén)

27 December at 7 a.m. (34)

Santiago Fernández González, 61, manual labourer, Belalcázar
José Paredes Ruiz, 30, farmer, Belalcázar
Manuel Pizarro Bravo, 55, farm worker, Belalcázar
Juan Valverde Castro, 25, farm worker, Torrecampo
Tomás Romero Enriquez, 29, bricklayer, Villanueva de Cordoba
Juan J Serrano Cepas, 33, shoemaker, Villanueva de Cordoba
Leopoldo Lucena de la Rubia, 33, farm worker, Porcuna
Emiliano Hidalgo Fernández, 61, businessman, Dos Torres
Valeriano Domenech Martinez, 32, farm worker, Montoro
Mateo Garcia Gómez, 51, cattle breeder, Montoro
Francisco Diaz Tintor, 44, manual labourer, Montoro
Juan Garcia Carrasco, 41, farm worker, Montoro
Francisco Navarro Majuelos, 39, farm worker, Montoro
Manuel Carmona Rastroyo, 25, farmer, Puente Genil
Fernando Molina Molina, 24, businessman, Puente Genil
Francisco Caballero Diaz, 40, farmer, Obejo
Martin Sánchez Bravo, 35, farmer, Alcaracejos
José Fernández Galán, 30, manual labourer, Alcaracejos
Lucas Centella Aranda, 40, farm worker, Castro del Rio
Rafael Moreno Bello, 28, farm worker, Castro del Rio
Rafael Rodríguez Gálvez, 34, bricklayer, El Carpio
José Román Romero, 29, farm worker, El Carpio
Lorenzo Gaitán Román, 27, chauffeur, El Carpio
Domingo Villalba Calvo, 32, manual labourer, Cañete de las Torres
Antonio Vázquez Navas, 50, farm worker, Fuenteobejuna
Rafael Pérez Román, 36, manual labourer, Adamuz
Juan Manuel Noguero Leal, 41, molder, Peñarroya
Juan Gutiérrez Cachinero, 37, farm worker, Azuel
Juan Calixto López Santiago, 40, farm worker, Valenzuela
Francisco Luque Morales, 32, farm worker, Espejo
Rafael Limones Caro, 33, bricklayer, Palma del Rio
Juan Abril Pardiñeiro, 61, miller, Espiel
Antonio Pavón Fernández, 46, manual labourer, Posadas
Juan Moya Carrillo, 56, manual labourer, Pedroche

1941

13 January at 6 a.m. (1)
    Manuel Fuillerat Lora, 34, shoemaker, Villa del Rio

20 January at 6 a.m. (1)
    José Suescun Moreno, 43, ironmonger, Villanueva del Rey

31 January at 6 a.m. **(25)**
    Félix Chaves Caballero, 53, manual labourer, Alcalde de Fuente la
    Lancha
    Antonio Vigara Regidor – *El Sabio*, 64, farmer, Belalcázar[xiv]
    Manuel Ruiz Fernández, 45, shoemaker, El Viso
    Vicente Rodríguez Ruiz, 44, manual labourer, Belalcázar
    Rafael Gómez Fernández,53, cattle breeder, Belalcázar
    Emilio Ruiz Rodríguez, 23, manual labourer, Belalcázar
    Lorenzo Rodríguez Tapias, 41, manual labourer, Belalcázar
    Manuel Hidalgo Gómez, 29, manual labourer, Belalcázar
    Isidoro Morales Cañamaque, 70, farm worker, Montoro
    Diego Valverde Ranchal, 26, manual labourer, Pedroche
    Matías González Calzadillo, 45, farm worker, Hinojosa del Duque
    Nicolás Vioque Caballero, 29, carrier, Hinojosa del Duque
    José Navarro Moreno, 24, manual labourer, Hinojosa del Duque
    Victoriano Murillo Platero, 28, farmer, Hinojosa del Duque
    Teófilo Morales Arellano, 50, manual labourer, Hinojosa del Duque
    Domingo Acedo González, 65, shoemaker, Hinojosa del Duque
    Vicente Ureña Villaseca, 24, cattle breeder, Hinojosa del Duque
    José Muñoz González, 35, muleteer, Palma del Río
    Marcos Luna García, 44, farmer, Villaralto
    Antonio Sánchez Puerto, 40, manual labourer, Villaralto
    Maximiliano Toril Fernández, 44, land owner, Villaralto
    Florencio Luna Fernández, 45, shepherd, Villaralto
    Luis Cabanillas Agredano, 27, manual labourer, Fuenteobejuna
    Manuel Expósito Gómez, 35, chauffeur, Fuenteobejuna
    Bernardo Fernández Santos, 20, manual labourer, Alcaracejos

1 May at 6 a.m. **(34)**
La Salud cemetery
    Manuel Sánchez Ruiz «El Perla», 33, farmer, Mayor of Montilla
    Blas Gómez Medina, 39, manual labourer, Villanueva de Cordoba
    José T Torralbo Expósito, 32, manual labourer, Villanueva de Cordoba

---

[xiv] An elderly socialist and very peaceful, President of the *Casa del Pueblo*, the community social
centre. Hid in his house for a year anLd a half until he was turned in to the authorities. His
son Agustín was executed soon afterwards.

José Mª Sánchez Jurado, 65, clerk, Villanueva de Cordoba
Pedro Padilla Moreno, 36, manual labourer, Villanueva de Cordoba
Agustin Vigara Garcia, 24, manual labourer, Belalcázar
Fernando Cano Yébenes, 47, farm worker, Morente
Manuel Ruano Borrego, 46, manual labourer, Cañete de las Torres
Gaspar Manrique Bejarano, 40, carpinter, Cañete de las Torres
Cristóbal Muñoz López, 45, farm worker, La Rambla
Rafael Garrido Marin, 51, farm worker, La Rambla
Juan Rivas Montilla, 26, farm worker, Valenzuela
Juan Cid Contreras, 22, baker, Bujalance
Bartolomé Parrado Serrano, 54, manual labourer, Bujalance
Mateo Castillo Rubio, 30, farm worker, Bujalance
Moisés López Sánchez, 34, cattle breeder, Villaralto
Augusto P Martin Fernández, 26, cattle breeder, Villaralto
Manuel Rojas Lara, 41, manual labourer, Montoro
Francisco Mora González, 39, manual labourer, Montoro
Vicente Lerena Iñiguez, 25, farm worker, Villa del Rio
Andrés Garcia Moreno, 23, farm worker, Castro del Rio
Arcadio Gordillo Monje, 69, farmer, Hinojosa del D
José Perea Cortés, 33, potter, Hinojosa del Duque
Cándido Garcia Arellano, 25, farm worker, Hinojosa del D
José Sánchez Salguero, 41, miner, Puertollano
Alfonso Regalón Román, 32, farm worker, Adamuz
Juan Pato Velázquez, 27, railway worker, Almodóvar del Rio
Antonio Guerra Almodóvar, 35, farm worker, Pedro Abad
Manuel Mena Molina, 38, manual labourer, Pedroche
Francisco Casado Pedrajas, 51, farmer, Pozoblanco[xv]
Florentino Moyano Fernández, 41, manual labourer, Fuente la Lancha
Rafael Alijo Torquemada, 36, manufacturing, Puente Genil
Francisco Ramirez Molina, 28, farm worker, Luque
Leoncio Gómez Fernández, 37, manual labourer, Villaralto

3 May at 6 a.m. (34)
San Rafael cemetery
Fernando López Muñoz, 31, farm worker, Bujalance
Francisco Garcia Pajuelo, 22, manual labourer, Alcaracejos
Francisco Muñoz Gutiérrez, 25, bricklayer, Montoro
Pedro Jurado Benavides, 47, tradesman, Montoro
Tomás Pizarro Rodriguez, 39, cattle breeder, Belalcázar
Francisco Nieto Zamorano, 38, farm worker, Pedro Abad
Gregorio Artero Rojas, 37, farm worker, Pedro Abad

[xv] This individual made the mistake of having his picture taken whilst sitting on the body of a dead right-winger in Pozoblanco, smoking a cigarette.

176

Juan Morales Millán, 43, farm worker, Pedro Abad
Mariano Morrugares Garrido, 38, farm worker, Pedro Abad
Fernando Lara Cuadrado, 23, farm worker, Pedro Abad
Manuel Cuenca Pelado, 29, railway worker, Villa del Rio
Rafael Piedrahita Jurado, 56, farm worker, Santa Eufemia
Bernardino Muñoz Castillo, 46, farm worker, Santa Eufemia
Florentino Redondo Serena, 36, farmer, Santa Eufemia
Aquilino Fernández Ruiz, 35, farm worker, Santa Eufemia
Manuel Daza Jurado, 45, farm worker, Santa Eufemia
Alberto Carrasco Garcia, 32, chauffeur, Hinojosa del Duque
José Fernández Luque, 48, farm worker, Hinojosa del Duque
Juan Barbancho Delgado, 36, bricklayer, Hinojosa del Duque
Alejandro Lima Fernández, 41, manual labourer, Villaralto
Antonio Fernández Sánchez, 35, farmer, Villaralto
José Ortigoso Moreno, 40, boiler maker, Belmez
Antonio Carisimo Prieto, 32, miner, Belmez
Vicente Blanco Garcia, 28, tradesman, Belmez[xvi]
Antonio Pizarro Valero, 41, manual labourer, Villaharta
Manuel Larias Fajardo, 30, railway worker, Guadalcanal
José Diaz Morales, 31, manual labourer, Fuente la Lancha
Antonio Gómez Alcántara, 24, farm worker, Castro del Rio
Alfonso Gómez Gutiérrez, 20, farm worker, Castro del Rio
Francisco Sánchez Mellado, 21, farm worker, Castro del Rio
Manuel Alejandre González, 34, labrador, Fuenteobejuna
Rafael Franco Anguita, 27, manual labourer, Palma del Rio
Manuel Ocón Fleitas, 31, farm worker, Adamuz
Antonio José Calero Tirado, 37, manual labourer, Pedroche

19 May at 5 a.m. (4)
Bernardo Rojas Navarro, 38, manual labourer, Hinojosa del Duque
Miguel Pérez Muñoz, 30, El Carpio
Antonio Castellano Guerrero, 29, manual labourer, Belalcázar
Diego Ruiz Medina, 24, manual labourer, Belalcázar

3 June (28)
San Rafael cemetery
Eduardo Bujalance López, 33, manual labourer, Hornachuelos[xvii]

[xvi] Attempted suicide in prison by cutting his wrists, because of the torture he had suffered. He was cured until he was well enough to be shot.

[xvii] Brother of Antonio Bujalance López, Frente Popular Member of Parliament, assassinated in Cordoba the first days of the coup. This was one of the most eminent Socialist families in Hornachuelos, all of the members of which were blacklisted for extermination, regardless of whether they were guilty of any crimes or not, as was Eduardo's case.

Pedro Torralbo Gómez – *Cuadrado,* 41, teacher, Villanueva de Cordoba[xviii]
Avelino Nevado Asencio, 23, cattle breeder, Villanueva de Cordoba
José Sánchez Torralbo, 39, manual labourer, Villanueva de Cordoba
Juan A Casado Muñoz <<El Ramo>>, 56, manual labourer, Villanueva de Cordoba
Francisco López Cejudo, 55, manual labourer, Villanueva de Cordoba
Gaspar Coleto Cabezas, 44, manual labourer, Villanueva de Cordoba
Alfonso Bujalance Gallego, 33, manual labourer, Villanueva de Cordoba[xix]
Ramón Javega Pozo, 40, manual labourer, Villanueva de Cordoba
Manuel Orellana Gómez, 28, cattle breeder, Villanueva de Cordoba
Francisco Illescas Palomo, 45, manual labourer, Villanueva de Cordoba[xx]
Bartolomé Viveros Torralbo, 29, farmer, Villanueva de Cordoba
Rafael Diéguez Montes, 32, mechanic, Cordoba
José Alvarado Borrull, 38, railway worker, Cordoba
Manuel Herrero Huertos, 31, manual labourer, Posadas
Antonio Luján Valenzuela, 29, manual labourer, Posadas
Francisco Villafranca Muñoz, 36, chauffeur, Bujalance
Juan Díaz Borrego, 50, farm manual labourer, Valenzuela
Juan Rodríguez Cobijar, 35, farm worker, Valenzuela
Pablo González Robles, 30, farm worker, Villanueva de la Serena
Lorenzo Márquez Quintero, 43, manual labourer, Castro del Río
Leonardo Ramos Perales, 34, manual labourer, Puente Genil
Francisco Pérez Cabello, 30, farmer, Puente Genil
Juán M. Cabrera de la Torre, 49, manual labourer, Montoro
Manuel Madueño Navarro, 29, bricklayer, Montoro
Ángel Trujillo Medina, 48, manual labourer, Villanueva del Duque
Miguel Domínguez Flores, 33, manual labourer, Palma del Río
Lucas Fortado Cañete, 39, chauffeur, El Pedroso (Sevilla)

9 June at 5 a.m. (9)
Blas Gajete López, 26, schoolmaster, Villafranca
Manuel Bonilla Castillo, 25, farm worker, Baena
Mariano Alcaide Aguilar, 23, bricklayer, La Carlota
Antonio Fernández Cruz, 29, farm worker, Torredonjimeno (Jaén)
Santiago Ramos Bazán, 27, mechanic, Villa del Río

[xviii] Leading member and founder of the PCE in Villanueva de Cordoba in 1921. Alderman 1931. Provincial Member of Parliament 1936. Served as Captain in the Garcés Battalion during the war.
[xix] Served as Major in the Republican army.
[xx] One of the great martyrs of Fascism in Villanueva, cruelly tortured in prison where a guard tore an ear off with his teeth. His wife and three sons died in 1939 and after his death, only one member of the family, a son named Francisco, survived.

Rafael Rojas Navarro, 35, farm worker, Pedro Abad
Francisco Olanda Garrido, 28, barber, Pedro Abad
Francisco Delgado Fernández, 22, baker, Montoro
Joaquín Antequera Gámiz, 22, farmer, Palenciana, near Pedro Abad

28 June at 5 a.m. (9)
San Rafael cemetery
Manuel Valle Expósito, 46, manual labourer, Montoro
Gumersindo Loro Expósito, 37, miner, Pueblonuevo
Nicolás D. Marchante Luengo, 37, miner, Pueblonuevo
Francisco Moya Gómez, 55, manual labourer, Pedroche
Teófilo Sánchez Delgado, 28, manual labourer, La Parrilla (Cordoba)
Ricardo Gómez Rivera, 30, miner, Villanueva del Duque
Manuel Gómez Ruiz, 43, manual labourer, Villaralto
José Caballero Expóito, 39, miner, Belmez
Carlos García Herrador, 28, fishmonger, Montilla

12 July at 5 a.m. (3)
Andrés González Cano, 52, manual labourer, Villanueva de Cordoba
Diego Garcia Castellón, 46, contractor, Villaviciosa
Antonio Jiménez Rojano, 45, farm worker, Aguilar

15 July at 5 a.m. (15)
San Rafael cemetery
Gumersindo Pérez Capitán, 25, farmer, Villanueva de Cordoba
Alfonso Ruiz Piedrahita, 33, stonecutter, El Viso
Juan Garcia Arriaza, 24, manual labourer, Fuente Carretero
Francisco Pedregosa Velasco, 39, farm worker, Valenzuela
Eduardo Murillo Murillo, 29, farm worker, Villanueva del Rey
Andrés Márquez Sillero, 26, farm worker, Villanueva del Rey
Sebastián Cantador Redondo, 39, farm worker, Adamuz
Rafael Pozo Marin, 33, manual labourer, Adamuz
Eulogio Carracedo Culebra, 23, farm worker, Obejo
Francisco Doncel Navajas, 35, farm worker, Castro del Rio
Alfonso Castilla Jiménez, 57, manual labourer, El Carpio
Emilio Garcia Lara, 37, shearer, Villa del Rio
Domingo Gil Izquierdo, 30, bricklayer, Villa del Rio
Benito Cantarero Ramirez, 39, boiler maker, Villa del Rio

8 August at 5 a.m. (2)
Pedro Robero Benitez, 60, manual labourer, Bujalance
Manuel Elias Sánchez, 24, manual labourer, Castro del Rio

20 August at 5:30 a.m. (8)
San Rafael cemetery

Rafael Deza Montero, 44, farmer, Puente Genil[xxi]
Benito Ceballos León, 24, manual labourer, Adamuz
Francisco Jiménez Amil, 59, farm worker, Adamuz
Francisco Garcia González, 22, potter, Hinojosa del Duque
Manuel Aljarilla Montilla, 24, farm worker, Valenzuela
Fidelio Gálvez Sánchez, 48, railway worker, El Hoyo (Belmez)
Antonio Morilla Torres, 45, manual labourer, Montoro
Antonio Zafra González, 40, farm worker, Villanueva del Rey

23 August at 5:30 a.m. (2)
Nicolás Sánchez Ramirez, 28, La Parrilla (Cordoba)
Antonio Acosta Navarrete, 25, La Rambla

25 August at 5 a.m. (4)
San Rafael cemetery
Manuel Lora Tejada, 26, cattle breeder, Pueblonuevo
Juan Blanco Luna, 33, farmer, Villaralto
Alfonso Ruiz Cachinero, 47, farm worker, Cardeña
José Rodriguez Rodriguez, 41, farm worker, Castro del Rio

30 August at 5:30 a.m. (4)
Martin Redondo Torralbo, 37, manual labourer, Villanueva de Cordoba
Antonio Risquez Medina, 27, farm worker, Añora
Juan José Castillo López, 49, farm worker, Valenzuela
José González Rodriguez, 22, manual labourer, Almodóvar del Río

12 September (11)
San Rafael cemetery
Juan Cantador Zamora, 50, manual labourer, Villanueva de Cordoba
Juan Lorenzo Cantador – *Cucharas,* 30, manual labourer, Villanueva de Cordoba
Francisco Muñoz Cabezas, 32, manual labourer, Villanueva de Cordoba
Juan Santofimia Muñoz, 70, Villanueva de Cordoba
Miguel Campos Toledo, 30, fromTorrecampo, resident Villanueva de Cordoba
Faustino García Calero – *El Peno,* 36, manual labourer, Pozoblanco[xxii]
Antonio Merino Guerrero, 44, from Valverde, resident Pozoblanco
Antonio Balbino Culebra, 27, Alcaracejos
Juan Sánchez Culebra, 28, Alcaracejos
Emiliano Ayala Navarrete, 28 Alcaracejos

[xxi] The Deza Montero family, socialists, were another of the most martyred families in Puente Genil. Three brothers were executed by Francoists: Justo, Marcos and Rafael.
[xxii] Served as Lieutenant in the Republican army.

Sergio Fernández Tenor, 30, Dos Torres

<u>29 September at 6 a.m.</u> (3)
San Rafael cemetery
    José Palomo Huertas, 59, farmer, Villanueva de Cordoba[xxiii]
    Juan Flores López, 51, businessman, Espiel
    Manuel López Toro, 39, farm worker, Bujalance

<u>11 October at 6:30 a.m.</u> (7)
San Rafael cemetery
    Antonio Machuca Molina, 46, Luque
    Pedro Ramos Navarro, 47, farmer, Hinojosa del Duque
    José Monje Tejero, 30, farm worker, Belalcázar
    Luis Martínez González, 26, manual labourer, Posadas
    Nicomedes de la Fuente Lanza, 22, farm worker, Villaviciosa
    Miguel Amor Jordán, 39, manual labourer, Adamuz
    Tomás Cuadrado Ruiz, 61, farm worker, Adamuz

<u>25 October</u> (2)
San Rafael cemetery
    Juan Fernández Utrero, 43, manual labourer, Badajoz
    Francisco Fernández Calderón, 35, manual labourer, Belalcázar

<u>6 November at 7 a.m.</u> (8)
San Rafael cemetery
    Juan Escoriza Segura, 44, manual labourer, Villanueva de Cordoba
    José Capitán Pozuelo, 47, manual labourer, Villanueva de Cordoba
    Juan Francisco Chuán Soto, 38, manual labourer, Villanueva de Cordoba
    Francisco Pamo Susin, 26, manual labourer, Valenzuela
    Leandro Benavente Murillo, 24, manual labourer, Villanueva del Rey
    José Domenech Martínez, 49, manual labourer, Montoro
    Francisco López Sánchez, 25, shoemaker, Alcaracejos
    Alfonso Castro Cruz, 37, manual labourer, Dos Torres

<u>17 November at 7 a.m.</u> (3)
San Rafael cemetery
    Antonio Baena Moreno, 37, schoolmaster, Pozoblanco[xxiv]

[xxiii] Together with his wife, Francisca Gómez Cuevas, leading Communist in Villanueva. The Palomo family was one of those blacklisted for elimination. His brother José Antonio was killed under the Law of Fugitives 8 June 1948 because he was listening to a clandestine radio station.

[xxiv] One of the most peaceful people who avoided strife at all costs, even acting in favour of right-wingers. He had three strikes against him: he was one of the most influential Socialists in Pozoblanco, he had chaired the War Committee and had served as a political

Jerónimo Jurado Carrillo, 28, electrician, Pozoblanco
Andrés Márquez Tamajón, 47, farm worker, Castro del Río

24 November at 7:15 a.m. (1)
San Rafael cemetery
José Cabello Béjar, 49, carpinter, Adamuz
25 November at 7 a.m. (1)
San Rafael cemetery
Miguel Lindo Serrano, 31, manual labourer, Adamuz[xxv]

10 December at 7:30 a.m. (10)
San Rafael cemetery
Luis Romero García, 29, farmer, Posadas
Manuel Martín Bovi, 35, manual labourer, Posadas
Miguel Fernández Navea, 25, peasant, Villa del Río
Juan Cívico Rincón, 47, peasant, Castro del Río
Fernando Sánchez Medina, 26, farm worker, Castro del Río
José Delgado Medina, 26, manual labourer, Villa del Río
Antonio Prieto Asensio, 27, metalúrgico, Villa del Río
Julián Claudio Carrillo, 35, farm worker, Pedroche
Francisco Carrillo Cobos, 39, farm worker, Pedroche
Juan Castilla Rivera, 26, farm worker, Pedro Abad

20 December at 7:30 a.m. (6)
San Rafael cemetery
Manuel Gómez Maratín, 42, manual labourer, Villaralto
Manuel Villegas Gómez, 29, manual labourer, Villaralto
Pedro Ranchal Alcaide, 28, manual labourer, Torrecampo
José Expósito Flores, 28, manual labourer, Obejo
Antonio Olmedo Molina, 30, manual labourer, Luque
Manuel Cepas Piedra, 40, manual labourer, Bujalance

1942

10 January at 7:30 a.m. (9)
San Rafael cemetery
Francisco Rojas Moreno, 24, manual labourer, Villanueva de Cordoba
Antonio Santofimia Ranchal, 23, farm worker, Pozoblanco
Juan Cazorla Muñoz, 30, hairdresser, Dos Torres

---

commisar with the VIII Army Corps and then as Commisar General for the Army of
Andalusia-Extremadura.
[xxv] Belonged to the famous Lindo family of AdaLLmuz, some of whom, Rafael and Diego
Luque Lindo, fled to the hills to fight with the Romera guerrillas, surviving until 1949 in
the surrounding mountains.

Juan Expósito Murillo, 35, farm worker, Hinojosa del Duque
Antonio Romero Alcudia, 30, bricklayer, Torrecampo
Rafael Aragonés Alcaide, 29, hairdresser, La Carlota
José Sabaquebas Martínez, 32, railway worker, Posadas
Manuel Aguilar Arance, 53, cordwainer, Bailén
José Rodríguez Calero, 22, manual labourer, La Granja de Torrehermosa

24 January at 7:30 a.m. (1)
San Rafael cemetery
Juan Valenatín Escribano, 31, manual labourer, Belalcázar

10 February at 7:30 a.m. (2)
San Rafael cemetery
José Gómez Flores, 29, manual labourer, Doña Mencía
Marcos Torres Cabanillas, 40, railway worker, Cabeza del Buey

25 February at 7:30 a.m. (4)
San Rafael cemetery
Bartolomé Martínez Peña, 57, manual labourer, Adamuz
Manuel Fernández Gómez, 54, manual labourer, Villaralto
Francisco José Fernández Ruiz, 37, manual labourer, Villaralto
Juan José López Casado, 43, metal worker, Hornachuelos

10 March at 7 a.m. (2)
San Rafael cemetery
Juan Amor Arvás, 30, manual labourer, Montoro
Joaquín Moreno Muñoz, 43, manual labourer, Baena

24 March at 7 a.m. (1)
San Rafael cemetery
Francisco Molina Toledano, 27, manual labourer, Obejo

9 April at 6:15 a.m. (1)
San Rafael cemetery
Juan Manuel de San Silvestre, 57, manual labourer, Posadas

11 May at 6:30 a.m. (1)
San Rafael cemetery
Antonio Ruiz Bejarano, 32, manual labourer, Pozoblanco

23 May at dawn (3)
San Rafael cemetery
José León Gómez, 45, manual labourer, Villaralto
Juan Liñan Suárez, 42, manual labourer, Adamuz
Manuel Mesa Rodríguez, 36, manual labourer, Montoro

<u>25 June at 6:15 a.m.</u> **(11)**
San Rafael cemetery
    Ambrosio Alcalde Bejarano, 30, manual labourer, Villanueva de Cordoba
    José Márquez Morales, 34, manual labourer, Hinojosa del Duque
    José Luna Aranda, 30, manual labourer, Hinojosa del Duque
    Antonio Pérez Murillo, 33, Hinojosa del Duque
    Alejandro Barbero Capilla, 25, debt collector, Espiel
    Bernabé Nevado Plaza, 46, manual labourer, Adamuz
    Antonio Izquiano Barea, 44, Adamuz
    Gerardo Muñoz Gómez, 31, electrician, Villaralto
    José Girón Villamón, 46, manual labourer, Pedroche
    Francisco Sánchez Castillo, 46, manual labourer, Pedroche
    Juan Ruiz Fernández, 49, Cabezarrubia

<u>3 July at 6:15 a.m.</u> (1)
San Rafael cemetery
    Francisco Rosales Rojano, manual labourer, Baena

<u>8 August at 6 a.m.</u> (7)
San Rafael cemetery
    Pedro Barea Higuera, 39, Villanueva de Cordoba
    Blas Fernández Díaz, 28, Dos Torres
    Juan Gutiérrez Peralvo, 28, Dos Torres
    Dámaso del Rey Cáceres, 38, Villanueva del Duque
    Andrés Lindo Pérez, 35, Adamuz
    Carlos Murillo Copé, 63, Belalcázar
    Juan Fernández Fernández, 33, Alcaracejos

<u>22 September at 6 a.m.</u> (2)
San Rafael cemetery
    Francisco Ceballos Cano, 43, shoemaker, Adamuz
    Agustín Sánchez Sánchez, 37, electriian, Alcaracejos

<u>2 October</u> (2)
    Ramón Lleida Gómez, 45, retired soldier, Valencia
    Manuel Galván Valdivia, 27, draftsman, Málaga

<u>7 November at 7 a.m.</u> (8)
    Rafael Zamorano Pella, 52, peasant, Espejo
    Juan Manuel Cáceres Oliva, 31, shoemaker, Palma del Río
    Saturnino Mulloz Luna, 31, cattle breeder, Villaralto
    Bartolomé Ayllón Quesada, 45, peasant, Adamuz
    Francisco Orgaz Pedregosa, 36, peasant, Adamuz
    José Hidalgo Acedo, 29, manual labourer, Dos Torres

Antonio López Moreno, 30, manual labourer, El Viso
Manuel Navarro Fernández, 41, nurse, Sevilla

9 November at 7 a.m. (1)
Juan Aguilera Ruiz, 40, manual labourer, Iznájar

24 November at 7 a.m. (4)
Bernabé Cano Delgado, 43, chauffeur, Adamuz
Pedro Crespo Alcaide, 36, farmer, Torrecampo

Antonio Montoro Ávila, 23, manual labourer, Montefrío (Granada)
Francisco Montoro Ávila, 26, manual labourer, Montefrío (Granada)

10 December at 7 a.m. (1)
Francisco Amor Cuadrado, 37, peasant, Adamuz

23 December (1)
Antonio Román Villamón, 25, baker, Pedroche

1943

23 January at 7 a.m. (3)
San Rafael cemetery
Rafael Pérez Expósito, 32, manual labourer, Montoro
Luis Lucena Plata, 29, manual labourer, Espejo
José Arévalo Villas, 43, welder, Belmez

10 March at 7 a.m. (3)
Francisco Ruiz Olalla, 38, Montoro
José Rodríguez García, 37, Montoro
Avelino Pedrajas Jaut, 32, Pozoblanco

25 March at 7 a.m. (5)
Juan Sánchez Pozuelo – *El de la Loma*, 27, manual labourer, Villanueva
de Cordoba
Joaquín Albacete Fernández, 29, manual labourer, Adamuz
Gregorio Sánchez Mulloz, 28, manual labourer, Cardella
Manuel Arroyo Rodríguez, 29, manual labourer, Baena
José Cuesta Melero, 28, manual labourer, Linares (Jaén)

9 April at 6:30 a.m. (2)
Feliciano García Castillo, 49, manual labourer, Balalcázar
Ceferino Lamelas Armesto, 44, sharpener, Orense

26 April at 6:30 a.m. (1)
  Agapito Fernández Sánchez, 34, farmer, Villaralto

24 May ata 6:30 a.m. (2)
  Andrés Mulloz Sánchez, 43, Villaralto
  Francisco Valcarreras Cambronero, 27, Pedro Abad

10 June at 6:30 a.m. (1)
  Pedro Marchena Molina, 41, Luque

9 July at 6:30 a.m. (1)
  Leopoldo Mulloz Jurado, 41, Espejo

9 August at 7 a.m. (2)
  Bartolomé Juan Garcia Dueñas, 36, cattle breeder, Pozoblanco
  Juan Zurita Solar, 51, businessman, Montoro

1944

25 January at 7:45 a.m. (2)
  Alfonso Ruiz Diaz, 46, peasant, Montoro
  Francisco Cabezas, 40, farmer, Puente Genil

21 June at 5:45 a.m. (1)
  Antonio José Castillo Benavides, 35, fishmonger, Montoro

19 October at 6:45 a.m. (13)
  Manuel Álvarez Agudo, 20, bank employee, Madrid
  Juan Vélez López, 32, plumber, Posadas
  Celestino Lara Ruiz, 39, cook, Cazorla (Jaén)
  Francisco Medina Rodriguez, 34, metal worker, Cordoba
  Antonio Fernández Cuenca, 29, tradesman, Brazil
  Alfonso Cerezo Regalón, 40, bricklayer, Adamuz
  Emilio Jiménez Rascón, 20, clerk, Cordoba
  Eusebio Gámez Guzmán, 32, manual labourer, Iznájar
  José Molero Berlanga, 32, telegraph operator, Espiel
  Rafael Medrán Navarrete, 33, miner, Alcaracejos
  Antonio Cobos León, 25, Army corporal, El Carpio
  Pedro Roldán Ortiz, 26, mechanic, Lucena
  Sebastián Caravaca Martinez – *El Niño del Dinero*, 20, peasant,
  Bujalance[xxvi]

[xxvi] Arrested at the end of 1943 when he came down from the mountains where he had been
fighting as one of the Los Jubiles guerrillas, to visit his family in Bujalance. It is not known

9 November at 7:30 a.m. (8)
    Antonio Sánchez Serrano – *El Chepa*, 42, railway worker, Llerena[xxvii]
    Francisco Garcia Rael, 22, manual labourer, Cordoba
    Pedro Gámez Machado, 25, manual labourer, Villa del Rio
    Sebastián Rivera Moyano, 25, manual labourer, Villa del Rio
    Bartolomé Canales González, 24, manual labourer, Villa del Rio
    Enrique Ramos Bazán, 34, bricklayer, Villa del Rio
    Juan Carmona Garcia, 27, manual labourer, Montoro
    Diego Bautista Caparrós, 36, manual labourer, Almeria

30 November at 7:30 a.m. (1)
    Vicente Resina Camino, 36, manual labourer, Montoro

1945

1 February 1945 at 7:30 a.m. (1)
    Justino Dominguez Mellado, 40, farmer, Espejo

21 February 1945 at 7 a.m. (1)
    Bartolomé Jurado Barrera, 39, manual labourer, Adamuz

TOTAL EXECUTED: 584

---

whether he was captured or whether he turned himself in. He was beaten unmercifully to force him to betray his comrades and then shot him.

[xxvii] Another member of the Los Jubiles guerrilla, arrested in September 1940 in Alcaracejos. They waited four years to kill him for some unknown reason.

APPENDIX V

CIVILIANS ASSASSINATED BY THE GUARDIA CIVIL UNDER THE LAW OF FUGITIVES JUST BEFORE & DURING THE 1947-1949 TRIENNIAL OF TERROR

Date	Name & Age	Place of Birth	Where killed
19-7-**1941**	Antonio Pizarro Illescas, 38	Vva. de Córdoba	Torrecampo
19-7-41	Juan Fernández García, 20	Pozoblanco	Espiel
19-7-41	Bernardino Mansilla Villarreal, 39	Pozoblanco	Espiel
19-7-41	Eusebio Vioque Sánchez, 38	Espiel	Espiel
19-7-41	Máximo Peralbo Caballero, 18	Villaralto	Espiel
19-7-41	Teodoro Sánchez Luna, 18, brother ↓	Villaralto	Espiel
19-7-41	Restituto Sánchez Luna, 22, brother↑	Villaralto	Espiel
19-7-41	Manuel Gómez Valverde, 33	Espiel	Espiel
19-7-41	Francisco Marabé Campos, 31	Pueblonuevo	Espiel
19-7-41	Baudilio Muñoz Márquez, 39	Pozoblanco	Espiel
19-7-41	Andrés Espinosa Martínez, 54	Pozoblanco	Espiel
19-7-41	Honorato Sánchez Gómez, 20	Pozoblanco	Espiel
19-7-41	Ángel Egea Risco, 28	Pozoblanco	Espiel
19-7-41	Eladio Rubio González, 27	Espiel	Espiel
19-7-41	Antonio Arévalo Fernández, 53	Pozoblanco	Espiel
19-7-41	Adrián Arévalo Bajo, 20	Pozoblanco	Espiel
27-7-41	Antonio Jurado Muñoz, 59	Dos Torres	Dos Torres
27-7-41	Genaro Cazorla Muñoz, 24	Dos Torres	Dos Torres
30-7-41	Pedro Romero Fernández, 23	Dos Torres	Dos Torres
30-7-41	José Talero Tapia, 60	Dos Torres	Dos Torres
30-7-41	Sebastián Lunar Rubio, 51	Dos Torres	Dos Torres
31-7-41	Florencio Rísquez Andújar, 29	Torrecampo	Torrecampo
31-7-41	Sebastián Pastor Romero, 41	Torrecampo	Torrecampo

1-8-41	José Romero Iglesias, 20	Dos Torres	Dos Torres
2-9-41	Rafael Parra	Córdoba	Vva de Córdoba
22-11-41	Alfonso Alharilla Morales, 19	Bujalance	Bujalance
22-11-41	José Gallardo Gómez, 19	Bujalance	Bujalance
22-11-41	Francisco Nieves Galiano, 18	Bujalance	Bujalance
18-5-**1943**	Andrés Cepas Luna, 45	Vva. de Córdoba	Vva. de Córdoba
3-8-**1946**	Diego García Cachinero, 43, (hung)	Obejo, Vva. Córdoba	La Candelera
26-10-46	Fernando Chacón Benito, 29	Villaviciosa	Villaviciosa
14-11-46	Miguel Esquina Carrión, 69 father↓	Hinojosa El Espartal	Pueblonuevo
14-11-46	Julián Esquina Barbarroja, 42 son↕	Hinojosa	Hinojosa
14-11-46	Andrés Esquina Barbarroja, 29 son↑	Hinojosa	Hinojosa
27-12-46	Manuel Sánchez Noceto, 51 father↓	Fuente Tójar	Fuente Tójar
27-12-46	Francisco Sánchez Moral, 31 son ↑	Fuente Tójar	Fuente Tójar
27-12-46	José Mª Leiva Pimentel, 36	Fuente Tójar	Fuente Tójar
27-12-46	Josefa Briones Molina, 58	Fuente Tójar	Fuente Tójar
1946	Francisco Sáncez López (beaten)	Vva. de Córdoba	Córdoba
18-1-**1947**	Juan J. Ortiz Castillejo, 57	La Cardenchosa	Hornachuelos
18-1-47	Diego Zújar Monterroso, 35	Cañada del Gamo	Hornachuelos
26-3-47	Daniel Gallardo Algaba, 49	Los Pánchez	Fuente Obejuna
26-3-47	Santiago Benavente Pérez, 58	Argallón	Fuente Obejuna
March-47	Ramón Oriego Salamanca	-	Baena
12-4-47	Antonio Capitán Pizarro, 33	Azuel	Cardeña
12-4-47	Antonio Vioque Alcalde, 33	Dos Torres	Cardeña
18-4-47	Miguel Fabios Amor, 19 (beaten)	Pozoblanco	Hospital/ Córdoba
17-6-47	Francisco Perea Gallardo	Fuenteobejuna	Fuenteobejuna
28-7-47	José Mª Jurado Zarnoza, 30	Vva. de Córdoba	Vva. de Córdoba
23-8-47	Pedro Molero Izquierdo, 24	Vva. de Córdoba	Montoro
26-8-47	Rafael Gómez Rivera, 18	Villaharta	Villalharta
25-1-**1948**	Rafael Muñoz Sánchez, 32, brother↓	Navas de Concepción	Km. 14, Navas
25-1-48	Manuel Muñoz Sánchez 34, brother↕	Navas de Concepción	Km. 14, Navas
25-1-48	Santos Modesto Muñoz Sánchez, br↑	Navas de Concepción	Km. 14, Navas

25-1-48	*El Conejo*'s father	-	Espiel
28-1-48	Antonio Caballero Fernández, 68	Villanueva del Rey	Vva. del Rey
8-3-48	Pedro Moya Tejada, 32	Pozoblanco	Pozoblanco
8-3-48	Juan Mejías Cerezo, 50	Adamuz	Pozoblanco
11-3-48	Enrique Muñoz Agudo, 33	Navas de Concepción	Hornachuelos
17-3-48	Antonio Salado Alonso, 39	Hornachuelos	Hornachuelos
27-3-48	Antonio Camacho Invernó, 38	Hornachuelos	Hornachuelos
18-4-48	Juan Ruíz Calero	Pozoblanco	Pozoblanco
18-4-48	Lucas Rodriguez Fernández, 34	Pozoblanco	Pozoblanco
24-4-48	Epifanio Delgado Hidalgo, 27	Obejo	Obejo
12-5-48	Pedro Gómez Jurado, 25	Rute	Hornachuelos
May - 48	Unknown man	Villanueva del Duque	Vva. del Duque
2-6-48	Andrés Cano Ruíz, 40	Villanueva del Rey	Belmez
8-6-48	Manuel Torralbo Cantador, 29	Vva. de Córdoba	Vva. de Córdoba
8-6-48	José A. Palomo Huertas, 48	Vva. de Córdoba	Vva. de Córdoba
8-6-48	Juan Romero Cachinero, 39	Vva. de Córdoba	Vva. de Córdoba
8-6-48	Isidoro Calero Pozo, 45	Vva. de Córdoba	Vva. de Córdoba
8-6-48	Andrés Díaz Gutiérrez, 58	Vva. de Córdoba	Vva. de Córdoba
8-6-48	Catalina Coleto Muñoz, 52	Vva. de Córdoba	Vva. de Córdoba
17-6-48	Juan García Serrano, 26	Vva. de Córdoba	Vva. de Córdoba
17-6-48	Pedro Coleto Días, 45	Vva. de Córdoba	Vva. de Córdoba
17-6-48	Genaro Ruíz Zamora, 27	Vva. de Córdoba	Vva. de Córdoba
5-7-48	Andrés Molero Redondo, 51	Villafranca	Obejo
5-7-48	Francisco Romero Huertas, 46	Vva. de Córdoba	Obejo
7-7-48	Pedro Rojas Serrano, 51	Montoro	Cardeña
8-7-48	Pablo Agenjo Rodríguez	Vva. de Córdoba	Cardeña
4-8-48	Juan Moyano Márquez, 23	Pozoblanco	Pozoblanco
4-8-48	Juan A. Fuentes Cardador, 25	Pozoblanco	Pozoblanco
31-8-48	Felipe González Torrico, 18	Hinojosa	Hinojosa
3-9-48	Antonio Gómez Soto, 43	Albuñán, Granada	Adamuz
3-9-48	Rafael Quesada Carvajal, 35	Villafranca	Adamuz
10-9-48	Amelia Rodríguez Lopez 49 mother↓	Pozoblanco	Pozoblanco
10-9-48	Amelia García Rodríg. 18 daughter↑	Pozoblanco	Pozoblanco
10-9-48	Isabel Tejada López, 60	Pozoblanco	Pozoblanco

10-9-48	Antonio Cabanillas Rodríguez, 34	Pozoblanco	Pozoblanco
12-9-48	Juan Cabello Moreno, 52	Vva. de Córdoba	Conquista
12-9-48	Andrés Gañán Calventos, 30	Conquista	Conquista
13-9-48	Sixto Fernández Gómez, 46	Villaralto/Cardeña	Cardeña
14-9-48	Cipriano Redondo Moreno 63 fath.↓	Obejo	Cardeña
14-9-48	Brígida Muñoz Díaz, 60 mother↕	Obejo	Cardeña
14-9-48	Juan Redondo Muñoz, 27 son↑	Obejo	Cardeña
24-9-48	Bernabé Sánchez Torralbo, 52	Adamuz	Adamuz
25-9-48	Fernando Gallego Pontes, 19	Villanueva del Duque	Vva. del Duque
28-9-48	Pedro Gómez Calero, 36	Vva. de Córdoba	Vva. de Córdoba
28-9-48	Miguel Fabios Dueñas, 59	Pozoblanco	Vva. de Córdoba
29-9-48	Matías Valero Aranda	Hinojosa	Vva. del Rey
29-9-48	Fernando Litón Cano, 54 father↓	Villanueva del Rey	Vva. del Rey
29-9-48	Jacinto Litón Cano, 27 son↑	Villanueva del Rey	Vva. del Rey
17-10-48	Ángel Sojo Llamas, 54	Fuentes de Andalucía	Hornachuelos
17-10-48	Fernando Antínez Bajo, 27	Navas de Concepción	Hornachuelos
26-10-48	Pedro Torrecilla Alias, 46	Adamuz	Adamuz
28-10-48	Pedro Márquez Rodríguez, 41	Pozoblanco	Pozoblanco
28-10-48	Juan Arévalo Calero, 39	Pozoblanco	Pozoblanco
28-10-48	Clemente Márquez Galán, 42	Ciudad Real	Pozoblanco
28-10-48	Manuel Fernández Fernández, 35	Alcaracejos	Pozoblanco
10-11-48	Andrés González Fernández, 62 bro↓	Villafranca	Villafranca
10-11-48	Diego González Fernández, 60 bro↑	Villafranca	Villafranca
11-11-48	Juan A. Redondo Monteagudo, 57	Adamuz	Adamuz
2-12-48	Pedro Herruzo García, 25	Pozoblanco	Pozoblanco
2-12-48	Pedro Caballero Olmo, 38	Añora	Pozoblanco
2-12-48	Antonio Olmo Caballero, 34	Añora	Vva. de Córdoba
2-12-48	Eufrasio Madero Expósito, 38	Vva. de Córdoba	Vva. de Córdoba
7-12-48	Joaquín Heredia Giménez, 39	Vva. de Córdoba	Vva. de Córdoba
7-12-48	Gaspar Martín Valverde, 45	Vva. de Córdoba	Vva. de Córdoba
19-12-48	Rafael Fernández Muñoz, 36	El Guijo	Pedroche
19-12-48	Juan Aperador García, 42	El Guijo	Pedroche

19-12-48	Pedro Castillo Fuente, 65	Pedroche	Pedroche
1948	Joaquim Chamizo Zoilo	Córdoba	Almodóvar
April – 48	Salado Alonso		Montoro*
May – 48	José Sánchez Cambrón	Hinojoja	Hinojosa*
May – 48	Maximiliano Ruíz		Hinojosa*
June – 48	Manuel Gutiérrez		Rute*
June – 48	Antonio Roldán		Cabra*
Sept. – 48	Francisco Revilla Martín		Montilla*
Undated	So-called Baltasar		Villaviciosa§
Undated	Enrique de la Fuente Arribas		Villaviciosa§
12-2-1949	Francisco Moreno Castro, 43	Hornachuelos	Hornachuelos
26-2-49	Manuel Zurita Cuadrado, 62	Fuenteobejuna	Fuenteobejuna
27-2-49	Higinio Diéguez García 43 brother↓	Fuenteobejuna	Belmez
27-2-49	José Diéguez García, 26 husband↕	Castillo Guardas	Belmez
27-2-49	Teresa Molina Sánchez, 26 wife↑	Espiel	Belmez
27-2-49	Antonio Medina Moreno, 59	Belalcázar	Belmez
5-3-49	Féliz Rubio Rojano, 46 cousin↓	Obejo	Hornachuelos
5-3-49	Rafael Santacruz Rojano 42 cousin↑	Obejo	Hornachuelos
6-4-49	Francisco Guijo Redondo, 22	Pozoblanco	Pozoblanco
10-4-49	Amador Cabanillas Castillejo, 69	Hornachuelos	Villaviciosa
12-4-49	Diego García Vázquez, 25	Fuenteobejuna	Villaviciosa
12-4-49	Juan Calero de los Ríos, 40	Villaviciosa	Villaviciosa
12-4-49	Rafael Ruíz Tirado, 38	Vva. del Rey	Vva. del Rey
17-7-49	Manuel Vigara Regidor (tortured)	Belalcázar	Belalcázar
27-7-49	Antonio Muñoz Fernández, 38	Vva. del Rey	Vva. del Rey
27-7-49	Pedro Manuel Cano Ruíz, 44	Vva. del Rey	Vva. del Rey
27-7-49	Antonio Sánchez Jódar, 46	Vva. del Rey	Vva. del Rey
10-9-49	Francisco Cebrián Fernández, 43	Adamuz	Adamuz
17-9-49	Rafael Rodríguez Carmona	Villafranca	Villafranca
27-9-49	Pedro Gómez Caro, 32	Valsequillo	Los Blázquez
27-9-49	Juan Menjíbar Murillo, 64	Castuera	Los Blázquez
27-9-49	Leoncio Rubio Sánchez, 54	Hinojosa	Los Blázquez
27-9-49	Lorenzo Gutiérrez Pérez, 23	Hinojosa	Los Blázquez
21-10-49	Isidoro Rodríguez Rubio, 29	Pozoblanaco	Pozoblanco
13-1-**1950**	Miguel Lira Cano, 48	Granja de T.	Belalcázar

13-1-50	Ángel Paredes Mansilla, 23	Belalcázar	Belalcázar
13-1-50	Pedro Benítez Medina, 27	Belalcázar	Belalcázar
27-6-50	Diego Porras Piedra, 39	Rute	Rute
27-6-50	Gumersindo Bueno Reina, 44	Rute	Rute

TOTAL civilians executed: 160

- incomplete information from official records
§ information from oral sources

Vva. stands for Villanueva, i.e., Villanueva de Córdoba

Missing from the above, Antonio Vargas Montes, born in Seville, a member of the Regional Committee of the PCE, murdered by the Guardia Civil in Belmez and buried in the local mass grave. Source: an email to Moreno Gómez from Francisco Espinosa, with the deceased's widow, María Luísa, testimony, dated 24-2-2007.

SOURCES CONSULTED – All volumes

Newspapers

ABC, Córdoba
ABC, Seville
Amanecer, Zaragoza
Córdoba, Córdoba
Diário Azul, Córdoba. Founded in 1936 as the official organ of the FET-JONS and published until 1941. Predecessor of today's Diário de Córdoba.
El Defensor de Córdoba
Heraldo de Aragón, Zaragoza
Villanueva, Villanueva de Córdoba

Documentaries

Albino Garrido's oral testimony can be heard as part of a 2011 documentary on Spanish TVE2 by Juan Sella and Rafael Robledo, *El pesadillo de Castuera Badajoz* (The nightmare of Castuera Badajoz), which includes multiple visual recordings of unnamed oral testimonies from survivors and relatives of disappeared prisoners at this concentration camp. Uploaded on YouTube 25 January 2014 by CGT Barcelona at: https://youtube/MAtWunQbbQM.

Carolina Gil Fonce. Interview with Judge Baltasar Garzón, 12 May 2008, on Radio Argentina. Can be downloaded at http://www.informam.nl.

Guerra de Gila. Caustic monologue by the comedian Miguel Gila Cuestas, where a soldier appears to have a phone conversation with 'the enemy'. *Is that the enemy speaking?* 2014. YouTube 17/08/2009. Available at: *https://www.youtube.com/watch?v=R7d4Aj4tFA4*.

Josu Martinez and Txsaber Larreategi, ETB. *Prohibido recordar* (Forbidden to Remember). Basque television documentary, Tentazioa Rec, 2010.

Juan Caunedo Domínguez. *Sombra, niebla y tiempo* (Shadow, fog and time). Free-lance producer. Documentary for the Madrid Forum for Memory.

Mariano Agudo Y Eduardo Montero. Directors. *Presos del Silencio* (Prisoners of Silence). Documentary produced by La Zanfoña Producciones, Canal Sur T.V. March 2009. Uploaded by Intermedia productions at: http://www.kaosenlared.net/noticia/presos-silencio-documental-fortaleza-historica

Marisa Paredes and José Luis Peñafuerte. *Los caminos de la memoria.* (The paths of memory). Documentary 2009. Available on the Internet at: http://cinepeliculasflv.com/21524-los-caminos-de-la-memoria-online-peliculas-gratis-hd-espanol.html.

Martin Jönsson and Carl Pontus Hjorthén. Documentary. *Maria Carmen España – The end of Silence.* 2011 Swedish TV Broadcast. Available on the Internet at: https://www.youtube.com/watch?v=wmlgo8uSXcg.

Montse Armengou & Ricard Belis. *Los niños perdidos del Francoism* (Franco's forgotten children]. Award-winning television documentary, Televisó de Catalunya, Barcelona, 2002.

Patxi Eguilaz. Documentary. *Desafectos. Esclavos de Franco en el Pirineo* (The disaffected. Slaves to Franco in the Pyrenees). Regarding a Workers' Battalion in El Roncal-Salazar, employed in the building of a road between these two towns, 1939-1941. Un-named survivors' oral testimonies. 2007. Uploaded to YouTube at: https://www.youtube.com/watch?v=OH89dek8hPk

Patxi Eguilaz. Documentary. *Nos quitaron todo* (They took everything from us). Produced and directed by Patxi Eguilaz, 85 min., Creative Commons, 2011. Distributed by Eguzki at Bideoak.geronimouztariz.com. Produced in collaboration with Professors César Laiana, Mirta Núñez, Emilio Majuelo, Miguel A. Rodriguez Arias, and José Miguel Gastón.

Guillermo Carnero Rosell and Carlos Ceacero, Producers and Directors. Documentary: *Una inmensa prisión. Imágines contra el olvido* (An immense prison. Images against oblivion). Sub-titled in English. By Impulso Records, 2005. Recording available to download from the Internet at: https://vimeo.com/111282336.

The Internationale. Hymn of the International Communist Party. Listen to in English with subtitles at: https://www.youtube.com/watch?v=3sh4kz_zhyo.

Calculation of the relative worth of 1939 peseta values vs. 2017 US dollars

The relative worth in 2017 US dollars for the peseta values given in the book were converted at the rate of USD 1$= 9.41 PTA in 1939. (In 1940, the relative worth of the peseta was 1.16, as compared to 1939.) Websites consulted: https://www.measuringworth.com/calculators/spaincompare/relativevalue.php
https://www.dollartimes.com/inflation/inflation.php?amount=1&year=1939.

BIBLIOGRAPHY - All volumes

Adriano Romero. *Eurocarrillismo y oportunismo* (Eurocarrillism and opportunism). Bilbao, 1984.

Alberto Reig Tapia. *Ideología e historia. Sobre la represión franquista y la guerra civil* (Ideology and history. The Francoist repression and the civil war). Madrid, Akal, 1984.

Albino Garrido. *Une longue marche. De la répression franquiste aux champs français* (A long march. From the Francoist repression to the French camps). Translated into French by his son Luís Garrido (France, Privat, 2011) and later published in the original Spanish, Lleida, Milenio, 2013.

Alfonso Yuste Álvarez. *84 años contradictorios* (84 contradictory years). Fernán Núñez, Ayuntamiento, 1989.

Ana Marcos. *El País Semanal*, Madrid, 19 February 1984.

Ana Messuti. *La querella argentina: La aplicación del principio de justicia universal al caso de las desapariciones forzadas.* (The Agentinian lawsuit: The application of the principle of universal justice to the case of the forced disappearances.). In Rafael Escudero Alday and Carmen Pérez González *Desapariciones forzadas, represión política y crímenes del franquiso* (Forced disappearances, political repression and crimes of Francoism.) Madrid, Trotta, 2013.

Ana Tudela. "Hambre, cartilla y estraperlo: España no come escrúpulos" (Hunger, ration cards and black market: Spain does not eat scruples). Article published on the Internet at www.Publico.es 2 April 2009.

Ángel B. Sanz. *De Re Penitenciaria (*prologue by Eduardo Aunós). Talleres Peniten-ciarios de Alcalá de Henares, Madrid, 1945, p. 181. Data reproduced by Halliday Sutherland, *Spanish Journey*, Hollis and Carter, London, 1948.

Ángel David Martín Rubio. *Paz, piedad, perdón... y verdad.* (Peace, piety, forgiveness... and the truth). Madrid, Fénix, 1997.

Ángel del Río et al. *Andaluces en los campos de Mauthausen* (Andalusians in the Mauthausen camps). Junta de Andalucia, 2006.

Ángel Hernández Sobrino. <<La joven Manuela>> ("Young Manuela"). Article kindly given to Moreno Gómez by the author, April 2013.

Ángel Suárez /Collective 36, *Libro blanco sobre las cárceles franquistas* (White paper on Francoist prisons). Planeta, Barcelona, 2012. (1st Edition, Ruedo Ibérico, 1976).

Ángel Viñas. *En el combate por la historia* (In the fight for History). Barcelona, Pasado & Presente, 2012.

Ángela Cenarro Lagunas. "Historia y memoria del Auxilio Social de la Falange" (History and memory of the Falangista Social Welfare Program.). In *Pliegos de Yuste,* numbers 11-12, 2010.

_____ "La institucionalización del universo penitenciario franquista" (The institution-ization of the Francoist prison universe), in *Una inmensa prisión* (An immense prison), Barcelona, Crítica, 2003.

Antonia González & Pablo Ortiz Romero. *Memoria y testimonio del campo de concentración de Castuera* (Memory and witness account of Castuera concentration camp). Minutes of the Congress on concentration camps and the world of the penitentiary in Spain during the civil war and under Francoism.

Antonio Bahamonde. *Un año com Queipo de Llano. (Memorias de un Nacionalista)* [A year with Queipo de Llano. (Memoires of a Nationalist). Espuela de Plata, Sevilla, 2005.

Antonio Barragán Moriana. *Control social y responsabilidades políticas. Córdoba (1936-1945)* (Social control and political responsibilities. Córdoba (1936-1945). Córdoba, El Páramo, 2009.

Antonio D. López Rodríguez. *Cruz, bandera y Caudillo. El campo de concentraión de Castuera* (Cross, flag and Caudillo. Castuera concentration camp). Badajoz, Ceder-La Serenam, 2006.

Antonio Elorza. "Genocides". In *Hispania Nova* (Online Contemporary History Magazine in Spanish) at http://e-revistas.uc3m.es/index.php/HISPNOV/index. Number 10, 2012..

Antonio Jaén Morente. *Estampas da Guerra.* [Sketches of the War]. Valencia, Izquierda Republicana, 1938. Moreno Gómez and Gorrell Jaén family archives.

Antonio Miguel Bernal, José Luis Gutiérrez Molina, Fernando Romero and Cecilio Gordillo et al.. *Proyecto Rapina* (Robbery Project). Seville, 23 January 2011. Investigation project created in Seville by the Recovery of the Historic Memory of Andalusia Group, with a view to studying the thefts, confiscations and seizures by Francoists beginning 18 July 1936.

Antonio Muñoz Molina. "Guerreros deseanados" (Apathetic Warriors). *El País. Cultura. 13* October 2012.

Arcángel Bedmar Gonzálves. *Los puños y las pistolas. La repressión en Montilla (1936-1939)* (Fists and revolvers. The repression in Montilla (1936-1939). Córdoba, Ed. Lucena, 2009.

_____ *La campiña roja. La repressión franquista en Fernán Núñez (1936-1943)* (The Red countryside. The Francoist repression in Fernán Nuñez). Lucena, Córdoba, Librería Juan de Mairena, 2003.

_____ *República, guerra y repressión. Lucena 1931-1939* (Republic, war and repression. Lucena 1931-1939). Lucena City Council, 2010. Revised edition.

_____ *Desaparecidos. La repressió franquista en Rute (1936-1950)* (The disappeared. The Francoist repression in Rute (1936-1950). Lucena, Córdoba, Rute City Council, 2004, Vol. 2.

_____ *Baena, roja y negra. Guerra civil y repressión (1936-1943)* (Baena, red and black. Civil war and repression). Lucena, Córdoba, Juan de Mairena, 2008. Revised edition 2013.

_____ *La Luz Sepultada* (The buried Light). Minutes of the I Congress on Historic Memory, Aguilar de la Frontera, 27 September-7 October, 2006.

_____ "El nacionalcatolicismo en Montilla y Lucena durante la guerra civil" (Nationalcatholicism in Montilla and Lucena during the civil war). In *La Luz Sepultada*, Aguilar de la Frontera, Sept.-Oct., 2006.

Archives of Territorial Military Court I, Military Government, Madrid. Case No. 128.712.

Arthur Koestler. *Diálogo con la muerte (Um testament español)* (Dialogue with death. A Spanish testimony.) Madrid, Amaranto, 2004.

Augustina Merino Tena. "La represión franquista en Villanueva de la Serena (Badajoz)". (The Francoist repression in Villanueva de la Serena – Badajoz). In *Memoria Antifranquista del Baix Llobregat. El genocidio franquista en Extremadura.*, number 12, 2012.

Baltasar Garzón and Vicente Romero. *El alma de los verdugos* [The soul of the executioners.], Barcelona, RBA, 2008.

Belalcázar Municipal Archives. Multiple documents.

Board of Trustees of the Reduction of Sentences through Work. *Memoria que eleva al Caudillo de España y a su Gobierno el Patronato de Redención de Penas por el Trabajo, de 1943* (Report from the Board of Trustees of the Reduction of Sentences through Work for 1943, to the Caudillo of Spain and his Government). Madrid, 1944.

Bulletí Oficial del Parlament de Catalunya - B.O.P.C. (Official Bulletin of the Parliament of Catalonia). 23 January 1940, reproducing the *Boletim Oficial del Estado* of 13 January, Year V, number 13.

Carlos Fonseca. *Trece Rosas Rojas* (Thirteen Roja Roses). Temas de Hoy, Mardid, 2005.

Carlos Jiménez Villarejo and Antonio Doñate Martín. *Jueces, pero parciales. La pervivencia del franquismo en el poder judicial.* (Judges, but partly so. The survival of Francoism in the judiciary.) Barcelona, Pasado & Presente, 2012.

Carmen Flórez Pérez, letter to Moreno Gómez denying him access to the Red Cross archives, 13 November 2013.

Causa General Archives, Spanish National Archives. Consulted on the Internet at: www.pares.mcu.org.

Casimiro Jabonero. *Diário del soldado republicano Casimiro Jabonero. Campo de prisioneros de Lavacolla. Prisión de Santiago de Compostela, 1939-1940* (Diary of Casimiro Jabonero, a Republican soldier. Lavacolla concentration camp. Santiago de Compostela Prison - *1939-1940*, Ed. Víctor Manuel Santidrián Arias, Ayuntamiento, Santiago de Compostela, 2004.

Charter of the International Military Tribunal. Article 6. "Crimes Against Humanity". Nuremberg Trial Procedings. Volume 1. Yale Law School. Downloaded from http://avalon.law.yale.edu/imt/imtconst.asp.

Corporal José Pérez Navarrete. *Diário de la guerra* (War Diary) dated 30 November 1939, Pozoblanco, unpublished.

Constanza de la Mora Maura, *Doble splendor* (Double splendor). Gadir, Madrid, 2004.

Crónica del Patronato Nacional de San Pablo (Chronicles of the National Council of Saint Paul). Ministry of Justice, Madrid, 1951, 379 pp.

Daily Operations Report of the Army of the South. (*Diario de Operaciones del Ejérito del Sur.) Partes oficiales de Guerra, 1936-1939*, Vol. I, Ejército Nacional (Official War Reports, 1936-1939, Vol. I, Spanish Army). Serviço Histórico Militar, Madrid, 1978. [2 Volumesl

Daniel Sueiro and Bernardo Días Nosty. *Historia del franquismo* (The history of Francoism). Madrid, Sedmay Ediciones, 1977.

Diego San José de la Torre, *De cárcel en cárcel* (From jail to jail). Do Castro, La Coruña, 1988.

Diógenes Cabrera. *Once cárceles y un destierro* (Eleven jails and one exile), Santa Cruz de Tenerife, 1980.

Domingo Rodriguez Teijeiro. "Excarcelación, libertad condicional e instrumentos de control poscarcelario en la inmediata posguerra (1939-1945)" (Prison release, conditional freedom and post-penal control in the immediate post-war period (1939-1945). University of Vigo. (No further source details known).

Eduardo Blanco Fernández. Unpublished private archives. Madrid.

Eduardo de Guzmán. *Sócrates Gómez, de la derrota a la represión.* (Sócrates Gómez, from the defeat to the *repression.*). *Tiempo de Historia,* number 62, January 1980.

Eric Hobsbawn. *Interesting Times: A Twentieth-Century life.* Spanish translation. Barcelona, Critica, 2002.

Ernesto Caballero Castillo. *Vivir con memoria.* (Living with memory). Córdoba, El Páramo, 2001.

Esteban Ibarra. *Xenophobia in time of crisis.* Madrid, 24 March 2011. Posted online by cristobalgomez at: https://movementagainstintolerance. wordpress.com/.

Eutimio Martin Garcia. *"El turismo penitenciario franquista"* (Franco Penitentiary Tourism), in *Historia 16,* number 239, 1996.

Fernando Mendiola Gonzalo and Edurne Beaumont Esandi (Associación Memoriaren Bideak). "Batallones Disciplinarios de Soldados Trabajadoares. Castigo político, trabajos forzados y cautividad" (Disciplinary Battalions of Soldier Workers. Political punishment, forced labour and captivity). In *Revista de Historia Actual,* number 2, 2004, and the documentary *Desafectos, Esclavos de Franco en el Pirineo* (Disaffected, Slaves of Franco in the Pyrenees), 2007.

Francisco Merino Cañasveras, *Castro del Río, del rojo al negro* (Castro del Río, from the red to the black). Terrassa, Barcelona, 1979.

Franciso Moreno Gómez. *Córdoba en la posguerra (La represión y la guerilla, 1939-1950)* (Post-war Córdoba. Repression and the guerilla, 1930-1950). Córdoba, F. Baena, 1987.

_____ *La Guerra Civil en Córdoba 1936-1939.* (The Civil War in Córdoba 1936-1939). Córdoba, 1985.

_____ *1936: El genocidio franquista en Córdoba. (1936:* The Francoist genocide in Córdoba.) Barcelona, Crítica, 2008.

_____ *La resistencia armada contra Franco* (Armed resistance against Franco). Barcelona, Crítica, 2001.

_____ *Victimas de la guerra civil* (Victims of the civil war). Madrid. Temas de Hoy, 1999.

_____ "Biography of Captain Blanco Pedraza". Villanueva de Córdoba, *Villanueva,* number 17, September 1981.

_____ with Juan Ortiz Villalba. *La masonería en Córdoba* (Freemasonry in Córdoba). Córdoba, F. Baena, 1985.

Francisco Morente Valero. *La Escuela y el Estado Nuevo. La depuración del Magisterio Nacional (1936 - 1943)* (The School and the New State. The purging of the national teaching professions (1936-1943). Valladolid, Ámbito, 1997.

Francisco Poyatos López. *Recuerdos de un hombre de toga* (Memories of a man who wore a jurist's robes). Córdoba, 1979. Self-published.

Francisco Ruiz Acevedo. *Memòria Antifranquista del Baix Llobregat. El genocidio franquista en Extremadura* (Anti-Francoist Written Report on the Baix Llobregat. The Francoist genocide in Extremadura). Number. 12, 2012.

Fuentes para la Historia de la 2ª República, la Guerra Civil y el Franquismo (Sources for the History of the 2nd Republic, the Civil War and Francoism): at http://fuentesguerracivil.blogspot.com

Gabriel Garcia de Consuegra, "La represión nacionalista en Pozoblanco" (Nationalist repression in Pozoblanco). In *Revista de Feria,* Pozoblanco, September 1985.

_____ with Angel and Fernando López López. *La repressión en Pozoblanco (guerra civil y posguerra)* (The repression in Pozoblanco. Civil war and post-war.). Córdoba, F. Baena, 1989.

Garcia de Consuegra. "The Nationalist repession in Pozoblanco" – Excerpt from the Diary of Sebastián Blanco Copado. Pozoblanco, *Revista de Feria*, September 1985.

General José Cuesta Moreno, Deputy to General Queipo de Llano in Sevilla. Documents. *Hechos ocurridos en los pueblos de la provincia de Córdoba* (Events in towns and villages of the province of Córdoba). Serviço Histórico Militar, Madrid. Undated

Gonzalo Amoedo López and Roberto Gil Moure. *Episodios del terror durante la guerra civil na provincia de Pontevedra. A illa de San Simón.* (Episodes of the terror during the civil war in the province of Pontevedra. San Simón island). Serais, Vigo, 2007.

Gregory H. Stanton. 1998. *Stop Genocide.* (Yale University Center). Translated by Diana Wang and presented as *Ocho estados de genocidio* (Eight stages of genocide) at the US Department of State, Washington, D.C., 1996.

Gutmaro Gómez Bravo. *"El desarrollo penitenciario en el primer franquismo (1939-1945"* (The penal development during the first period of Francoism (1939-1945). In *Hispania Nova*, number 6, 2006.

_____ I Congress of Victims of Francoism, Rivas Maciamadrid, Madrid, April 2012.

Hartmut Heine. *La oposición política al franquismo* (Political opposition to Francoism). Grijalbo, Barcelona, 1983.

Herbert R. Southworth. *Myth of Franco's Crusade.* Translated into Spanish and French. Paris, France, Ruedo Ibérico, 1963.

Hilari Raguer. *La pólvora y el incienso. La Iglesia y la guerra civil española (1936-1939),* (Gunpowder and Incense. The Church and the Spanish Civil War (1936-1939). Barcelona, Península, 2001.

Historical Archives of the Army of the Air (AHFA). Ministry of Defence, Madrid. Archive A2035.

International Criminal Court, *Legal Texts and Tools.* Article 7(e). Consulted at:

https://www.icc-cpi.int/NR/rdonlyres/ADD16852-AEE9-4757-ABE79CDC7CF02886/283503/RomeStatutEng1.pdf

Inspección de Campos de Concentración y Prisioneros - ICCP (Concentration Camp and Prisoners Inspectorate), Memorandum, 1937.

Isabel González and Agustina Gonzalez. *A dos voces* (Two voices). Self-published. Córdoba, 2011.

Jacinta Gallardo Moreno. *La guerra civil en La Serena*. (The civil war in La Serena). Badajoz, Diputación Provincial, 1994.

Javier Rodrigo. *Los campos de concentración franquistas, entre la historia y la memoria*. (Francoist concentration camps, history and memories). Madrid, Siete Mares, 2003.

Jerónimo Mansilla Escudero and Luís Miguel Montes Oviedo. *El crimen de El Contadero. Los nueve asesinados de Chillón – 3 de junio de 1939* (The crime of El Contadero. The nine murdered in Chillón – 3 June 1939.) Ciudad Real, 2009.

Jesús Maria Romero Ruiz. *Recuperación de la memoria histórica de La Rambla* (Recovering the historic memory of La Rambla). La Rambla, City Council, 2010.

_____ *Que el 20 de febrero de 1936, cuando los sucesos del jardín* (It happened in the garden 20 February 1936). Ayuntamiento, La Rambla, 2010.

Joan Llarch, *Campos de concentración en la España de Franco* (Concentration camps in Franco's Spain). Barcelona, Producciones Editoriales, 1978.

Joe Monks. *Con los rojos en Andalucía* (With the Reds in Andalucia). Seville, Renacimiento, 2012.

José Ángel Etxaniz Ortlñez and Vicente del Palacio Sánchez, "Dossier. Morir en Gernika-Lumo" (Dossier. Dying in Gernika-Lumo), *Aldaba* magazine, issue 122, April-May 2003.

José Espejo Ruz. *Memoria fértil* (Fertile memory) & Romero Ruiz, Jesús María. *Recuperación de la memoria histórica de La Rambla* (Recovering the historic memory of La Rambla). La Rambla, Córdoba, City Council, 2010.

José Francisco Luque Moreno. *Montemayor, 1900-1945. Cuestión social, República, Guerra y Represión* (Montemayor, 1900-1945. Social Issue, Republic, War and Repression). Córdoba, Provincial Council, 2011.

José López Gavilán, *Aquellos duros tiempos. Anecdotario,* Córdoba, 2004.

José Luis Casas Sánchez. *"La memoria histórica del exilio republicano. El caso del canónigo Gallegos Rocafull"* (The historic memory of the Republican exile. The case of Canon Gallegos Rocafull". In *La Luz Sepultada,* Minutes I Congress on Historic Memory, Aguilar de la Frontera, 2006.

José M. Gallegos Rocafull. *La pequeña grey. Testimonios religiosos sobre la guerra civil española.* (The small congregation. Religious Testimony on the Spanish civil war). Barcelona, Península, 2007.

José Manuel Sabín Rodríguez. *La dictatura franquista (1936-1975). Textos y documentos.* (The Francoist dictatorship (1936-1975). Texts and documents.) Madrid, Akal, 1997.

José María García Marquez and Miguel Guardado Rodríguez. *Morón: Consumatum est. 1936-1953. Historia de un crimen de guerra.* (Morón: 1936-1953. History of a war crime.) Morón de la Frontera, Seville, Planta Baja, 2011.

_____ *Las víctimas de la represión militar en la provincia de Sevilla (1936-1963)* (The victims of the military repression in the province of Seville 1936-1963). Aconcagua, Sevilla.

José María Lama. *Una biografia frente al olvido: José González Barbero, alcalde de Zafra en la II República.* (A forgotten biography: José González Barbero, Mayor of Zafra during the 2nd Republic). Badajoz, Imprenta de la Diputación de Badajoz, 2000.

José Maria Romero Ruiz, *Recuperación de la memoria histórica de* La *Rambla* (Recovering the Historic Memory of La Rambla). Ayuntamiento, La Rambla, Córdoba, 2010.

José Moreno Salazar. *El guerrillero que no pudo bailar - resistencia anarquista en la posguerra andaluza* (The guerrilla who could not dance – post-war anarchist resistance in Andalusia). Silente, Ed. Victoriano Camas, 2004.

Josep M. Solé i Sabaté. *La repressió franquista a Catalunya, 1938-1953.* (The Francoist repression in Catalonia, 1938-1953). Barcelona, Edicions 62, 1985.

José Subirats Piñana. *Pilatos 1939-1941. Prisión de Tarragona* (Pilate 1939-1941. Tarragona Prison). Madrid, Ed. Pablo Iglesias, 1993.

_____ *Entre Vivències* (Memoires). Viena, 2003.

José Torralba Rico. *Vidas secretas. Memòries d'un militant clandestí.* (Memoires of a clandestine militant). Mansesa, Barcelona, Centre d'Estudis del Bages, 2009.

Juan José del Águila Torres. "La jurisdicción militar de guerra en la represión política: Las Comisiones Provinciales (CPEP) y Central de Examen de Penas (CCEP), 1940-1947" (Wartime military jurisdiction and political repression: The provincial committees (CPEP) and the Center for the Examination of Sentences (CCEP). IX Congress of Contemporary History, Murcia, 17-20 September 2008, 27 folios. Guadalajara General Military Archives.

Juan Sánchez Vallejo. *La locura y su memoria histórica.* (Madness and its Historic Memory). Ediciones Atlantis, Madrid, 2013.

Juan Simeón Vidarte, *Todos fuimos culpables.* (We were all guilty). Barcelona, Grijalbo, 1978. Vol. 2.

Juana Doña. *Desde la noche y la niebla (mujeres en las cárceles franquistas)* (From the night and the fog. Women in Franchoist jails)., La Torre, Madrid, 1978.

Julián Casanova. *La Iglesia de Franco* (Franco's Church). Annotated edition, Barcelona, Crítica, 2005.

_____ with Rufino Ayuso Fernández. *Morir, matar, sobrevivir. La violencia en la dictadura de Franco* (Death, killing and survival. Violence during Franco's dictatorship). Barcelona, Crítica, 2002.

Julio González Gil "El último testimonio de Unamuno" (Unamuno's Last Will). Uploaded to Youtube 2 November, 2007.

L. M. Montes Oviedo. "70 años después. Ley de Memoria rcelHistórica" (70 years later. The Historic Memory Law.) *Feria y Fiestas,* Alamdén, 2009.

L. M. Sánchez Tostado. *Historia de las prisiones en la provincia de Jaén. 500 años de confinamiento, presidios, cárceles y mazmorras.*(History of the penitentiaries in the province of Jaén. 500 years of confinements, imprisonments, jails and dungeons). Jaén, 1997.

Luís García Berlanga. *La Vaquilla.* Movie, 1985.

Manuel García Muñoz. *Los fusilamientos de la Almudena.* (The Almudena executions). Madrid, História del Siglo XX, 2012.

Manuel Morente Diaz. *La depuración de la enseñanza pública cordobesa a raíz de la Guerra Civil* (The purging of public education in Córdoba as a result of the Civil War). Córdoba, El Páramo, 2011.

_____ *La mala semilla. Depuración de libros y bibliotecas en Córdoba.* (The bad seed. Purging of books and libraries in Córdoba). Córdoba, ECO magazine, number 8, 22 June 2011.

Manuel Reyes Mate Rupétez, *Memoria de Auschwitz* (Memory of Auschwitz). Trotta, Madrid, 2003.

Manuel Rubio Díaz y Silverio Gómez Zafra, *Almendralejo (1930-1941). Doce años intensos.* (Almendralejo (1930-1941). Twelve intense years.) Los Santos de Maimona, Badajoz, 1987.

Margalida Capellá i Roig. *"Represión política y derecho internacional. Una perspective comparada* (1936-2006)" (Political repression and international law. A comparative approach (1936-2006).) in *La memoria histórica en perspectiva jurídica (1936/2006)* (Historic memory from the legal viewpoint – 1936/2006) by Margalida Capellá and David Ginard, Documenta Balear, Palma de Mallorca, 2009.

Maria Victoria Fernández Luceño and José Maria Garcia Márquez. *Fallecidos en el campo de concentración de Las Arenas (La Algaba, Sevilla),* (Deaths in the Las Arenas, La Algaba, Sevilla, concentration camp). *El Mundo*, Seville, 2013.

Marino Ayerra Redin. *Maldito seais! No me avergoncé del evangelio* (Be damned! I was not ashamed of the Gospel). Buenos Aires, Periplo, 1958.

Matías Romero Badía. *Memorias* (Memories). Madrid, A-Z Ediciones, 1996.

Matilde Eiroa. Article on the commutation of death sentences. *Hispania Nova* online newspaper, number 10, 2012. http://hispanianova.rediris.es/

Martin Torrent. *Que me dice usted de los presos?* (What do you have to say about the prisoners?), Talleres Penitenciarios de Alcalá de Henares, 1942.

Memoria que eleva al Caudillo de España y a su Gobierno el Patronato Central para la Redención de Penas por el Trabajo, de 1943. (Memorandum from the Caudillo of Spain and his Government regarding the National Council for the Redemption of Sentences Through Work., 1943). Madrid.1944.

Michael Ricards. *Un tiempo de silencio. La guerra civil y la cultura de la repressión en la España de Franco, 1936-1945* (A time of silence. The civil war and the culture of repression in Franco's Spain, 1936-1945). Crítica, Barcelona, 1999.

Michel Leiberich. *"El món concentracionari europeu"*. International Congress on Concentration Camps and Penitentiaries in Spain under Franco, Barcelona, October 2002.

Miguel Gila. *Y entonces nací yo. Memorias para desmemoriados.* (And then I was born. Memories for those who have forgotten). Madrid, Temas de Hoy, 1995. In Isáis Lafuente. *Esclavos por la patria. La explotación de los presos bajo el franquismo* (Slaves for the Fatherland. Exploitation of prisoners under Francoism). Madrid, Temas de Hoy, 2002.

Miguel Hernández. *Obra completa. III Prosas. Correspondencia* (Complete work. III Prose. Correspondence). Madrid, Espasa-Calpe, 1992.

_____ *Cartas escritas en la prisión de Orihuela, entre septiembre y octubre de 1939)* Letters written in the Orihuela jail between September and October 1939).

Ministry of Justice. *Breve resumen de la obra del Ministerio de Justicia para la pacificación espiritual de España.* (Brief summary of the work of the Ministry of Justice for the spiritual pacification of Spain). Published in 1946.

Minutes of the *I Jornadas para la Recuperación de la Memoria Histórica* (I Conference on the Recovery of the Historic Memory). Posadas, Ayuntamiento, 2010.

Minutes of the Meeting of the Villanueva de Córdoba City Council, 28 March, 14 July and 19 December 1939.

Mirta Núñez Diaz-Balart et al.. *La gran repressión. Los Años de plomo del franquismo* (The great repression. The sombre years of Francoism). Madrid, Flor del Viento, 2009.

Mónica Orduño Prada. *El Auxilio Social (1936-1940). La etapa fundacional.* (Social Welfare. 1936-1940. The foundation). Madrid, Libreria Libre Editorial, 1996.

National Basque Archives and Sabino Arana Foundation. *Informe sobre presos vascos en el Penal del Puerto de Santa María. (*Report on Basque prisoners in the Puerto Santa Maria penal complex). Manuel Martínez Cuadrado, in *El Penal de El Puerto de Santa María, 1886-1981 (*Puerto Santa María Penitentiaries 1886-1981). Cádiz, 2004.

New Larousse Encyclopedia. In Spanish.. Vol. 8. Barcelona, Plante, 1980.

Óscar Rodríguez Barreira.. *El franquismo desde los márgenes* (Francoism seen from the sidelines). University of Lleida, 2013.

Pablo Uriel. *Mi guerra civil.* (My civil war). Introduction by Ian Gibson. Self-published, Valencia, 1988.

Patricia Campelo. 'Sin muertos, tampoco hay culpable' (If there are no dead, there also are no guilty). In: *Memoria Pública*, Villanueva de Odra,27 March 2012.

Paul Preston. *El gran manipulador. La mentira cotidiana de Franco* (The great manipulator. Franco's daily lies.) Barcelona, Ediciones B., 2008.

Pedro Garfias. *Heróes del Sur* (Heroes of the South). Mexico, 1941.

Pedro Pascual, "Campos de concentración en España" (Concentration camps in Spain). *Historia 16*, Year XXV, number 310, February 2002.

_____ "Campos de concentración en España y Batallones de Trabajadores" (Concentration camps in Spain and Forced Labor Battalions). Minutes of the Congress on Concentration Camps and the Penitentiary World in Spain during the Civil War and Francoism. Barcelona, Crítica, 2003.

Peter Anderson. Conference at the Universidad Complutense of Madrid 11 November 2011. Author of *The Francoist Military Trials. Terror and Complicity, 1939-1945.* Routledge, London, 2009.

Pozoblanco Municipal Archives. Document provided courtesy of Fernando López. 1939.

Rafael Bedmar Guerrero. November 1983. Unpublished memoires. A second version of these: *1936: Memorias de una guerra* (1936: Memories of a war.) was self-published, Córdoba, 2007.

Rafael Escudero Alday and Carmen Pérez González *Desapariciones forzadas, represión política y crímenes del franquiso* (Forced disappearances, political repression and crimes of Francoism.) Madrid, Trotta, 2013.

Rafael Espino Navarro. *La tiza roja* (Red chalk). Asociación para la Recuperación de la Memoria Histórica de Aguilar de la Frontera, published on the social media.

Rafael García Contreras. *Susurros de libertad. Memorias.* (Whispers of freedom. Memories). Córdoba, Puntoreklamo, 2008.

Raphael Lemkin. Vth International Conference for the Unification of Penal Law, Madrid. October 1933. Representing Poland.

_____ *Axis Rule in Occupied Europe: Laws of Occupation - Analysis of Government - Proposals for Redress.* Carnegie Endowment for International Peace, Washington, D.C., 1944, Part II, chapter IX.

_____ *Axis Rule in Occupied Europe*, Columbia University Press, New York, 1944.

_____ "Genocide", *American Scholar,* April 1946.

Rafael Sánchez Guerra, *Mis prisiones* (My imprisonments). Buenos Aires, Alaridad, 1946.

Ramón Serrano Súñez. *Entre el silencio y la propaganda, la historia como fue.* (Between silence and propaganda; history as it was). *Memorias,* Planeta, Barcelona, 1997.

Regional Court of Political Responsibilities. Seville. Sentence of the Court: Eugenio Jurado Pozuelo. January 14 1942.

Renzo Stroscio. *"Hacia una tipologia de los campos de concentración y exterminio nacionalsocialistas"* (Regarding a feature of the Nationalsocialist concentration and extermination camps), Minutes of the *Congress on The concentration camps and the penitentiary world in Spain during the civil war and Francoism,* Crítica, Barcelona, 2003.

Reyes Mate, *Memoria de Auschwitz* (Memory of Auschwitz). Trotta, Madrid, 2003.

Ricard Vinyes. "El universo penitenciario durante el franquismo"(The prison universe during Francoism). In: *Una inmensa prisión (*An immense prison). Barcelona, Crítica, 2003.

Rufino Ayuso Fernández. Field work given to Moreno Gómez in 2002. An enthusiastic supporter of groups dedicated to recovering the historic memory, he was a policeman by profession and died very young. The author refers to this research in greater detail in "Huidos, guerrilleros, resistentes. La oposición armada a la dictadura" (Fugitives, volunteer militia and freedom fighters. Armed opposition to the dictatorship.) In *Morir, matar, sobrevivir. La violencia en la dictadura de Franco. (*Death, killing and survival. Violence during Franco's dictatorship.) Collaborative book coordinated by Julián Casanova. Barcelona, Crítica, 2002.

Tomás de Boada, Count of Marsal. *Carta del Presidente del Patronato de Presos y Penados (1945) (*Letter to *The Times* from the President of the Brotherhood of Saint Paul for the Imprisoned and Punished), London, dated 5 October 1945.

Tomasa Cuevas Gutiérrez. *Testimonios de mujeres en las cárceles franquistas.* (Testimonials of women in Franco's prisons). Instituto de Estudios Altoaragoneses, Huesca, 2004 (1ˢᵗ Edition, Casa de Campo, Madrid, 1982).

Territorial Military Archives II, Seville.

Todos Los Nombres. All the Names. Internet project asking for information regarding the whereabouts of missing relatives from the civil war period. Link to website: http://www.todoslosnombres.org/enlaces.

United Nations Working Group on Enforced or Involuntary Disappearances. Preliminary report of its visit to Madrid, Spain. 30 September 2013.

Vicente Fajardo. Short field work given to Moreno Gómez, a colleague of his at the Institute.